GOOD TEMPERED FOOD

Tamasin Day-Lewis
GOOD TEMPERED FOOD
Recipes to love, leave, and linger over

Photography by David Loftus

WEIDENFELD & NICOLSON

DEDICATION

For the three loveliest children in the world, Miranda, Harry and Charissa

Contents

6 Introduction 12 A Slow Start – 'reuniting with your sense of pleasure in the kitchen'. 84 Time to Cook – 'how the simplest dishes can transport, relax and infuse one with a degree of pleasure'. 168 The Advance Party – 'food that you can cook a bit of now, a bit later, prepare today for tomorrow, or the next day or even next week, tinker with, macerate, freeze, finish or reheat'. 232 A Lingering End – 'savour them, enjoy them, afford them the time and respect they deserve, they are more than what life is about, they are life itself'. 282 Suppliers 283 Index

Introduction

IT SEEMS TO ME THAT THIS PASSAGE tells us as much about what's wrong with our attitude towards food today as it does about what, at best, it should be. We are not prepared to 'tarry'. In fact in modern doctrine, the very idea of tarrying is stigmatic. We worship at the altar of the instant, we are governed and seduced by the words 'easy', 'fast', 'quick', 'simple'. Leapfrog the process, vault over the preparation, skim, short cut and bypass the stages that true cooking rather than assembling is all about, and you have bought into the culture that Pandarus was warning Troilus against around 400 years ago. In the absence of patience, of tarrying, fast food is your reward.

Look, I am no purist hardliner. There are days, if not weeks, when I crave easy food; a quickly frazzled bacon sandwich dribbling unsalted butter; pasta with handfuls of fresh herbs and raw broad beans from the garden thrown after them; a crab and avocado salad spritzed with lime, for which Phil my fishmonger has done the picking and dressing; a one-pan, flame-coloured piperade or Spanish omelette oozing a tangle of oily wilted onion and spinach and yesterday's potatoes. But none of these quite fits our notion of fast food, which is as much about provenance, or the lack of it, as it is about speed and convenience, two words which fill me with the same sense of gloom as hygiene when applied to food.

The very expression 'fast food' is a misnomer, an insult, an indicator of something inferior – mere fuel to be ingested at speed, to provide energy, be convenient, serve a purpose. Does this equate with pleasure, goodness, love, care, attention, nurture? To the scents and smells of a fresh yeasted loaf cooling on a rack, a stock simmering, a chicken roasting, a stew stewing quietly and unobtrusively in its own juices, the bitter whiff of January's Seville oranges filling the kitchen as they osmose to marmalade, clots of strawberries bubbling into jam, the raw depths of a garlicky aïoli, toast toasting, biscuits baking. Food cooked slowly isn't better by definition, but every process, from conception, gestation, seeding, fruiting, to picking, plucking, peeling, paring, preparing is also about waiting. As is cooking itself. The alchemy of food, its transformation from raw to cooked or raw to plate is about our transforming touch. Once we are no longer involved with that part of the process, once we know not how to perform the simple but satisfying tasks that even basic food demands, we are no longer cooks, nor are we heir to the traditions that food has been about since man first cooked it.

Somehow we have fallen for a myth, the notion that food that isn't fast prepared and fast cooked is inherently more difficult, more time consuming, more of a sweat, almost not worth the effort or, at least, only worth the effort some of the time.

I lay the blame first at the feet of the supermarkets and fast-food outlets whose interests, and by that I mean profits, this is in; second, with the consumer, easily led, lazy, wanting to spend less rather than invest in quality, better nutritional value, taste and sustainable methods of production; third, with the food manufacturers whose advertising, as dishonest as it is, is often brilliantly executed and faultless in its powers of seduction; and fourth, with the television chefs who are force-feeding their audience a diet that perpetuates the myth, telling people how quick and easy everything is, and choosing recipes that make-believe technique is unnecessary, time a luxury you can't afford, patience and attention to detail a curious anachronism from the past.

Well I'm here to tell you that slow-cooked food, and what I like to call 'good-tempered food,' food that you can cook a bit of now, a bit of later, prepare today for tomorrow, or the next day or even next week, tinker with, macerate, freeze, finish or reheat in another life, add to, subtract from, reincarnate, is what proper cooking is REALLY all about. In fact, it's the chief pleasure of cooking, and if you find cooking pleasure enough to read about, buy into and experiment with, you're being short-changed if the writer is advising you exactly how to get the whole thing over and done with as fast as pulling a tooth, so the pain is past tense, and you can get on with the things that really give you pleasure.

This book is about reuniting you with that sense of pleasure in the kitchen; about setting aside time, just THINKING about what you want to cook and eat. This is a hugely underrated pleasure in its own right – as can be the planning, shopping, reading cookery books, deliberating, telephoning a friend for a recipe, or even that most evanescent of things, inspiration; checking out the cupboard, the larder, the fridge, the vegetable garden.

Sometimes it is a chore, how could it not be? At domestic level, feeding a

family is like a prolonged, never-ending military campaign; if one bit of the advance preparation goes AWOL or is forgotten, DISASTER, or, at least, a complete change of strategy is needed. But it's what you probably cope with already at least once a week. And what do you need most in a tricky culinary impasse? Time and imagination, though just one of these should do. And the knowledge that most food lends itself to this sort of crisis, even if it's 'empty fridge' syndrome or 'there's-nothing-I-feel-like-cooking,' or an extra battalion has invited itself to supper.

Cooking is an exam without the paper, the questions or the answers, in the sense that you, the cook, are constantly trying to please a disparate bunch of people who most often, being family, will not hold back on the criticism. You are coping with other pressures – budgetary constraints, an imperfect kitchen, no kitchen slaves to scrub, chop, wash up; but still, something as simple as a clove of garlic sizzling in good olive oil, podding a tightly packed pea pod, smelling the readiness of the simplest of dishes can transport, relax, infuse with a degree of pleasure that the smallest of things can so cunningly do with the greatest of impact. Take the lid off a fat piece of belly pork that has been idling in the oven doing time for five, maybe six, maybe seven hours, steeped in its gluey juices, black breathed with the sweetness of molasses, raw brown sugar, star anise, and you should feel not far short of paradise.

Decide not to feel guilty if you are still slamming cupboard doors and searching for a 20-minute supper to cook when your children are mutinous with post-homework hunger and you are scanning the darker recesses of your memory and your fridge for a one-pot supper. I did just that last week, after four days in New York, arriving back jet lagged to a yawningly empty kitchen and a lack of inspiration equalled only by my intense hunger. But I just didn't want to have to think or cook. The result: I picked the tiniest green embryos of broad beans from the garden, with handfuls of chives, mint, chervil, and thyme. I roasted some tiny, rather overripe, tomatoes in olive oil until split and deliciously weeping. Found some goat's cheese and mozzarella lurking at the back of the fridge. Cooked some penne. Threw the tomatoes and their juices whole into the drained pasta, followed by chunks of the cheeses, more verdant olive oil, the very finely chopped herbs, salt, pepper, some zested lemon and the raw broad beans. We ate it warm rather than piping hot. It didn't feel like cooking, but it made me want to cook again. My youngest daughter Charissa eulogized over what felt like almost cheating, and thus was my appetite for the stove rekindled. It is, after all, appetite that induces pleasure and inspiration, and which, on contemplating the creating of something out of nothing, is all the better stimulated. The elaborate and the refined have their place too, but food was always a necessity before it was a luxury, so maybe it is down to some ancient atavistic urge that the most satisfying of dishes are usually those that excite through their very simplicity and through the power of memory.

Let us not forget the simple art of roasting; and those of baking, poaching, pickling, bottling, preserving. More than that, that the greatest gift we can bestow on the next generation is educating them in the art, science, lore, tradition and pragmatic experience of the kitchen. The quiet, unhurried, unchaotic ritual of preparation for the table, its simple repetitions, its satisfying processes, and its accompaniments – conversation, music, a glass of wine – savour them, enjoy them, afford them the time and respect they deserve. They are more than what life is all about, they are life itself.

TAMASIN DAY-LEWIS

Sologa – a perfect starter.
The contrasting textures and
brilliant colours make a feast for
the eye as well as the taste buds.
Assemble all the ingredients in
advance and arrange the dish
when you are ready to eat.

a slow start

I

A spectacularly beautiful yet simple dish that I first ate at my Swedish friend Kristina von Wrede's house. The combination of sweet, sour, astringent and salt, of textures from smooth to crisp and fresh, and the brilliance of the colours, make this dish both startling and original.

'Sun's Eye', or Sologa

FOR EACH SERVING:

3–4 anchovies, preferably the salted ones, rinsed and dried
1 tbsp capers or cornichons, chopped
1–2 tbsp white onion, finely chopped
2–3 tbsp pickled beetroot, and I do not mean the throat-gagging kind pickled in malt vinegar; white wine vinegar please
2–3 tbsp flat-leaf parsley, chopped
1 raw egg yolk
a few drops of lemon juice (optional)

Chop all the ingredients one by one, keeping them separate. Arrange each plate, starting with a small circle of anchovies in the middle, so that all you can fit inside it is the egg yolk later. Then do the same with the capers or cornichons, so that the circle abuts the anchovies, and outside that, the onions then the beetroot then the parsley, over which you may sprinkle a bit of lemon juice. Finally put the egg yolk in the middle.

You eat the dish by breaking into the yolk and mixing it into the other ingredients. Would I be foolish in imaging this to be a good hangover cure if your hands were steady enough to make it? Serve with a home-made wholemeal or caraway roll.

Wholemeal Caraway Rolls

MAKES ABOUT 20
preheat oven to 220°C/425°F/Gas 7

50g/2oz butter
350ml/12oz milk
50g/2oz fresh yeast
200g/7oz organic stoneground
    wholemeal flour to mix with
    350ml/12fl oz boiling water
1½ tsp sea salt
2 tbsp molasses sugar
300g/10oz organic stoneground
    wholemeal flour
250g/9oz organic strong
    unbleached white flour
a handful of caraway seeds
    (optional)

Melt the butter in a pan. Pour in the milk and heat to lukewarm. Crumble the yeast into a bowl, pour in the liquid and stir until the yeast has dissolved. Add the flour and boiling water mixture, the salt and sugar, the 300g/10oz of stoneground flour and most of the white flour. Mix everything together into a pliable dough, then cover the bowl with a tea towel you have rinsed in boiling water and squeezed out and leave the dough in a warm place to rise for about an hour.

Using the rest of the white flour, knead the dough with determination for about 7 minutes on a floured surface, then separate into two pieces. Cut each piece into 10 and shape them into rolls. Place them on two greased baking sheets, cover with tea towels and leave for a further 30 minutes.

Bake in the middle of the oven for 10 minutes, then let the rolls cool on a wire rack under a tea towel. Serve warm.

Last year I purchased half a Berkshire pig and armed with a copy of Jane Grigson's reissued classic *Charcuterie and French Pork Cookery*, I dreamed of raised pies, galantines, trotters, snouts, pigs' tails and tongues. The pig came with a proper fatty overcoat, ideal for things like brawn and terrines since the greatest enemy of the terrine is dryness, and good back fat and belly is of the essence. If you don't possess a mincer, any good butcher will mince the ingredients for you. Other than remembering how important the proportions of fat to lean, bacon to offal are, this is a simple and utterly beguiling old-school dish, about as unlike the grey, chewy offerings of an inferior deli or the hideously pink commercial pâtés as you could imagine. When you turn out your browned, pink-middled, coarse-textured wonder, you will glow with pride.

Country Terrine

SERVES 10–12
preheat oven to 150°C/300°F/Gas 2

450g/1lb onions
70g/2½oz unsalted butter
450g/1lb belly pork, rind and
   small bones removed, and
   coarsely minced through the
   largest hole of the mincer
350g/12oz unsmoked streaky
   organic bacon, minced
450g/1lb pig's liver, minced
175g/6oz pork back fat, minced
50ml/2fl oz Cognac
50ml/2fl oz dry sherry
4 cloves of garlic, peeled and
   finely chopped
flat-leaf parsley, chopped
2 tsp olive oil
sprig of rosemary, finely chopped
a few sprigs of thyme
1 egg
½ tsp ground allspice
sea salt and white pepper

Peel and roughly chop the onions. Cook them in the butter gently until softened and golden (about 30 minutes), then put them on a plate to cool. Thoroughly mix all the minced meats and fat together with your hands in a big bowl, until well amalgamated. Warm the alcohol in the pan you cooked the onions in, then set light to it with a taper and allow the alcohol to burn off.

Throw the onions and alcohol into the bowl of minced meat with the garlic and parsley. Heat the olive oil in a small frying pan, throw in the rosemary and thyme, and allow them to soften (a couple of minutes). Pour them over the minced meat, add the beaten egg and the allspice, then season generously.

Scrape the mixture into a 1-litre/1¾-pint terrine, cover with foil, and place in a roasting tin. Fill the tin three-quarters full with boiling water, then put into the oven for an hour. Uncover and check with a skewer poked down to the middle of the terrine. After 10 seconds, see if it is hot on your tongue. The meat juices should be pink. Leave the foil off and return the tin to the oven for 15–30 minutes for the terrine to brown.

Remove from the oven, replace the foil or lid and leave to cool. Place in the fridge until you want to eat it. It tastes even better if it is left for a couple of days.

This is one of the simplest and most delicious titbits of a dish that I have ever cooked. It should be eaten straight from a communal plate, or even the frying pan, your fingers oozing the pinkly sticky, buttery spicy juices, while you clutch a cold glass of something good with your free hand. The spices can all be ground an hour or so in advance and stirred together with the flour in the mortar. You may also de-vein the chicken livers in advance, leaving them whole, so that all you need to do when your guests arrive or your family descend like gannets to the kitchen, is roll the livers in the spiced flour, heat your olive oil or butter and cook them for about a couple of minutes a side. Beware, the spices spit, and do not allow the centres to turn from rosy softness to firm greyness. Tip hot with their oily juices on to a plate, and devour!

Spiced Chicken Livers

SERVES 4—6
as a starter with drinks, depending on greed and what's to follow

450g/1lb organic chicken livers. I'm afraid I take a purist line here – only organic will do, since chemical residues collect in the liver and kidneys
1½ heaped tsp cumin seeds
1 tsp coriander seeds
the tip of a tsp of cayenne
1 tsp sea salt crystals
1 tsp black peppercorns
1–1½ tbsp plain flour
olive oil or a good-sized knob of unsalted butter

Temper the cumin and coriander in a small frying pan over a gentle heat for 30 seconds to a minute, until the spices exude their scent. Tip into a mortar and crush with the sea salt and peppercorns. Add the cayenne, then the flour, and stir well together. Set aside.

Clean and de-vein the livers, keeping them whole, and removing any green patches. Pat them dry and keep in the fridge until about 30 minutes before you want to cook them.

Just before cooking, roll each liver in the spice mixture in the mortar and put on a plate. Heat a good knob of unsalted butter or olive oil, whichever you prefer, in a frying pan – I err on the side of butter, with a tiny addition of oil to discourage burning. Throw in the livers when the fat is hot. Allow one side to spit and crisp for a couple of minutes, turn over and repeat, then test with a knife point. When gorgeously oozily pink, shunt the contents of the pan on to a white plate and consume.

This is a magical starter that I dreamt up as everyone was sitting down to dinner one night. I had already invented the spiced livers for a previous party. This time I offset their heat and spice with the bitter-sweet endives softened in what amounts to a warm salad dressing. You can serve the dish hot or warm. I cooked it in three or four minutes while people took their pews.

Spiced Chicken Livers on Wilted Endives

SERVES 6
the ingredients for the chicken livers
as on page 19, plus:

3 endives
4 tbsp best olive oil
1 tsp molasses sugar
sea salt and black pepper
lemon juice to taste

While you fry the livers, cut the base off the endives, core them and strip them into leaves. Heat the olive oil gently in a pan with the molasses sugar, then throw in the endives and stir them in the warm oil. They will begin to wilt pretty quickly. Season, remove from the heat and spritz on the lemon to taste.

Pile a few leaves on to each plate, add a few livers with their juices, then serve.

Look on grilled peppers as a base or foundation that can withstand pretty serious cosmetic enhancement and be easily transmogrified into something more glamorous if the need should arise. In the meanwhile, you can prepare pounds of red or yellow peppers, organic if possible – I am no fan of the hideous hydroponically grown numbers that the Dutch send us – when they are cheap and in season, and keep them in the fridge in jars *sott'olio*, under oil, for two or three months. Then you can use them as is as a starter, layer a vermilion or yellow seam of them in sandwiches or bruschetta with a lovely goat's cheese like Ragstone or Golden Cross, or use them as an accompaniment to cold pork. If you are going to serve them on their own, the following sauce, in which you can also abandon the peppers for up to a week, defines the word alchemy.

Grilled Peppers

SERVES 4 OR SO

4 red or yellow organic peppers
3 salted anchovies or 6 anchovy
   fillets
2 cloves of garlic
a handful of flat-leaf parsley
1 small, seeded dried chilli
sea salt
best olive oil, Seggiano or Ravida
   if you can lay your hands on
   them

Grill or char your peppers in the usual way. I only have an erratic overhead grill, so I keep turning mine over with tongs until they are uniformly blackened and softened. Leave them to cool, then the skins should peel away easily. I am not of the plastic bag school of pepper peeling, it is unnecessary, and I hate the idea of hot plastic melting into healthy organic peppers. Halve, core and seed the peppers, then cut them lengthwise into thin strips.

Desalinate the salted anchovies if you are using them, by running them under the cold tap. Pound them in a mortar with the garlic, parsley, chilli and a little bit of salt, or chop them all together finely with a sharp knife or mezzaluna.

Put the mixture into a small pan with 4–5 tablespoons of olive oil, and heat very gently, mashing the mixture down as you go. Spoon over the peppers and let them marinate for at least 4 hours. Here's the best bit: the longer you leave them the better they get, up to a week in the fridge is just fine. You need good bread with a proper crust on it to accompany them.

Rillons are the big brother to rillettes, being whole rather than shredded. Like goose or duck legs in the classic confit, large cubes of belly pork, which I buy from my organic butcher Swaddles Green Farm, are cooked slowly in seasoned fat. When they have been cooled, they can be stored for months beneath their snowy mantle of fat.

Rillons, or Confit of Belly Pork

SERVES 6—8
preheat oven to 200°C/400°F/Gas 6

1–2kg/2¼–4¼lb pork belly, the
   ribs removed
a generous tbsp of lard
some sprigs of thyme
2–3 cloves of garlic, bruised with
   the back of a knife (optional)
a large glass of red wine
a small glass of water
sea salt and black pepper

Cut the belly pork roughly into large cubes about 5cm/2in square, leaving the skin on. Heat the lard in a roomy pan and throw in the meat. Brown fast and hard, turning occasionally, then transfer to a large ovenproof dish in which, ideally, the pieces should fit snugly in a single layer. Add the other ingredients, and put in the oven. Check on it every 10 minutes, turning the pieces as you do. After about 30 minutes, the fat rendered from the pork should be at least half way up the meat, which will be browning nicely.

Turn the oven down to 170°C/350°F/Gas 3 and cook the rillons for at least another hour, turning them once or twice. They are done when the skin is soft enough to chew without much effort.

Unlike most things, rillons are best served cold, straight from the fridge with some extra sea salt. Great with a glass of iced fino, my favourite is Valdespino, which you can buy at wine merchants Lea and Sandeman. Home-made granary bread toasted is all the accompaniment you need.

Store the rillons for months in a sealed jar in a cool place, but if you think you are going to eat them within a couple of weeks, a plastic container in the fridge will do. The fat will help to keep them moist, but if you don't like the taste of it, you can wipe it off before you use them. This fat will set to a highly flavoured lard, perfect for roasting potatoes and parsnips.

I have tried pork, duck, goose and rabbit rillettes. All are delicious, as verified by the good people of the Sarthe region of northwest France, renowned for their extraordinary consumption of this delicacy. At 12.5 kilograms/27½ pounds per person per year, it is a hundred times higher than the national average.

Rillettes de Tours

SERVES 4—6
as a starter or lunch dish,
or 8—10 as part of a cold table
preheat oven to 10°C/225°F/Gas1¼

1kg/2¼lb belly pork
1 wineglass of dry white wine
4–6 cloves of garlic, crushed
nutmeg
salt and pepper
450g/1lb pork fat

Take the rind off the belly pork and put it to one side. Remove and discard the bones and cut the meat into 2.5cm/1in chunks. Put them into a Pyrex or non-aluminium dish. Pour the wine over them, then add the crushed garlic, a suspicion of nutmeg and the seasoning. Cover and bake for at least 5 hours, or until the meat is virtually falling to pieces. , Meanwhile, sprinkle the rind with salt and roast it in a hot oven, 200°C/400°F/Gas 6 until crisp. Leave to cool on a rack set over a plate to catch any residue.

Chop the rind finely. Melt the pork fat and strain it. Shred the meat roughly using two forks and mix it with its juices and the garlic; mix in the chopped, roasted rind and its juices. Pour into small pots or jars, or into one larger earthenware dish. When cool, pour the pork fat over it to seal the top. Like the rillons, rillettes can be stored for months in a sealed jar in a cool place, or if you are going to eat them within a couple of weeks, you can keep them in a plastic container in the fridge.

Serve with a good crusty bread, some glossy green or black olives, a few cornichons and a good bitter lettuce such as escarole or radicchio.

Everyone knows this wonderful northern Italian dish. I add crumbled feta and a sprig of thyme and serve quarters of the peppers like warm boats transporting their cargo of salt anchovy, garlic, olive oil and herbed cheese. The perfect ambulant pre-dinner starter served with a glass of iced manzanilla sherry or rosé. You can prepare the *petits bateaux* in advance, then put them in the oven just before your guests arrive. Hot, warm or cold, all are equally delicious.

Piemontese Peppers

SERVES 4
preheat oven to 180°C/350°F/Gas 4

2 organic red peppers
2 large organic tomatoes
4–6 good-quality anchovies
best olive oil
a generous knob unsalted butter
a sprig of thyme
3 cloves of garlic
some crumbled or cubed feta
   cheese, the best sheep's milk
   one you can find
sea salt, pepper

Halve the peppers, remove the seeds and innards, then halve them again and place them on a flat roasting tray like small boats. On each deck, place two tiny chunks of tomato, three thin slices of garlic, half a chopped anchovy in tiny bits, a sprinkling of thyme and a splosh of best olive oil. Season, add a dot of butter, and bake in the oven for 40 minutes, or until the peppers are tender but slightly resistant.

Add some crumbled bits of good feta cheese to the boats while still hot. Cool to whatever temperature you wish to serve them at and make sure you spoon back any escaped juices.

The therapeutic stuffing and rolling into parcels of this dish is as pleasurable as the eating, either hot, warm or cold. You can eschew the meat and do a vegetarian version if you would rather. The soaking and draining of the vine leaves is hardly time consuming, and very much worth the effort. You can make the dish hours before you want to eat it and serve it at room temperature. The other joy is that you can use leftover cooked rice.

Stuffed Vine Leaves

MAKES 45—50
serve 4 per person for a starter, about
double for a main course, or serve a few
with drinks alongside other dishes

1 jar of vine leaves in brine
100g/3½oz organic basmati rice,
    cooked and drained
225g/8oz raw minced organic
    lamb
2 tomatoes, skinned, seeded and
    chopped
1 small onion, peeled and very
    finely chopped, almost minced
3 tbsp each of finely chopped
    mint, flat-leaf parsley and
    celery leaves
50g/scant 2oz pine nuts
¼ tsp ground cinnamon
¼ tsp ground allspice
2 tbsp concentrated tomato purée
6 cloves of garlic, cut into slivers
150ml/5fl oz good olive oil and the
    same quantity of water
juice of 1½ lemons
sea salt and freshly ground black
    pepper

Drain the vine leaves and put them in a bowl. Cover them with boiling water and soak for 20 minutes. Repeat the process twice more, but with cold water, before a final drain.

In a large bowl mix together the rice, minced lamb, tomatoes, onion, herbs, pine nuts, spices and tomato purée. Season. Place a vine leaf on your work surface, vein side up, the stem edge nearest to you. Put a heaped teaspoon of the mixture in the centre of the leaf near the stem. Fold up over the filling, then fold both sides of the leaf towards the middle, and roll into a little cigar. Do the same with the remaining 49. Children are very adept at this sort of repetitive action if you have any on hand to bribe, but I find some comfort and relaxation in the leisurely performing of this sort of task, which is not going to ruin if the telephone rings.

Line a heavy-bottomed casserole with a single layer of unstuffed vine leaves, slightly overlapping, so that they come about a third of the way up the sides of the pan. Pack in the stuffed vine leaves, snuggled tightly together and one or two layers deep, placing occasional slivers of garlic between them. Add the olive oil, water and lemon juice, and weight down with an upturned plate and a couple of weights.

Cook very gently on top of the stove for about 2 hours, until tender when pierced with a skewer. Check the liquid level after the first hour, you may need to add a bit more water. The sort of unhurried, uncomplicated but tremendously satisfying cooking that brings forth memories of the best kind of Greek taverna.

One of those delightfully old-style-trat dishes that is as substantial as you could wish for as a starter or main course. Why do things fall from fashion, only to be resuscitated as the emperor's new clothes? All I can say is there is always a place in my repertoire for a classic such as this, where there is a true marriage of texture and flavour, and not one ingredient too many.

Parmigiana di Melanzane

SERVES 4
preheat oven to 200°C/400°F/Gas 6

1kg/2¼lb aubergines
sea salt
1 buffalo mozzarella (do not buy the supermarket elastic band kind on the grounds that no one will notice once it is cooked)
a few tbsp of good olive oil
400g/14oz tin of whole plum tomatoes, coarsely chopped, without their juice
1 clove of garlic, peeled and bruised with the back of a knife
handful of basil leaves
vegetable oil for frying, a non-intrusive-tasting one like ground nut oil
black pepper
50g/2oz Parmesan cheese, freshly grated
2 eggs, hard boiled

Peel the aubergines, and cut them lengthwise into 5mm/¼ inch slices like long tongues. Sprinkle them with sea salt and let them drain in a colander for a couple of hours before rinsing them and patting them dry on kitchen paper.

Chop the mozzarella into tiny cubes. Heat a splosh of olive oil in a pan and add the tomatoes, garlic and basil leaves, which you have torn by hand. Season and cook down at a brisk heat for a few minutes, before puréeing through the coarse disc of a food mill or food processor, making sure that the basil gets through the holes.

Heat 2.5cm/1in of vegetable oil in a roomy heavy-bottomed frying pan and test by dropping in a tiny corner of bread; it should sizzle immediately. Then put in a single layer of aubergines and fry until golden brown on both sides, about 5 minutes. This method of salting, drying and cooking in hot oil prevents the aubergines from absorbing copious quantities of fat and ending up hideously greasy, I promise.

Drain the aubergines on kitchen paper. Brush the bottom of a gratin dish with good olive oil, cover with a layer of aubergines, spread some of the tomato sauce on top, and dot with mozzarella. Season with black pepper and strew with some freshly grated Parmesan. Then top with a few slices of egg before repeating the process. Finish the dish with a layer of aubergine, on to which you dribble a bit of olive oil before baking for 25–30 minutes.

Allow to cool for a few minutes before serving – this dish emerges molten and bubbling from the oven and too hot to taste.

My first trip to Sicily this year was to the heights of Erice, a mountainous village shrouded in swirling mists, through which, when a skein occasionally parted, the valley floor and sea would appear far below. I was at a conference on molecular gastronomy, with a group of international physicists, chefs, food technologists and writers, a sort of cross-cultural soup which was at once inspiring and huge fun. Unfortunately, we had no time to travel the island and taste its legendary food, so much of which arrived with the Saracens. But a couple of visits to Trapani for good fish and the daily fresh ricotta brought in by two of the most delightful scientists I have ever met, Ugo and Beatrice Palma, with wine from their estate, did more to encourage my taste for Sicilian food than the famous Sicilian lemons I have always bought whenever I come across them. This Sicilian dish is great as a starter or main course, or accompanies game or cold roast meat with brio. Make it in advance, and eat it warm or cold.

Peperoni alla Siciliana

SERVES 4

4 red peppers
1 onion, finely sliced
2 cloves of garlic, chopped
½ an organic vegetable bouillon cube
3 tbsp best extra virgin olive oil
2 tbsp best balsamic vinegar, and by that, I mean an aged, velvety black number that is mellow rather than sharp. Mine is a 20-year-old.
a small bunch of fresh oregano
18 best glossy black olives, halved and stoned
2 salted anchovies, rinsed and boned, or 4 anchovy fillets in olive oil
1½ tbsp salted capers rinsed under a cold tap
sea salt and black pepper

Grill or char your peppers until they are uniformly blackened and softened. Leave them to cool, then the skins should peel away easily. Cut the prepared peppers into long strips.

Cook the onion, garlic and olive oil gently in a covered pan, with a bit of salt and a couple of tablespoons of water. You want the onion to be softened to a purée. Remove the lid, and carry on cooking until the onion is golden, which will take about 40 minutes. Add the strips of pepper, the crumbled bouillon cube and the balsamic vinegar. Cook uncovered for a further 30 minutes, stirring occasionally. You can always add an extra tablespoon or two of water if the mixture seems to be drying out.

Add all the other ingredients, and carry on slow cooking for 20 minutes at a very low temperature; anything more and the anchovies will turn bitter.

Serve the peppers warm or at room temperature, with good crusty bread or with game or cold roast meat as above.

Capers are a classic with skate and a black butter sauce. This is another Sicilian dish, a great accompaniment to a plain poached wing of skate, or served spooned out into some hollowed-out Pugliese bread or alongside it, as either a starter or picnic. It's that sweet-sour combination that does it for me. You can make the caponata a day in advance – indeed, it tastes better if you do – and leave it out of the fridge overnight to serve at room temperature. If you want to make it even further in advance, it will happily tolerate being kept in the fridge for a few days and then brought back to room temperature before serving.

Caponata

SERVES 6

1.4kg/3lb aubergines
sea salt and black pepper
vegetable oil for frying
olive oil
1 heart, or 3 sticks of celery
1 large onion, sliced
2 tsp molasses sugar
1 clove of garlic, chopped
400g/14oz tin of plum tomatoes
4 tbsp red wine vinegar
85g/3oz salted capers, rinsed
85g/3oz good green olives, pitted
a handful of flat-leaf parsley,
    roughly chopped

Peel the aubergines, cut them into 2cm/¾in cubes. Sprinkle them with salt, weight them down with a plate and leave them to drain in a colander for an hour. Squeeze them out, and dry them on kitchen paper.

Pour the vegetable oil into a frying pan so you have a layer about 2.5cm/1in deep. When it is hot, drop in the cubes of aubergine and fry until brown all over, watching that they don't burn. Drain them on kitchen paper. Cut the celery into matchstick strips and fry them in the oil until they are crisped and golden.

Heat a splosh of good olive oil in another pan and throw in the sliced onion, garlic and a teaspoon of the sugar. Cook for about 5 minutes until the onions begin to colour, then add the tinned tomatoes, the rest of the sugar and season to taste. Cook briskly for a couple of minutes before adding the vinegar and capers. Halve the pitted olives and add them and the aubergines and celery to the tomato mixture. Cook gently for about 30 minutes, adjust the seasonings, and leave to cool.

When just warm and jammy, scatter over some roughly chopped parsley and serve, or keep as suggested above.

Smoky Aubergine and White Bean Purée

SERVES 6

as a starter, more as part of a mezze

1 aubergine

olive oil

2 cloves of garlic

400g/14oz tin of cannellini beans,
   or cook your own

1 tsp cumin and 1 tsp coriander
   seeds, roasted for 30 seconds in
   a pan until they exude their
   scent, then crushed in a mortar

1 tsp sea salt

½ tsp fresh chilli paste, or make
   your own by crushing a seeded
   red chilli with a bit of sea salt in
   a mortar

1 heaped tsp tahini

juice of half a lemon

a handful each of fresh mint and
   coriander leaves

olive oil

pepper

Cut the aubergine in half lengthwise, make slits diagonally in the flesh and brush with olive oil. If you have a griddle, brush oil over it lightly, then place the aubergine halves on it cut side down with the whole, unpeeled garlic. If not, cook them on a lightly oiled baking tray in a moderate to hot oven. Cook until soft and beginning to char.

Scoop out the flesh of the aubergine and the garlic cloves into the food processor along with all the other ingredients, process until smooth, and check the seasoning. Serve with some hot, griddled pitta bread.

The word 'glut', so emotive in its conjuring up a surfeit, a superabundance, the natural world gone mildly but irresistibly and deliciously out of control, was almost invented for the tomato. The correlation between the last flaming days of late summer and the arrival of this most versatile of fruits, their splash of scarlet a seasonal sunset or epilogue, should inspire you to make a home-made ketchup, a real Bloody Mary, jars of fresh tomato sauce or a piperade, one of the glories of the Basque country.

Piperade, or Piperrada

SERVES 4

500g/a generous 1lb of organic red peppers
500g/a generous 1lb of ripe, organic tomatoes, skinned and seeded
8 large organic eggs
olive oil
1 onion, chopped
1 clove of garlic, chopped
4 slices of ham, Bayonne, pata negra or prosciutto
sea salt and black pepper

Grill the peppers in the normal way, turning them every few minutes until the skins are charred all over. Allow the peppers to cool before peeling, removing the cores and seeds and chopping them.

Heat a couple of tablespoons of olive oil in a frying pan and gently sauté the chopped onion over a gentle heat until golden, adding the chopped garlic towards the end. Chop the tomatoes, remove their cores, and add them to the pan with the peppers, cooking them down until you have a meltingly soft texture. Beat the eggs, season with pepper – I never add salt to eggs at the raw stage as it turns them watery – and pour them over the sauce, stirring everything together to make a sunset-coloured mixture. Be patient, worry the eggs a bit and cook very slowly until soft and slightly runny.

Fry the ham separately in a bit of olive oil until crisp, and serve it atop the eggs. I think warm with a hunk of good bread is preferable to hot.

An unshowy and versatile dish which you can eat in its own right as a starter or light lunch, or can equally well partner a grilled chicken or a pork chop as a more substantial main course. If you look snobbishly down on the much maligned stuffed tomato, think again. I know you will reconsider if you try this dish. You can prepare the tomatoes several hours in advance before cooking.

Tomatoes Baked with Olives, Mustard and Gruyère

SERVES 4
preheat oven to 220°C/425°F/Gas 7

8 ripe medium-sized organic
   tomatoes
sea salt and pepper
1 tbsp Dijon mustard
1 tbsp black olive paste, the best
   are Seggiano and Carluccio
a sprig of fresh thyme
125g/4oz Gruyère, grated
a handful of breadcrumbs made
   with day-old bread, white or
   wholemeal
olive oil
16 glossy, best black olives

Cut the tomatoes in half horizontally and scoop out the seeds and core with a teaspoon. Place them cut side up on a baking tray, season and plop a pitted olive inside each half.

Rub a few thyme leaves from their sprig with your fingers into the olive paste, then stir in the mustard and brush it over the tomatoes. Mix the breadcrumbs with half the grated Gruyère and stuff the tomatoes. Put the rest of the grated cheese on top and pour a slug of olive oil over each tomato half.

You are now ready to bake, but you can leave these prepared tomatoes for a few hours before cooking them if it suits you. Bake for 20 minutes and serve warm, with a good hunk of bread or a roll if you feel like it.

Why? Because it's worth it. And don't say a Bloody Mary isn't a starter. It's the best precursor to a fine sirloin of beef with the undercut that I know, and it is my pre-Sunday lunch, post 8-mile-run-and-bath ritual, which I would have to be shaken not stirred out of to consider giving up. My most recent convert was my best friend Janie while filming a 15-part television series *Tamasin's Weekends*. Actually, that is only partly the truth. The whole crew and production team were instantly seduced. Janie, in her inimitable way, showed somewhat insulted and shocked surprise that for so many years she had been unaware of the heights this drink could reach and vowed to try it out on her husband as soon as she got home. Remember that a good Bloody Mary's strength is down to the individual. Janie's first comment when I asked her what mine needed was 'more vodka'. I am not sure whether she regretted saying that since the alcohol is so successfully masked by the strength of the other ingredients. Once you have made the real McCoy, you will never go back to your old habits.

A Home-made Bloody Mary

Makes 6—8 glasses

1.2kg/2½lb ripe organic tomatoes
2 small stalks of celery from the
    heart, with their leaves
a small bunch of fresh coriander
a sprig each of thyme, flat-leaf
    parsley and rosemary
1 tsp grated horseradish, or a
    proprietary brand that is pure
    horseradish
1 tsp grated onion
juice of 2 lemons
a pinch of molasses sugar
a pinch of sea salt
a few drops each of Tabasco and
    Worcestershire sauce
vodka, about a third of a bottle for
    this quantity should do
half a tray of ice cubes

If you have a pretty glass jug, put it in the deep freeze for 30 minutes before you make your Bloody Mary – and the glasses if you have room. That way, everything has a rime of frosting when you serve it; quite beautiful.

Cut the tomatoes into halves or quarters, depending on their size. Liquidize everything but the alcohol in the food processor or blender, then push as much as you can through a sieve into a bowl, forcing it down hard with the back of a wooden spoon. Pour the cold vodka into the cold jug, add the contents of the bowl and mix well. Adjust the seasoning and serve the Bloody Mary in the cold glasses.

If there are any would-be virgins among you, keep back some of the Virgin Mary before you jug it and add the vodka.

I discovered a wonderful source of quail in Devon the other week, from The Ark Chicken Company, who do the rounds of the farmers' markets and will send you quail, guinea fowl and chickens. All are organically reared, sensitively slaughtered and properly hung, the guinea fowl for a week, uneviscerated, to help break down the flesh and allow the gamey flavour to develop. See page 282 for details if you would like to have an order sent to you.

Grilled Quail Flavoured with Balsamic Vinegar

SERVES 4 AS A STARTER,
2 FOR A MAIN COURSE

4 quail
olive oil
sea salt
black pepper
best aged balsamic vinegar
chicken stock

This is almost not a recipe it is so simple; the sort of dish you can cook in front of friends over drinks and eat as an ambulant starter together, inspiring the conviviality of the table before you even get to it. Dunk a bit of bread in the sweet-sour juices, balsamic is perfect for small game, and do eat with your fingers – quail and cutlery don't go. I cook mine 'long leg,' that is, with the trail still inside them, but if you are squeamish, don't.

Preheat the grill. Place the birds on their sides in a large gratin dish, brush with olive oil and rub with sea salt and black pepper. Cook for 5 minutes, then repeat the process with the other side. Finally, splosh a dessertspoon of best aged balsamic vinegar over each bird, add a tablespoon of chicken stock per bird to the dish and blast the quails under the grill for a final 5 minutes. Gently pull a leg away from the body and pierce here to check the quail are cooked through, then rest them, turning them in their juice for 5 minutes before eating.

When blood oranges are in season, they make a thrillingly beautiful Sauce Maltese, but better still is the sharpness of a Seville orange. The sauce is, after all, just a delectable version of a hollandaise, so perfect with fish. The sweet-with-sweet leeks and scallops is a fine marriage, sharpened by a puddle of the unctuous and glossy sauce.

Scallops and Steamed Leeks with Sauce Maltese

SERVES 4

2 large or 3 smaller scallops per
　person
3 tbsp white wine or tarragon
　vinegar
2 tbsp water
10 white peppercorns
3 large organic egg yolks
175g/6oz best unsalted butter,
　l'Escure or d'Isigny are my
　favourites
sea salt
Seville orange or orange and
　lemon juice to taste
1 fat leek or 4 slim wands of baby
　leeks per person, depending on
　the season

Trim the scallops, leaving their coral whole and separate. Slice the whites into three discs if the scallops are large, two if they are smaller. Season just before you griddle them.

Put the vinegar, water and peppercorns into a small pan and boil down to about a tablespoon of liquid, then pour it into a bowl and leave it to cool for a few minutes. Beat the egg yolks into the reduced liquor, then place the bowl over a pan of barely simmering water and stir, adding small knobs of butter, bit by bit, as they melt in. If by any ghastly chance the mixture curdles, the remedy is the same as it is for mayonnaise: first hold your nerve, then try to bring it back by stirring in a tablespoon of scalding water. If that doesn't work, start with another egg yolk, whisk it, then add a tiny trickle of the curdled sauce, starting drop by drop, whisking hard as you go, until all is well. Once the sauce looks as thick and glossy as newly washed hair, remove from the heat, season with salt and add the juice to taste. You can leave the sauce for an hour or so before you want it, then heat it through over barely simmering water, making absolutely sure you don't overheat it. Scrambled eggs is not the idea.

I steam my well-washed whites of leek whole if they are the baby ones. If it is later in the season and they are thicker, either ruthlessly peel off any tough outer layers and steam them whole, or slice them finely to steam. You want them soft right through to the point of a knife. Keep them hot while you cook the scallops.

Cook the scallop whites on a hot griddle you have lightly brushed with oil before heating, or in a frying pan prepared the same way – a minute a side until just stiffened and opaque should do, introducing the whole corals for 30 seconds a side. Scatter the scallops over the leeks and hand round the sauce in a jug or pour it over each plate, according to your taste in such matters.

Poor man's food they may be – in the west of Ireland, when my friend John Kilcoyne was growing up, 'herring choker' was an abusive term used by those in the town who thought their country brethren were not as well endowed as they were, intellectually speaking – but that does not stop herrings from being one of the jewel's of the sea's harvest.

Grilled Herrings
with Sweet Smoked Paprika and Coriander

SERVES 2
preheat the grill

Allow 1 herring per person as a
    starter, 2 as a main course, and
    ask your fishmonger to fillet
    them for you
coarse sea salt
1 tbsp coriander, finely chopped
1 small clove of garlic, finely
    chopped
2 pinches sweet, smoked paprika
lemon juice

Place the herrings, butterflied out and skin side up, on the grill rack and scatter over a good sprinkling of coarse sea salt. Put the pan as close as you can get it under the preheated grill. The skin will bubble up, and the salt will spit. Leave for about 3 minutes. Turn over the fillets, they should be almost tender when pierced with a skewer, and place back under the grill for only 30 seconds or the flesh will dry out.

Remove the herrings and place them on serving plates. Scatter a tiny pinch of the smoked paprika, some coriander and a morsel of garlic on each one, spritz with lemon juice and serve. With brown bread and butter.

I have always found it curious how oily fish – mackerel, smoked salmon, smoked eel – are made less rich by brown bread and butter. Curious but true.

This dish should be marinated for 18–24 hours before you serve it, leaving only the potato salad to do a couple of hours beforehand. It is really a fish 'tartare' perfectly pickling the fish without cooking it, and the effect of the white wine vinegar is to ameliorate the oiliness of the fish. A wonderful starter if you are cooking for huge numbers, since it cooks itself and you can make it in advance.

Marinated Mackerel with Potato Salad

SERVES 6

6–8 mackerel fillets (ask your
    fishmonger to skin and fillet
    them of all bones)

For the marinade:
125ml/4fl oz good green olive oil
125ml/4fl oz dry white wine
50ml/2fl oz white wine vinegar
125ml/4fl oz water
2 tbsp Pernod
1 lemon, sliced
1 bay leaf
a few sprigs of parsley, dill and
    thyme
1 carrot, finely sliced
1 stick of celery, peeled and finely
    chopped
1 shallot, finely chopped
a generous pinch of molasses
    sugar
salt and pepper

For the potato salad:
450g/1lb waxy salad potatoes such
    as Pink Fir Apple or Anya
1 shallot, finely chopped
4 tbsp good olive oil
1 tbsp white wine vinegar
2 tbsp of flat-leaf parsley, chopped
sea salt and black pepper

Cut the mackerel into long, thin strips, 7.5 x 1.25cm/3 x ½in. Put all the marinade ingredients together in a bow, add the strips of fish and submerge them. Cover the bowl with cling film and refrigerate for at least 18 hours. Bring to room temperature before you serve.

An hour or two before you want to eat, prepare the potato salad. Boil the potatoes and skin them while still as hot as you can bear. Pour the various components of the dressing – shallot, olive oil, white wine vinegar, parsley and seasoning – over the potatoes while they are still hot and turn them gently to coat them in the dressing. Place a layer of the potato salad on each plate, or on one large plate. Then place some mackerel with its accompanying juices, vegetables and herbs on the potato summit.

Short of catching them myself, as I do in the west of Ireland, the only shrimps I would consider using for this stupendous, timeless classic of a dish are Morecambe Bay brown shrimps. Local fishermen have been catching them off the Cumbrian coast for over 100 years, and you can buy them at London's Borough Market or by mail order. The stockists are Furness Fish, Poultry and Game Supplies – see page 282 for details. The secret is all in the spicing: too much discretion and it will be invisible; too much flamboyance and all subtlety is lost, just like life. And it is the balance and quality of the spices that is important, no one should predominate, indeed, you should be nudged into awareness of each of them individually. They should be proper blades of mace and fresh nutmegs that you use, alongside a restrained measure of cayenne. You want it to hit but not hurt. Lecture over. This is a dish that will happily stand to attention in the fridge overnight or over two nights, and can then be turned out with its halo of set clarified butter and deep pink flesh to be eaten with warm granary toast and a glass of ice-cold Valdespino fino sherry.

Potted Shrimps

SERVES 6

up to 175g/6oz best unsalted
    butter, l'Escure or d'Isigny if
    possible
a small blade of mace
cayenne
nutmeg
600ml/1 pint peeled, cooked
    brown shrimps
salt, pepper, lemon juice

First clarify the butter: melt it slowly in a pan, leave it a couple of minutes, then pour the buttercup-yellow pure residue minus the milky curd-like solids into two small pans, half into each.

Crush the mace in a mortar and add it with the tip of a teaspoon of cayenne and a grating of nutmeg into one half of the warm butter. Taste and adjust the spicing, remembering that it has a bit of competing to do once you add the shrimps. Leave to infuse for 5–10 minutes, then stir in the shrimps. Season, spritz with a little lemon juice and put the mixture, packed tightly down, into 6 ramekins. Cool, then put in the fridge to set.

When set, pour a layer of clarified butter over the top of each ramekin, and return to the fridge to set again. Take the ramekins out of the fridge about 20 minutes before you want to serve them. Using a fine-pointed knife dipped in hot water, turn out each ramekin on to a plate. Serve with hot granary toast.

I will not be moved on the subject of salmon. I will not buy and will never knowingly eat the farmed stuff. The breeding methods, cocktails of chemicals and antibiotics, danger to the wild fish when the farmed ones escape and breed with them (thus weakening the gene pool), and the horrors of sea lice upon these poor, caged apologies of creatures, whose taste and texture is limp, greasy and flabby, is enough to make me determined that salmon should remain a special, albeit expensive, SEASONAL – that heretical word in supermarket quarters – treat. Once a year is fine by me, although I usually manage a couple of extra salmon caught by obliging friends in the west of Ireland in the summer. But it beats me why we have to pretend that salmon is not a luxury food and that it should be available all the year round. Thus are bad eating habits, greed and expectation manipulated by the food giants. Here is my recipe for fantastic ceviche, uncooked but pickled and preserved in its winey, citrusy marinade. To be eaten alongside a sambal of cucumber, fennel and avocado, with or without brown bread and butter.

Ceviche of Wild Salmon
with a Cucumber, Fennel and Avocado Sambal

SERVES 6—8

700g/1½lb wild salmon cut from
   the centre where it is fattest,
   skinned and filleted, which
   operation your fishmonger
   should perform willingly
175ml/6fl oz dry white wine
juice of 1 lime
juice of half an orange
juice of half a lemon
1 small onion, sliced into
   thin rings
1 clove of garlic, sliced thinly

Using a very sharp knife, carve the salmon, taken straight from the fridge, into slices 5mm/¼in thick and put them into a container that has a lid, an old plastic ice cream container is ideal. Add all the other ingredients, cover and refrigerate. Turn the salmon over from time to time.

It will be ready to eat after 8 hours, but keeps well for 2 days if you remember to remove the onion and garlic after the first day so that they don't overwhelm the flavour.

To serve, strain off the marinade and put a tablespoon of the sambal alongside the fish. Accompany with good wholemeal or soda bread if you like.

Cucumber, Avocado and Fennel Sambal

MAKES ENOUGH FOR 6-8

half a cucumber
half a red pepper
the flesh of an avocado
1 bulb of fennel, cored
lemon juice
a tiny bit of sugar
olive oil
black pepper
dill, finely chopped

This works well with a crab soufflé or fishcake too. Simply skin and seed half a cucumber and half a red pepper and chop them, with the inside of a cored bulb of fennel, as finely as you can, so that they are somewhere between dolls' sized and minced.

Chop the flesh from an avocado into slightly bigger cubes, then sprinkle over lemon juice, a tiny bit of sugar and turn in olive oil to taste. Finally add some black pepper and finely chopped dill.

At the sharp-aired turn of the season, this dish, beloved of the Swedes, with its earthy-sweet beetroot, sharp herring and crème fraîche, and combination of raw, cooked and pickled, captures and reflects the autumn to winter shift. In medieval England such dishes were known as 'salemine', which meant salty or highly seasoned, and referred to game as well as fish. They have transmuted over the centuries through 'salmagundi' to the more modern 'salmi.' Rollmops are not the answer. Either pickle your own herring with the very simple recipe given below or buy the Swedish pickled herrings in jars from Swedish Affar in Crawford St, London W1 or from Ikea. If you are salting your own herring and pickling your own beetroot, you need to start this dish three or four days before you want to eat it. If you've already pickled your beetroot and the herring is shop bought, start 24 hours before you want to serve it. Do not buy beetroot pickled in malt vinegar; it is too crude a substitute for white wine vinegar.

Sillsalad

SERVES 6

300g/10oz pickled herring fillets
4–6, depending on size, waxy-
  fleshed salad potatoes like Pink
  Fir Apple or Anya, cooked,
  skinned and cooled
4 medium-sized pickled beetroots
2 tart eating apples, preferably
  Coxes
2–3 large cornichons or 4–5
  smaller ones
1 small onion, finely chopped
crème fraîche
fresh dill

TO PICKLE HERRING: Put the fish in a plastic bag with one cup of coarse sea salt to 1kg/2¼lb of herring and store in a cool dark place for 1–4 days. Remove the backbone, fillet, and soak thoroughly in water to desalinate for 6–8 hours.

TO PICKLE BEETROOT: Put the whole cooked beetroots in a jar and pour over white wine vinegar and sugar, 4:1, to cover. Add one clove of garlic, a teaspoon of mustard seed and 6 cloves. Screw the lid on and the flavour will be absorbed after 2 days.

TO MAKE THE SALAD: Cut all the ingredients into rough 1cm/½in cubes and mix them together in a bowl. Add freshly ground pepper. Cover the salad and let it mature in the fridge for 24 hours.

When you're ready to serve, mix in the crème fraîche and chopped dill. Pile the salad on a serving dish, sprinkle with some more chopped dill and serve with some thinly sliced rye bread and butter.

As the author of *The Art of the Tart*, I have made my, and several other people's, fair share of tarts, to the extent that my publisher referred to me, during the gestatory period of the book, as 'the Queen of Tarts'. After the book was complete, I took a sabbatical. Neither a pudding nor a savoury crossed the threshold of my cooker, over or under pastry, for many months. Gradually the craving crept up on me, and first in line were these fabulous tomato and prosciutto tarts. I eased my way back into pastry making gently, by buying a sheet of the best puff pastry from Baker and Spice – see page 282 for details. L'Escure butter, French flour and a hand with a feather-light touch conspire with the recipe, which allows you to assemble the tarts before your guests arrive, to create as near a culinary heaven of a savoury, ambulant starter to be consumed with drinks as this side of paradise allows. So the only indulgence I crave is in repeating the recipe in this book.

Tomato and Prosciutto Tarts

MAKES 8 SMALL TARTS
preheat oven to 190°C/375°F/Gas 5

1kg/2¼lb sheet of Baker and Spice puff pastry, of which you will need 300g/10oz or so for this recipe and the rest you can freeze; or use a brand that is all butter, nothing else will do

8 slices prosciutto, San Daniele if possible

150ml/5fl oz best extra virgin olive oil

3 cloves of garlic

black pepper

10 plum tomatoes or about 40 organic cherry tomatoes

a handful of fresh basil and the same of either thyme or rosemary

Start with 300g/10oz of puff pastry. Roll it out, and stamp it out into eight 10cm/4in circles. Place them on a greased baking sheet and leave them in the fridge until you need them.

Tear the prosciutto roughly and put it in the food processor with half the olive oil, the garlic cloves and the pepper. Blitz for a few seconds to make a rough purée. Slice the plum tomatoes or halve the cherry tomatoes. Tear the basil leaves and add them to the remaining olive oil, but not more than 20 minutes before you are going to use them, or they will blacken.

Spoon a mound of the prosciutto mixture on to each tart base, leaving a good-sized edge free. Place a circle of tomatoes on top, brush with a little of the oil and basil mixture and sprinkle with chopped thyme or rosemary. Cook for about 15 minutes, until the pastry is puffed up, golden and cooked through. Put the tarts on a rack, brush with more of the oil and basil mixture and serve them warm.

Slow-roasted Tomato Tart

SERVES 6

For the pastry:
125g/4oz plain white flour
50g/2oz unsalted butter
pinch of sea salt
ice-cold water, about 2–2½ tbsp
1 egg white

For the filling:
1.4kg/3lb ripe plum tomatoes
6 cloves of garlic, sliced wafer thin
5 tbsp olive oil
2 tbsp balsamic vinegar
salt and black pepper
a little sugar
3 egg yolks
150ml/5fl oz crème fraîche
2 handfuls of basil leaves

Make the pastry in the usual way. Place in a 23cm/9in tin and chill for at least 30 minutes before baking. Preheat the oven to 190°C/375°F/Gas 5. Bake the pastry blind for 15 minutes, then remove the beans and return to the oven for 5 minutes. Brush egg white over the pastry and leave it to cool. Turn the oven down to 150°C/300°F/Gas 2 to bake the tart.

Place the tomatoes in a bowl and pour boiling water over them. Spike each one with the point of a knife and drain after a minute. Pour cold water over them and drain it off immediately; they will now be cool enough to handle. Slip the tomatoes out of their skins, slice them in half vertically and place them cut side up in a roasting dish. Lay the garlic slices inside the tomato halves. Dribble the olive oil and balsamic vinegar into the halves and sprinkle with the salt, pepper and a little sugar. Roast in the oven for about an hour, until shrunken and brown around the edges.

Arrange the roasted tomatoes in the pastry case, adding any juices from the roasting dish. Mix together the egg yolks and crème fraîche and tear in the basil leaves. Season with salt and pepper and pour the mixture over the tomatoes. Bake for 30–40 minutes, until the custard is set and lightly browned. Leave to stand for 10 minutes before turning out and serving.

This is a brilliant stand-in-the-kitchen-and-eat dish, which you can prepare in advance, cook in front of your friends and serve straight from the pan with drinks. It is a dish most suited to a fish or vegetarian main course. I, for one, do not advocate meat-heavy dinners. You raise the temperature with the spice, then cool it with the guacamole, all in one mouthful.

Spiced Pork Meatballs with Guacamole

SERVES 8—10 AS A DISH-
WITH-DRINKS

1.2kg/2½lb minced organic pork,
    fatty enough to stop the
    meatballs from drying out
    during the cooking
sea salt
1 red chilli, finely chopped
    with its seeds
1 tbsp root ginger, grated
1 tbsp flat-leaf parsley, chopped
1 tbsp fresh coriander, chopped
1 tsp fresh thyme, chopped
1 tbsp Dijon mustard
zest of a lemon

Throw everything into a large bowl and mix together well with your fingers, making sure that you don't rub your eyes afterwards; chilli is lethal. Form into small balls, the size of walnuts. At this point, you can leave the meat for an hour or two until you need it. Remember, if you cover the meatballs and put them in the fridge, don't cook them until they have come back to room temperature.

I cook mine on a griddle with no fat – there is enough in the meatballs – until crusted and crisped all over and cooked through to the stage where there are no pink juices flowing out of the meat when you test it with a skewer.

The guacamole can be chilled for up to an hour before you want it, so all you need to do is spoon it over the meatballs, cold with hot, when they are cooked.

Guacamole

SERVES 8—10

3 ripe organic avocados
juice of 3 limes
1 chilli, finely chopped,
    with its seeds
sea salt
a handful of fresh coriander
    leaves, chopped

Mash the avocados on a plate with a fork until they are smooth but with the odd lump for texture. Stir in the lime juice, and the chillies and salt. Scrape into a bowl, cover and chill for an hour. Stir in the coriander, taste and adjust the seasoning and citrus to taste. Lob spoons of it on to the pork meatballs hot from the griddle. If you want to eat this as a main course, you can make the pork balls into large, flat burgers, grill them in the same way, top them with guacamole and put them over and under a good floury bap or tortilla.

I hate English pumpkins. They are fibrous, watery and about as anaemic as you could never wish to be. If Anna del Conte and Richard Corrigan refuse to cook with English pumpkins, that's good enough for me. Richard at his brilliant Soho restaurant, Lindsay House, uses French, and Anna makes her *gnocchi di zucca* with butternut squash and sweet potato when she's in England, since they are the nearest approximation to the Italian pumpkin. This is a perfect autumnal dish, timely for the confluence of squash and porcini or chanterelles if, like me, you go out fungi foraging. If you don't, you can use organic chestnut or Portobello mushrooms.

Roasted Butternut Squash with Wild or Chestnut Mushrooms and Cream

SERVES 4
preheat oven to 180°C/350°F/Gas 4

2 butternut squash, allow half a
    squash per person
butter and olive oil
2 cloves of garlic, crushed
    in a mortar with some
    sea salt to a paste
pepper
2 tsp rosemary or sage leaves
300ml/10fl oz organic double
    cream, unpasteurized if you
    can get it
400g/14oz fungi, but stick to one
    kind; to dilute the porcini or
    chanterelles with another
    fungus is sacrilege
a handful of flat-leaf parsley,
    chopped

Cut the squash in half around their circumference and seed. You will find that the seeds are contained in only one of the halves, but scoop out some space in both cavities. Put a generous lump of butter and a splosh of best olive oil in each cavity, with a bit of the garlic paste, the finely chopped rosemary or sage and some ground black pepper. Reserve half the garlic for the mushrooms. Roast until the flesh is soft, 30–40 minutes.

Brush the earth off the porcini, or clean the mushrooms with a damp cloth, before slicing them and frying them in a bit of olive oil until they begin to weep with juice. Add the garlic and cream and allow it to bubble, stirring as you go. Scatter over the parsley, season and tip the contents of the pan into the squash cavities, stirring in the cream with the butter. Allow to cool for a few minutes before you bring the squash to the table.

Richard Corrigan included this unusual, delicately spiced dish on the St Patrick's Day menu we devised this year. It is beautifully uncheffy, and most of the preparation can be done the day before, so all you need to do on the day of eating is mix the cheeses and minced shallot and arrange the plates with slices of wild smoked salmon. A lovely starter or lunch dish.

Smoked Salmon with Saffron-braised Fennel

SERVES 4
preheat oven to 200°C/400°F/Gas 6

2 bulbs of fennel with the
　　root left on
100ml/3½fl oz water
200ml/7fl oz olive oil
3 star anise
a handful of green olives
　　preserved in good olive oil,
　　not brine, pitted and halved
a pinch of saffron
salt and pepper
8 slices of smoked salmon,
　　preferably wild
2 tbsp cream cheese
2 tbsp mascarpone cheese
1 tbsp shallots, very finely
　　chopped

Cut each fennel bulb in half, then each half into quarters or slices, depending on their size. Put them in a roasting tin or gratin dish with the water, olive oil, star anise, olives, saffron and seasoning. Bring slowly to the boil, then cover with tin foil and cook in the oven until tender. Check with a skewer after 20 minutes. Cool and refrigerate – this can be done the day before.

　　Mix the cheeses with the finely chopped shallot. On each plate, arrange the fennel with a mound made out of a couple of the slices of smoked salmon, then add a spoonful of the cheese mixture. Serve with Irish soda bread.

Nothing last-minute about this dish, which makes a perfect cold starter or one of a series of dishes to serve at an al fresco lunch in the summer. My friend Brigid has brought it over to me in the casserole before now, the artichokes from her garden.

Globe Artichokes in an Overnight Balsamic and Shallot Dressing

SERVES 4

4 globe artichokes
half a lemon
2–3 shallots, peeled and finely chopped
good olive oil
balsamic vinegar, the best aged vinegar you can find, mellow and glossily black
sea salt and black pepper

Bring a large pan of water to the boil and acidulate it with half a squeezed lemon. Throw in your artichokes and cook without a lid at a rolling boil until you can easily pull an outside leaf away from its parent stem, about 25–30 minutes. Remove and drain.

In a small pan, heat the finely chopped shallot very gently in some good olive oil until it is softened. Remove from the heat and whisk in the balsamic vinegar and seasoning to taste. Pour the warm dressing over the artichokes, and leave for as long as you can, preferably overnight. Before serving, spoon some of the escaped dressing over the artichokes.

Said to have been invented by a peasant for a hungry king, this dish has been cooked in Spain for at least 400 years. Every tapas bar seems to serve tortilla, with glasses of chilled fino or manzanilla, and although the classic rendering is made with potato, you may substitute onion, prawns, peppers, spinach, chard or what you will. I think tortillas make the perfect mouthful to accompany drinks, so absorbent are they, like blotting paper, arresting initial hunger pangs and any light-headedness concomitantly. The great thing, too, is that there is really no time of day I wouldn't serve a tortilla — late breakfast or brunch, lunch, on a picnic, in the early evening with drinks, or dinner itself. Tortilla can be served hot, warm or cold.

Tortilla Española

SERVES 4

450g/1lb potatoes, peeled and cut
    into small dice
6 large organic eggs
125ml/4fl oz best olive oil
sea salt and freshly ground pepper

Do not use a voluminous frying pan, you are making a cake of eggs, not a flat omelette. Heat the olive oil, and when it is hot, throw in the potatoes and coat them all over in the oil. Lower the heat and turn them gently every so often until they are cooked through. Remove the potatoes with a slotted spoon and drain them on kitchen paper in a bowl.

Heat the olive oil in the pan again, with a bit extra if you need it. Meanwhile, beat the eggs with the pepper and pour them over the potatoes, then pour the mixture into the hot oil in the pan and cook at a high heat for a minute before turning the temperature down. Add salt and cook until there is no sign of liquid egg at the top of the mixture. Cover with a plate and flip the tortilla over on to it, add a splosh more olive oil to the pan, then slide the tortilla back into the pan and cook for a further couple of minutes.

Serve hot or warm with a tomato sauce, on its own or with some Navarrico piquillo peppers, roasted over beech wood and imported by Brindisa. Or eat it cold and cut into wedges with a tomato salad. Once cooked, a tortilla will keep for a couple of days, and reheats well in a tomato sauce.

On my first night in Jerez, after flying into a pistachio green and smoked salmon sunset with Mark Sainsbury and Sam Clark of the lovely Moro restaurant in Clerkenwell, London, we were whisked off by our wonderful guide Bartolome Vergara to a tiny tapas bar. There we swiftly downed our glasses of chilled fino with dishes of tiny red mullet no bigger than leaves, and broad beans with Serrano ham, a wonderful combination.

Broad Beans with Serrano Ham

SERVES 6

1kg/2¼lb broad beans, fingernail sized, not the giant toughies
175g/6oz Serrano ham, prosciutto or organic green back bacon
4 tbsp good olive oil
175g/6oz onion, a mild one, very finely chopped
1 clove of garlic, finely chopped
4 large organic eggs
sea salt and black pepper
a handful of flat-leaf parsley, chopped

Cut or tear the ham into small strips and sauté it gently in the hot olive oil in a pan with the chopped onion until the onion is softened. Add the garlic and soften briefly. Throw in the broad beans, cover, turn down the heat and cook until they are tender, about 6–7 minutes.

Hard boil the eggs for about 7 minutes – I do not favour them being cooked until there is a grim black ring around a dried up planetary orb – then peel them and chop them.

Season the ham and beans, stir in the chopped egg and parsley and serve warm.

A lovely Provençal hors-d'oeuvre, black, oily, salt – perfect to whet the most recalcitrant of appetites. Serve with a glass of cold rosé.

Hard-boiled Eggs with Tapenade

SERVES 6 OR MORE IF
THERE ARE OTHER
DISHES

6 large organic eggs
24 stoned black olives,
   the good Mediterranean
   ones kept in olive oil
6 salted anchovies,
   desalinated and de-spined,
   or 10 fillets of anchovy
   in olive oil
2 tbsp salted capers,
   desalinated on a slotted spoon
   under a cold tap
50g/2oz best tinned tuna,
   Ortiz is fantastic
a scant teaspoon of
   Dijon mustard
olive oil
lemon juice
a few drops of eau de vie, Marc
   de Provence if you have it,
   or Cognac
pepper

Hard boil the eggs. Cut them in half lengthwise and scoop out the yolks to use in the tapenade.

Pound the egg yolks, black olives, anchovies, capers, tuna and mustard together in a mortar. Then gradually amalgamate a couple of tablespoons of olive oil into the mixture, followed by a spritz of lemon and a breath of spirit. Season with pepper to taste; you will not need salt because of the salt ingredients.

With a teaspoon, fill the white egg cavities with the black tapenade. Serve cool. The tapenade will keep well for days and is equally good spread like a pâté on fingers of warm toast to be served with drinks.

This is an elaborate version of a Provençal anchoiade with the strength of a tapenade – magical, particularly on a hot day. Serve it with fingers of country bread, Pugliese or Boule de Meule are ideal, which you have brushed with olive oil and baked in the oven.

Anchoiade de Croze

SERVES 8

1 dried red chilli
12 whole blanched almonds
6 salted anchovies,
   desalinated and de-spined,
   or 12 anchovies in olive oil
3 dried figs, roughly chopped
1 small onion, quartered
2 cloves of garlic, chopped
2 fronds of fennel
50g/2oz mixed parsley,
   chives and tarragon
olive oil
lemon juice
up to 1 tbsp orange flower water

Put the chilli, almonds, anchovies, figs, onion, garlic, fennel and herbs in the food processor. Process to a thick paste, pouring in the olive oil in a steady stream, then adding the lemon juice and any extra olive oil to taste. Finally add the orange flower water, a dessertspoon to start with, it must scent not overwhelm.

Instead of serving the anchoiade on baked bread, you can oil the bottom of the bread, spread the anchoiade on the top and bake in a hot oven for 10 minutes.

Tinned simply will not do. I am not saying ever, but texturally you will not accomplish this dish unless you cook them yourself. After all, soaking and cooking chickpeas has nothing to do with skill and time and everything to do with bothering, then leaving well alone. The effect of the libation of grassy, peppery olive oil upon hot, cooked chickpeas, or any other vegetable for that matter, is stimulant enough to the senses, releasing the scent of both and uniting them at the same time. When you stir in the chopped onion and parsley you complete the circle, scents and textures conjoined.

A Salad of Hot Chickpeas

SERVES 6

225g/8oz organic chickpeas
an onion stuck with a
    couple of cloves
1 carrot, chopped
1 stick celery, chopped
a sprig of thyme
a couple of fresh bay leaves
olive oil
a sprinkle of wine vinegar
sea salt
black pepper
1 small onion, finely sliced into
    rings
a little finely chopped red chilli or
    225g/8oz spinach (optional)
flat-leaf parsley, roughly chopped

Soak the chickpeas overnight in cold water. Next day, rinse them and just cover with fresh water in a large earthenware casserole. Add an onion stuck with a couple of cloves, a chopped carrot and stick of celery, a sprig of thyme and a couple of fresh bay leaves, bring to the boil, skim for your life, then cover and allow to simmer at a mere burble for 2 hours.

Drain the chickpeas, turn them into an earthenware serving dish and douse immediately with your best olive oil, a sprinkle of wine vinegar and sea salt, which you must never add during the cooking, since it will toughen the skins irredeemably. Add a good scrunch of black pepper and the onion, so finely sliced that the rings are papery thin and will wilt on contact with the hot chickpeas.

You may also add some finely chopped red chilli if you feel like it or some spinach, the baby leaves called pousse if possible, which you throw in raw so that they wilt into the warm assembly. Finally the parsley, a good green confetti of roughly chopped leaves. What could be simpler yet more delicious?

A delicate summer starter or lunch that you can leave in the fridge to set the night before you want it. How old fashioned are the connotations of a cold mousse, but a light touch with the gelatine, the creaminess, the cucumber crunch, and the pale, sappy green of the finished dish are timeless and should not be consigned to the folklore of an earlier culinary era. At the last minute, peel some ribbons of cucumber with a potato peeler, sash length if possible, and drop them into the centre of the mousse.

Cold Cucumber and Ricotta Mousse

SERVES 8

1 organic cucumber, peeled, seeded and diced small

1 heaped tsp sea salt

3 tbsp tarragon vinegar

15g/½oz packet of gelatine or the equivalent in leaf gelatine, my preference, see the packet for instructions

300ml/10fl oz organic double cream

500g/1lb 2oz fresh ricotta if you can get it, strained overnight through a sieve lined with muslin or a J-cloth, or a tub of ordinary ricotta from a supermarket which doesn't need straining

black pepper

a generous handful of chopped chives, parsley and spring onion

Mix the cucumber, salt and vinegar thoroughly in a bowl. Turn the mixture into a colander, put a plate on top and leave to drain for at least an hour. Remove the plate, and press down gently with a cloth.

Dissolve the gelatine in 6 tablespoons of very hot water, or as per the leaf gelatine instructions in cold water, and cool to tepid. Make sure the gelatine is thoroughly dissolved, then whisk in the cream gradually until the mixture is smooth and very thick but not stiff. Add the ricotta by passing it through the small disc of a food mill to aerate it as you go, then stir it in with the cucumber. Taste, and add a touch more tarragon vinegar and salt if you think it needs it, but do not make the taste too strong. Grind in the black pepper, then stir in the herbs and spring onion. Turn into an oiled mould, and set in the fridge overnight.

Turn out on to a large plate just before you want it, by slipping the mould into a basin of boiling water very briefly, then going round the edge of the mould with the point of a knife that you have dipped in hot water. Serve with some wholemeal or caraway rolls (see page 16).

An old-fashioned ring mould is the thing I like best for making this tomato cream in. You can heap some tiger prawns grilled with chilli, garlic and olive oil in the middle, or add some tepid broad beans that you have stewed in olive oil adding a spritz of lemon and some chopped chives at the end or simply some chopped tomatoes and cucumber. Or you can surround the dish with eggs stuffed with tapenade (see page 58). Another forgotten dish that should reassert itself in the culinary canon. A sort of tremblingly set Virgin Mary if you think of the ingredients.

Tomato Cream

SERVES 8

organic tomatoes of a kind that
    really taste, although I
    shouldn't have to say that
gelatine
225ml/8fl oz whipping cream
sea salt
Tabasco
Worcestershire sauce
sugar

Skin, process and sieve enough tomatoes to give you 400g/14fl oz. Mix in the gelatine, dissolved as in the recipe on page 62 or as per the instructions, then add salt, Tabasco, Worcestershire sauce and a little sugar to taste. The flavour should be strong, since the cream will mute it. You could also add some chopped tarragon, parsley and spring onion, or some chopped basil.

Chill until the mixture has thickened to the consistency of egg whites, then fold in the cream which you have whipped to stiffness but not rigidity.

Check the seasoning again, scrape into an oiled mould, and set in the fridge overnight. Turn out and serve with some chopped tomatoes dressed with herbs and oil.

The combination of garnet-hued beetroot, ivory sour cream and green snipped chives is as beautiful as it is delicious. The tomatoes add a sour note to the earthy sweetness of the beetroot.

Chilled Beetroot Soup

SERVES 6

1.4 litres/2½ pints chicken stock
about 500g/1 and a bit lb small
    beetroots, cleaned, their
    whiskery bits left intact
3 or 4 good-sized organic
    tomatoes, chopped
salt and fresh black pepper
lemon juice
150ml/5fl oz soured cream
2 tbsp chives, chopped

Bake the beetroots in individually wrapped foil parcels in a hottish oven until just tender when pierced with a skewer. Peel and cube them and add them to the hot stock, keeping one or two back to perk up the colour later. Add the chopped tomatoes, and keep the temperature at a blip for 20 minutes. Liquidize and sieve the soup, then let it cool and chill in the fridge.

Grate the remaining beetroot. Season the soup to taste, add a spritz of lemon juice, and pour into bowls. Add a spoon of grated beetroot and one each of sour cream and chives to each bowl.

Iced Broad Bean Soup

SERVES 4

125g/4oz onion, chopped
50g/2oz unsalted butter
1 litre/1¾ pints chicken stock,
    really concentrated and jellied
    if possible
450g/1lb shelled weight of tiny
    broad beans
sea salt, pepper, sugar
cream
a few leaves of lovage, finely
    chopped, or sage if you don't
    have lovage

Soften the onion gently in the butter in a heavy-bottomed casserole, sprinkling on some sea salt to draw out the moisture. Add three-quarters of the beans, stir for a minute and tip on the boiling chicken stock. Cook the soup at a simmer until the beans are done, about 5 minutes. Season with more salt, pepper and a tiny scrap of sugar.

Cook the rest of the beans even more briefly, by throwing them into boiling salted water for a couple of minutes, draining and refreshing in cold water, then peeling them. Fiddly, but worth it — the baby emerald embryos lurking like jewels in the soup make all the difference. Liquidize the soup, sieve it, then throw in the shelled beans and allow it to cool in a bowl before leaving the fridge for several hours before you drink it. You can stir in a bit of cream if you want a rich soup, I prefer not to. Sprinkle some lovage over each bowl when you serve it. You can eat this soup hot, in which case try frying the lovage leaves in a bit of butter until crisp, and then scattering them over the hot soup.

My cousin Deborah was horrified when she discovered I'd finished the manuscript for this book and she didn't feature. She has contributed to each of my books so far, and, more importantly, to my cooking and eating life since we were small, extremely greedy children. She remains one of the handful of people I most like to cook with, a rare attribute. We are totally simpatico in the kitchen, can communicate in shorthand and can totally trust one another to come up with the goods with no fuss and plenty of fun. We have always joked that if our careers were scrapheaped, we'd always be able to earn a crust cooking a good dinner together. If it came to it, we would! This is the first of her three recipes for this book.

Green Salad Soup

SERVES 6

1 medium potato
50g/2oz butter
1 medium onion
250g/9oz organic rocket
450g/1lb baby spinach
250g/9oz bunch watercress
300ml/10fl oz milk
600–900ml/1–1½ pints chicken or
    vegetable stock
salt and milled black pepper to
    taste
a few toasted almonds (optional)
single cream (optional)

Peel and chop the potato into small dice. Chop the onion finely. Melt the butter in a large saucepan and sweat the onion and potato until soft and transparent over a low heat for 5 to 10 minutes.

Add all the green leaves and sweat with the butter and onions until they have collapsed – about 5 minutes. Give them a stir from time to time. Add the stock and milk and simmer on a low heat for 10 minutes. Blitz the soup until you have a smooth purée and add salt and pepper to taste.

Garnish with a few toasted almonds and a swirl of single cream on each bowl before serving. The soup can be served hot or cold, and with or without the garnish

Predating Roman times, this ancient soup is said to have as many versions as there are mortars and pestles. If you are making it at the last minute, it can be whacked into the freezer for a 30-minute freeze down. If you have time, make it the day before you need it, keep it in the fridge overnight and allow the intense flavours to mingle. On the day, just add a jug of cold water and stir to the desired texture and strength. I serve mine in glasses, but if you want to add little bits of chopped egg, olive, pepper, onions or jamon, serve the soup in bowls and let people spoon in the accompaniments. Do use organic vegetables if you can.

Gazpacho

SERVES 6—8

450g/1lb tomatoes, use organic
  tinned tomatoes with their
  juice if you can't get good
  tomatoes
2 slices stale white bread without
  the crusts
1 small onion, cut into chunks
2 cloves garlic, chopped
1½ red peppers
1 cucumber, half-peeled,
  quartered lengthwise and
  seeded
2 tbsp best sherry vinegar
2 tbsp best olive oil
sea salt and cayenne
600—900ml/1—1½ pints very cold
  water straight from the fridge

Chop the tomatoes. I don't bother to skin them – you may prefer to – but I do halve and seed. Hold the bread under the cold tap, then squeeze out the water and put it in the food processor with the onion, garlic, a teaspoon of sea salt, the olive oil and cayenne. The soup is meant to be piquant not hot, so start with the tip of a teaspoon of cayenne, and correct at the end if it is not quite right. Blitz briefly to a pulp.

Add the cucumber, pepper, vinegar and tomato and blitz until liquid. The mixture will be coarse rather than puréed. Pour into a bowl, cover and chill as above. Just before serving, dilute with the fridge-cold water, stirring and tasting to the required texture and flavour, adjust the seasoning and serve in tall glasses or bowls.

Dating back more than a thousand years to when the Moors ruled much of Spain, this is one of my favourite soups. Utterly unusual and subtle, it has an extraordinary ability to cool the imbiber on the hottest of days.

White Gazpacho, or Ajo Blanco con Uvas de Malaga

SERVES 4

125g/4oz organic Spanish almonds, I use Rapunzel which you can get at Planet Organic and good health food shops
225g/8oz day-old organic white bread, the crusts removed
2 cloves of new season's garlic, peeled
sea salt
2–3 tbsp best olive oil
2 tbsp sherry vinegar, Valdespino if you can get it
600ml/1 pint water you have chilled in the fridge
a handful of seedless green grapes

Blanch the almonds briefly in hot water and pop them out of their skins. Process the almonds until ground or do it yourself in a mortar yourself if you are feeling purist and energetic.

Wet thick slices of bread under the cold tap, then squeeze it out. Tear it into chunks and throw it into the blender with the chopped garlic, salt and olive oil. Purée, then add the vinegar and almonds and slowly pour in the cold water with the blender running. Process until smooth and creamy, then refrigerate for several hours.

Ladle into bowls and toss a few halved seedless green grapes into each one.

Sally Edwards, whose alternative River Café – the Taunton, not the London emporium – closed this summer, robbing a bunch of hard-line lunchers of the only star-in-the-diadem in what is a culinary desert, gave me this recipe when I wrote about her plans to go solo with a new café. They should have come to fruition by the time you read this book. In the meantime, several of her stunning recipes grace these pages and help the withdrawal symptoms for me at least, who now has no escape from the stove of a Saturday lunchtime. Sally makes her soup with a vegetable stock; I made my version with chicken stock. Experiment.

Thai Lettuce and Pea Soup

SERVES 6

1 tsp coriander seeds
1 tsp cumin seeds
2 medium onions,
    roughly chopped
1 tbsp olive oil
2 cloves of garlic,
    peeled and chopped
1 thumb fresh ginger, peeled
    and chopped or grated
½ tsp fresh chilli paste, Sally uses
    Bart's Spices fresh hot chilli in
    sunflower oil, or you can use
    some seeded red chilli crushed
    in the mortar with a bit of salt
1 medium potato,
    peeled and cubed
1 vegetable stock cube,
    organic if possible, dissolved
    in 900ml/1½ pints of hot water
400ml/13fl oz tin coconut milk
300g/10oz fresh or frozen peas
1 lettuce

Roast the coriander and cumin seeds briefly in a frying pan for only 30 seconds or so until they exude their scent; any longer and they burn.

Sauté the onion gently in a little olive oil. Add the garlic, ginger, spices and chilli and sauté for a few more minutes until softened and translucent. Add the potato and stock, then simmer together for 25–30 minutes.

Add the coconut milk, bring back to a simmer. Add the peas and lettuce and bring it back to a simmer before removing from the heat. Process in the blender, season and serve.

With its swirl of vermilion rouille, this corn-yellow soup is a picture of autumn and a bowl of balance: strong colours and flavours that neither suppress nor overwhelm each other.

Sweetcorn Soup with a Rouille

SERVES 6

6 corn cobs
40g/1½oz unsalted butter
1 medium onion, peeled and
    finely chopped
1 leek, white part only, washed
    and chopped
1 small carrot, peeled and diced
2 cloves of garlic, peeled and
    finely chopped
1.2 litres/2 pints chicken, duck or
    vegetable stock
6 tbsp double cream
salt, pepper, sugar and lemon
    juice
fresh coriander, chopped
    (optional)

For the rouille:
200g/7oz jar pimentos, I prefer
    Brindisa's piquillo peppers
1 clove of garlic
2 red chilli peppers, seeded
2 tbsp olive oil

Strip the kernels from the corn cobs with a sharp knife. Melt the butter, add the onion and stew gently with the leek and carrot in a heavy-bottomed pan until translucent. Add the garlic about 10 minutes into the cooking. Pour over the hot stock, and carry on simmering for 10 minutes.

Add the kernels of corn, bring the soup back to the boil, then take the pan off the heat. Leave the pan for 5 minutes before puréeing in your blender. It will need a good 2 or 3 minutes before it is liquidized enough for you to push it through a sieve. Then stir in the cream and season to taste with sugar and lemon as well as salt and pepper. If the corn is young and sweet enough, you will not need any sugar.

Make the rouille by simply placing the pimentos, garlic, chilli and olive oil in the blender with some seasoning and whizzing them to a scarlet paste to be dropped into the centre of the corn yellow soup. Add a scattering of coriander leaves over the summit if you feel like it.

What an amenable root the parsnip is. It is enhanced by spicing, so makes a stunning curried soup. It also allows its sweetness to be offset by a good, sharp cooking apple. I used the windfalls from under my apple tree in this autumnal concoction.

Parsnip and Baked Apple Soup

SERVES 6

1 small onion, peeled and finely chopped
750g/1lb 10oz parsnips, peeled and diced
1 large cooking apple
50g/2oz unsalted butter
1.2 litres/2 pints chicken stock or vegetable stock if you're a veggie
6 sage leaves, tied in a bundle with string
150ml/5fl oz cream (optional)
salt, pepper, flat-leaf parsley

Score the cooking apple around its circumference, core it and bake it on a tray with 1cm/½in of water. Bake in a hot oven until tender right through when pierced with a skewer.

Sweat the onion and parsnip in the butter gently for about 10 minutes, seasoning early on, then pour in the stock and sage and simmer until tender. Remove the sage, liquidize the soup, adding the apple that you have peeled when it comes out of the oven, ensuring that there are no nasty toenaily bits around the core.

Check the seasoning, reheat with the cream, or without, and serve with a scattering of chopped parsley.

Cabbage and Bacon Soup

SERVES 4–6

25g/1oz butter
1 small onion, chopped
125g/4oz organic smoked back
  bacon, snipped into strips
450g/1lb head of cabbage, cored
  and shredded
1 potato, peeled and diced
1.2 litres/2 pints chicken stock
salt and pepper
a few tbsp of single cream

Melt the butter and gently soften the onion and bacon. Stir in the cabbage and potato, then add the stock and bring to the boil. Simmer gently until the cabbage and potato are soft, about 30 minutes. Season, liquidize, reheat, adjust the seasoning and stir in a few tablespoons of cream.

Sweet Potato and Coriander Soup

SERVES 6

2 large onions, peeled and diced
1cm/½in fresh ginger, grated
4 tbsp vegetable oil
4 large sweet potatoes, pink
  tinged if possible, peeled and
  diced
1.5 litres/2½ pints chicken or
  vegetable stock
225ml/8fl oz coconut cream
a handful of fresh coriander,
  chopped
sea salt and black pepper

Heat the oil in a large pan and sweat the onions and ginger until softened but not coloured. Add the sweet potatoes and stock and bring to the boil. Simmer gently until the sweet potatoes are tender, then add the coconut cream, coriander, salt and pepper to taste. Purée the soup in a blender or food processor, gently reheat and adjust the seasoning before serving if necessary.

It seems that every nation but the English has a version of one-pot soup-stew; think of ribollita, pot au feu, borscht, for which you simmer in water whatever meat you happen to have and any pulses and vegetables you can find. The following recipe is Scottish, not English; a soup of substance and address that is not really asking for anything to follow it. Quite the reverse, it is almost saying 'I bet you can't eat anything after this'.

Barley Broth

SERVES 8

1.5 kg/3lb 5oz neck of lamb or
   mutton
125g/4oz organic barley
125g/4oz split peas
2 carrots, diced
1 turnip, diced
1 swede, diced
2 onions or fat leeks, diced
salt and pepper
a handful of flat-leaf parsley,
   chopped

Put the meat in the bottom of a large, heavy-bottomed pot, add 2.2–2.8 litres/4–5 of pints of water, then the barley and peas. Bring it to the boil slowly, skim until clear, then simmer slowly for an hour if it's mutton, 30 minutes if it's lamb. I mean so slowly that a bubble barely breaks the surface. Add the vegetables and continue simmering until the meat is really tender. This could take as long as an hour.

When the meat is cooked, remove it and the vegetables, barley and pulses from the pot. Boil down the broth until you have a more intense flavour. Season, remove the meat from the bones if you feel like a modicum of refinement and return everything to the pot to heat through. Throw a good handful of chopped parsley into the pot and serve.

The mealy sweetness of sweet potato, with its beautiful orange flesh, and the sharp acidity of the cherry tomatoes with a smidgen of molasses sugar to add minerally, treacly back notes, is an unexpectedly good combination in a soup. And the colour is like an extravagantly unbelievable sunset.

Baked Sweet Potato and Roasted Cherry Tomato Soup

SERVES 6
preheat oven to 200°C/400°F/Gas 6

6 medium-sized orange-fleshed
    sweet potatoes
1 onion
450g/1lb or so of organic cherry
    tomatoes
a sprig of thyme
olive oil
a scrap of chilli
a sprig of rosemary
1 litre/1¾ pints chicken stock
1 heaped tsp molasses sugar

Cut the sweet potatoes, in their skins, into chunks, about 3 per potato. Cut the onion into large chunks, and place both on a roasting tray. Splash over a little olive oil, scatter over some thyme leaves, some finely chopped rosemary, a scrap of finely chopped, seeded red chilli, sea salt and black pepper and turn the vegetables in the mixture to coat. Bake for about 30 minutes, they will not be hard when you test them, but they will not have reached softness through and through either.

Slide in the tomatoes, and a bit of extra olive oil if it looks as though there isn't enough to gloss them, and return the vegetables to the oven for 15–20 minutes, when everything should be done: the tomatoes weeping their luscious juices and beginning to split at the seams, the onion caramelized and the sweet potatoes totally tender.

Skin the sweet potatoes while still as hot as you can stand and throw them into a food processor with everything else, including the stock which you have brought to the boil, and the molasses sugar. Bring back just to the boil and taste for seasoning and sweetness. If the tomatoes have made the soup too sharp, add a little more sugar and serve.

Every so often, only mild and delicate will do. There are times when I just do not feel like a gutsy, deep-flavoured soup, but something pure and one note, reassuring in its simplicity and in the fact that it tastes of itself and its strength of character can stand alone. Florentine fennel with its slightly medicinal astringency is one such flavour that can support a pale but interesting soup. A much underused and undervalued vegetable.

Cream of Fennel Soup

SERVES 4

3 fennel bulbs, with their wispy fronds, but ruthlessly robbed of their tough skinned layers, chopped
1 small onion, chopped
olive oil
butter
1 tsp of dill seeds
900ml/1½ pints chicken stock
salt, pepper
lemon juice
a few tbsp single cream

Heat the oil and butter, a splosh of one, 30g/1½ oz or so of t'other, in a heavy-bottomed pan. Add the fennel and onion, with the dill seeds, about a teaspoon, and some salt and pepper and soften gently with a lid on for 15–20 minutes, peeking occasionally and giving an encouraging stir. Then add the hot stock and simmer until the vegetables are soft, about 15 minutes, before you push everything through the coarse disc of a mouli-légumes, my preference, or liquidize and sieve if you haven't got a mouli.

Add a few tablespoons of cream, taste, adjust the seasoning and cream and add a tiny spritz of lemon if you feel like cutting the creaminess a little. Reheat to boiling point, but do not let it boil, and serve.

You could, if you like, serve this soup with Parmesan crisps, or just *au natur* with a good roll or a ficelle with fennel and poppy seeds, such as they make at Baker and Spice.

This soup does have guts, though they be vegetarian guts, and will quite happily stand alone as a main course. The flavours of chickpea, rosemary and tomato predominate and then you add, at the last minute, some tiny pasta such as ditalini and finish with a sprinkling of grated Parmesan cheese. You can make the soup up to the point of cooking the pasta two or three days in advance and keep it in the fridge. You then reheat it, cook the ditalini and serve with a bowl of Parmesan and a pile of soca.

Chickpea Soup with Pasta

SERVES 6

300g/10oz dried chickpeas, soaked overnight in plenty of water and a dsrtsp of bicarbonate of soda

2 litres/3½ pints vegetable stock, either home-made with 2 bulbs of fennel, 2 stalks of celery, a couple of onions and carrots, a leek and a bunch of parsley and its stalks tied with a bay leaf, or an organic stock cube, or water

2 large sprigs of rosemary

6 cloves of garlic, peeled and bruised with the back of a knife

best olive oil

300g/10oz organic tomatoes, skinned and seeded, or a 400g/14oz tin if there aren't any good ripe ones

175g/6oz tiny pasta like ditalini

freshly grated Parmesan cheese

salt and black pepper

Drain and rinse the chickpeas, put them in a large enamel pot and cover them with the vegetable stock or water. Add the sprigs of rosemary, preferably inside muslin since they are not the easiest thing to fish out by their needles at the end, the garlic, and 2 tablespoons of olive oil. Put the lid on the pan and bring to the boil, then lower the heat to an unpersistent simmer and cook for 2 hours before you check to see if the chickpeas are soft. They will harden if you lift the lid early in the cooking or salt them before they are cooked.

When they are cooked, remove the garlic and rosemary and add the tomatoes, which you have put through a mouli-légumes or processed. Season and simmer a further 10 minutes. Cook the pasta separately and add to the pan when it is *al dente*.

You may omit the pasta if you feel like it, in which case, you could purée half the soup for texture before returning it to the pan. It would be too thick to serve like this with pasta.

Serve the soup in hot bowls, with a bowl of freshly grated Parmesan cheese to hand round.

These little pancakes, made from chickpea or gram flour, are simple to make and perfect to accompany the chickpea and pasta soup opposite. Gram flour is available from Indian food stores, health food shops and good supermarkets.

Soca

MAKES 12

125g/4oz chickpea or gram flour
1 tbsp fresh rosemary or sage,
    finely chopped
olive oil
300ml/10 fl oz of water
sea salt

About 40 minutes before you want to serve the soup, mix the chickpea flour with a pinch of sea salt, a couple of teaspoons of rosemary and a tablespoon of olive oil. Add enough water to give the mixture the consistency of single cream when you have whisked it well. Let it stand for 30 minutes.

Whisk again, then brush the bottom of a heavy frying pan with olive oil. Heat until beginning to smoke, then drop a ladleful of the mixture into the pan, tilting the pan as you go to get a uniform covering. Sprinkle immediately with a little more chopped rosemary, fry for 2 to 3 minutes, then flip over and cook the other side.

Slide the cooked pancake on to a warmed plate and keep warm in a warming oven while you make the other 11.

Another meal in a bowl, or precursor to something light, say steamed or poached fish. It is one of the few dishes that never falls from favour with all three of my children, a distinct plus when one spends a lot of one's life feeling a little like a jaded short-order chef, struggling to keep up with the whims and mercurial fads of one's dependents.

Lentil and Pasta Soup with Smoked Bacon

SERVES 6

3 tbsp olive oil
2 small onions, finely chopped
6 cloves of garlic, finely chopped
2 sticks of celery, peeled and finely chopped
125g/4oz organic smoked streaky bacon, snipped small
225g/8oz Puy or Umbrian lentils, each the ultimate from their respective birthplaces
2 x 400g/14oz tins organic tomatoes
1.4 litres/2½ pints chicken or vegetable stock, or water
3 sprigs of thyme and 2 fresh bay leaves
225g/8oz small, tubular pasta, but not as minute as ditalini
sea salt and black pepper
a handful of flat-leaf parsley
125g/4oz Parmesan cheese, freshly grated

Heat the oil in a large, heavy-bottomed casserole, add the onions, celery and bacon and cook slowly until softened and translucent. Introduce the garlic after about 10 minutes, so it doesn't become bitter. Add the lentils and stir to coat them in the oil and bacon fat. Add the tomatoes, chopping them down into the juice with a sharp knife, bring up to a bubble, then pour over the hot stock or water. Add the thyme and bay, and bring to the boil. Cover and simmer for about 40 minutes, until the lentils are cooked. If the lentils are absorbing too much liquid, and beginning to look too thick for a soup, add a ladleful more of water whenever necessary. Season when the lentils are cooked through.

Cook the pasta separately until *al dente*, then add it to each soup bowl when ready. If you have enough soup left over to reheat, you need to cook fresh pasta for it, since pasta goes very soggy if it is left in soup and then reheated.

As with chickpea soup on page 80, this can be made a couple of days in advance, up to the point where you cook the pasta, and kept in the fridge until needed.

This is a classic Spanish soup, whose peasant ingredients and apparent simplicity belie its fragrance and subtlety. Garlic, chorizo, bread and eggs – nourishment to the soul enlivened with sweet smoked paprika.

Sopa de Ajo

SERVES 4

a few tbsp of fruity olive oil

4 bulbs of garlic, broken into cloves in their skins

85g/3oz small organic chorizo, Swaddles Green Farm make a lovely one

a sprig of thyme

the tip of a tsp of sweet smoked paprika; it is as easy to overdo it as it is with cayenne, beware

1.2 litres/2 pints chicken stock

4 organic eggs

4 slices of country bread, Pugliese or sourdough, toasted and torn into rough bits

sea salt and black pepper

Heat 3–4 tablespoons of oil in a heavy-bottomed pan, then add the garlic and cook gently for about 20 minutes until the skins are golden and the flesh inside softened. Remove, and squeeze out the innards as soon as the cloves are cool enough. Crush to a purée in a mortar with a little salt. Cut the chorizo into matchstick strips and fry in the oil until browned, then strip off the thyme and add it for a few seconds, followed by the garlic.

Add the paprika and then pour over the hot chicken stock. Bring to the boil, then turn down to a simmer, and season.

About 2 minutes before serving, add the toasted bread, drop the eggs into the soup to poach, then serve immediately.

Golden saffron-infused liquor, ready for cooking a wonderful monkfish dish served with a spicy romesco sauce. Nothing complicated here but a spectacular result.

time to cook

2

It had to be good. The marathon culinary weekends undertaken by me and my friend George Morley when she comes to stay for the weekend have a lot to live up to. She is an outstanding cook, and as outstanding a scavenger of good recipes as I have come across, but then neither of us is entirely uncompetitive in that particular department. Last time she came to stay, I was in the throes of making a series for the BBC's new digital UK Food channel. A team of 15 was filming my weekends – alarmingly, every day became a weekend for 16 days. For once, I couldn't wait for Monday to mean Monday. George HAD to figure, she is one of the few cooks with whom it is a real pleasure to share a kitchen. On equal terms. Unfazed as ever, she arrived with her new-found recipe for bitter orange ice cream. Enough to make you swoon, despite the stress of it. In turn, she was treated to this dish and added a swag of her own, the most divine crushed Jersey potatoes with olive oil and thyme. I added the thyme – that is how things evolve when we start cooking. The result, we agreed, was up to standard, and that, in our most critical joint case, means quite something. Sunset-coloured saffron and romesco, ivory potato, courgettes fried with pine nuts, sultanas and lemon juice. A feast of a dish. And her bitter orange ice cream, accompanied by tiny home-made hazelnut and orange biscuits (mine), was a triumph.

You can make the gaudily brilliant sunset of a sauce an hour, even a day ahead, to dollop on top of the crocus-coloured fish, which can be served hot, warm or cold. Any left-over sauce can be kept for several days, versatile as it is, to eat with pork, chicken, vegetables or fish. The fish needs 30 minutes or so to soak in its saffrony milk bath.

Monkfish Steeped in Saffron Milk with a Romesco Sauce

SERVES 5

For the sauce:

25g/1oz whole blanched almonds

25g/1oz whole roasted hazelnuts

225g/8oz skinned and seeded
  tomatoes, or the equivalent
  from a tin, with juice

2 cloves of garlic, finely chopped

6 tbsp best olive oil

a slice of stale bread, brown or
  white

2 tbsp red wine vinegar

4 tbsp fino sherry

1 red chilli, seeded and finely
  chopped, or cayenne to taste

For the monkfish:

a 1.2kg/2½lb piece of monkfish
  tail, taken from the thick end,
  on the bone

a generous pinch of saffron
  stamens

a few tbsp of milk

olive oil

sea salt and freshly ground pepper

FOR THE SAUCE: Roast the almonds briefly in a moderate oven until pale gold. Heat 4 tablespoons of the olive oil in a pan slowly, with the chopped garlic. When the oil is hot, remove and reserve the garlic and fry the bread briefly on both sides until crisp and golden. Remove from the pan, add 2 more tablespoons of oil and then the tomatoes and chill and stir until they are reduced and jammily thickened. About 10–15 minutes. Grind the nuts in a food processor, or a mortar for a better texture, then add the bread and garlic and continue to pound with the vinegar and sherry. Stir in the cooled tomato sauce, and serve in the mortar.

FOR THE MONKFISH: Cut the monkfish away from the bone, then cut each fillet into slices 5mm/¼in thick. Warm a few tablespoons of milk, then take the pan off the heat, add the saffron, cover and leave to infuse for around 30 minutes. Put the fish in a single layer in a large dish and cover with the saffron milk. Heat some olive oil in a frying pan, add the pieces of fish and cook for a couple of minutes or so on each side. The point of a skewer should find the fish consistently soft right the way through when it is cooked. Season and keep the fish warm on a plate in the oven while you cook the the copious saffron-hued liquor to reduce it by about a half. Pour it over the fish, and serve with the romesco sauce and the vegetables on the following page.

Griddled Courgettes

SERVES 4—6

6 small to medium courgettes
olive oil
lemon juice
sea salt and black pepper

Slice the courgettes lengthwise into long, thin tongues and brush both sides with olive oil. Heat your griddle, having oiled it first, slap on the courgette tongues and cook for a few minutes on each side until just resistant and branded with brown stripes. Remove, season and spritz with a bit of lemon juice. Good served hot, warm or cold.

Crushed New Potatoes with Olive Oil and Thyme

SERVES 4—6

1.2kg/2½lb new potatoes, Jersey
    for preference, scraped
best olive oil
2 or 3 sprigs of thyme
sea salt and crushed black pepper

Steam the new potatoes until tender. Tip them into a large earthenware dish or heavy pot with a few tablespoons of really verdant, grassy olive oil and crush briefly with a masher. Aim, as you wouldn't for mash, for a lumpy texture. Add the stripped thyme leaves and seasoning, then some more olive oil, and stir with a wooden spoon until softly lumpy and amalgamated.

The potatoes should taste of the oil, so it really is essential not to just use any old commercial olive oil, I use Seggiano or Ravida for this sort of dish. Both are available at many of the good, independent food shops and delis, or by mail order from The Fine Cheese Company in Bath (see page 282).

Left: *Monkfish Steeped in Saffron Milk, with Griddled Courgettes*

This is wonderful with the monkfish and with much else besides. It is really a courgette salad – it can be served as part of a vegetarian lunch or supper and eaten hot, warm or cold. I serve it with the tomato and goat's camembert tart from my book *The Art of the Tart*, or with pork, veal or chicken. Don't worry about the courgettes being unevenly cooked. That, according to my friend George, is part of the charm of the dish – some are browned, some firm, some almost cooked to a pale green pulp.

Courgette, Pine Nut and Sultana Salad

SERVES 4–6

6 medium courgettes
olive oil
2 cloves of garlic, peeled and
   finely chopped
a handful of sultanas
a handful of pine nuts
lemon juice
sea salt and black pepper

Slice the courgettes into what my children refer to as money courgettes, and throw them into a heavy-bottomed frying pan in which you have heated a few tablespoons of good olive oil. Cook, stirring as you go, until they are no longer completely firm and resistant. I hesitate to offer a time, as size and heat are the deciding factors, but around 7 minutes.

Then add the sultanas, pine nuts, garlic and plenty of seasoning. Let the pine nuts brown slightly before adding lemon juice to taste – use at least one whole lemon and possibly more. Cook everything together briefly to marry the flavours, then turn out on to a serving dish, preferably one of a contrasting colour to show them off best.

There are movable feasts and interchangeable feasts. The next four dishes are the latter. You may use guinea fowl or pheasant instead of chicken. Just pay attention to the cooking times accordingly: jointed pheasants, say, are smaller than jointed chicken. If it is a whole bird you are cooking, always pierce the bird right through the leg with a skewer and wait for the juices to run clear.

I jointed a plump, small organic chicken from The Ark Chicken Company to make this deliciously simple but festive dish, and included the wings for succulence and glueiness. The sharpness of the vinegar was bubbled away and mellowed with a bit of molasses sugar. I added little bits of butter at the end to gloss the sauce to a shiny caramel colour. You do not always need to add wine to a stewed dish; indeed, the wine vinegar makes this dish less rich, but allows the flavour of the chicken and its exceptionally good texture to come through.

Pollo alla Cacciatore, or
Chicken Cooked with Red Wine Vinegar and Herbs

SERVES 4

1 organic chicken, about
    1.4kg/3lb weight
50g/2oz organic smoked streaky
    bacon (I use Swaddles Green
    Farm's because they cure
    without nitrites)
a sprig of rosemary, 4 sage leaves,
    2 fresh bay leaves and a little
    bunch of thyme
olive oil and unsalted butter
4 or 5 Navarrico piquillo peppers,
    cut in strips, or 1 dried chilli
2 large cloves of garlic, peeled and
    bruised with the back of a knife
100ml/3½ fl oz good red wine
    vinegar
1 tsp sugar
50g/2oz butter
sea salt and pepper

Joint the chicken so that you have 4 pieces of leg, 4 pieces of breast and 2 wings. Snip the bacon into small strips. With a mezzaluna or sharp knife, chop all the herbs together really finely and roll them into the bacon.

In a large, heavy-bottomed casserole that will fit all the chicken pieces in a single layer, heat a generous splosh of good olive oil with a lump of butter, about 50g/2 oz. Gently sauté the bacon and herb mixture with the dried chilli if you are using it, and the cloves of garlic. Remove the chilli and garlic once you sense the aroma of them has been released into the dish. Add the pieces of chicken, season and brown properly on both sides for a total of 15 minutes. Add the strips of piquillo pepper at this stage if you are using them. Raise the heat and add the red wine vinegar, then let it bubble furiously for a minute or so before adding 150ml/5fl oz of hot water.

Reduce the temperature to a gentle simmer, cover with a lid and cook for a further 30 minutes, by which time the chicken will be tender when pierced with a skewer. Remove the chicken with all the herbs, peppers and bacon to a heated dish and keep warm.

Boil down the juices for a few minutes with a teaspoon of sugar until they become more syrupy. Add some small pieces of butter to make the sauce glossy, check the seasoning and pour the sauce over the chicken. Everyone can have half a breast and a piece of leg, and you still have the wings to suck on. I served this with brown jasmine rice and steamed ruby chard.

Organic guinea fowl, reared by the Ark Chicken Company (see page 282) are around 1.2–1.4kg/2½–3lb in weight, and Jason Wise will hang them for you for up to a week, uneviscerated, which is just how I like mine. That way, the flesh begins to break down and tenderize, and the gamey flavour emerges without overwhelming. I threw both feet and giblets into the pot to help the juices along. I cooked this whole dish in about 45 minutes and it was sensational, the organic smoked streaky bacon adding flavour to the earthy lentils, and the Marsala, which I added in lieu of port, sweetening and fortifying the pan juices. Puy lentils are the best of the French, Umbrian the best of the Italian.

Guinea Fowl with Puy Lentils, Lardons and Marsala

SERVES 4

1 guinea fowl, hung for a week,
  with its giblets and feet
olive oil
a knob of butter
sea salt and black pepper
a glass of Marsala (or port)
225g/8oz Puy or Umbrian lentils,
  unsoaked
a fat clove of garlic, skinned and
  crushed with the back of a knife
a bay leaf
a bunch of fresh thyme
125g/4oz organic smoked streaky
  bacon, cut into thin strips
  without the rind
3 large organic carrots, peeled and
  finely sliced
12 shallots, peeled, optional
a bit of double cream, optional

Heat a good-sized knob of butter and a generous splash of olive oil in a heavy-bottomed casserole. When they begin to bubble, put the whole guinea fowl in the pot and brown it first on one side, then on the other for about 4 minutes a side.

In the meantime, wash the lentils and place them in another heavy-bottomed pot. Add the garlic, bay leaf, bunch of thyme, bacon and a good scrunch of pepper, just cover with water and bring to the boil. Skim, turn the heat to a simmer, cover with a lid and continue to cook at a mild simmer, checking the pot from time to time, and adding a bit more water if the level gets too low.

After 20 minutes, bury the carrots and shallots, if you are using them, in the lentils and continue to cook until everything is softened and cooked through. Add some butter to the little bit of remaining liquid, season with salt and pepper, add a splosh of double cream if you are feeling so inclined, which I was, and keep the lentils hot.

Returning to the guinea fowl, brown each breast for 2 minutes before turning the bird over and sitting it on its back on the bottom of the pot. Season well and continue to cook gently for about 10 minutes. Add the giblets, feet and Marsala, turn the bird on to its side again, cover the pot with a lid, and continue to cook for another 7 minutes a side, followed by another few minutes breast up.

Pull a leg gently away from the bird sufficiently to see whether it still looks faintly raw and stick a skewer in to see if the juices still run red. If the answers are 'no' and 'no', pour the juices from the cavity into the pot as you remove the bird to a carving board, and let it rest for a few minutes. Place a shovelful – sorry, I am allergic to the word 'bed' – of lentils on each plate. Give everyone half a leg and some breast, then pour over the pan juices. Mashed potato, and plenty of it, is a *sine qua non*.

There are dishes whose pedigree is so unimpeachable you cannot alter them one iota, they are true thoroughbreds. This particular one came into my hands through two generations of top-drawer cooks, Tim Withers of The George and Dragon at Rowde in Wiltshire, whose dish it is, via the illustrious chef and food writer Simon Hopkinson. As Simon has noted, '50 grams of tarragon may seem a lot but, believe me, it makes all the difference.' I cannot implore you enough to try this dish: it is as good as it gets and there is no difficulty in its execution. Even if there were it would be worth it. Worthy of your most serious or celebratory of occasions.

Chicken Savoyarde

SERVES 6

For cooking the chicken:
1 x 2kg/4¼lb organic chicken
2 onions, peeled, and one of them
    stuck with 2 cloves
2 carrots, peeled and sliced in half
    lengthways
3 sticks of celery, chopped in half
2 leeks, trimmed and well washed
2 bay leaves and 2 sprigs of thyme
salt

For the sauce and to finish:
50g/2oz butter
50g/2oz flour
400ml/14fl oz poaching stock
300ml/10fl oz dry white wine
250ml/8fl oz double cream
100g/3½oz Gruyère cheese, grated
1tbsp Dijon mustard
50g/2oz tarragon leaves, chopped
salt and pepper
50g/2oz breadcrumbs
25g/1oz Parmesan cheese, grated

Put the chicken in a large pot, add the vegetables and herbs and salt. Poach very gently for around an hour and a half, skimming off any scum that comes to the surface. Once cooked, lift out the bird and allow to cool. Strain the stock through a fine sieve and discard all solids. Leave to settle and lift off any surface fat using several sheets of absorbent kitchen paper.

Remove all meat from the chicken carcass (discarding skin and also removing all sinews from the drumsticks) and cut into large, bite-sized pieces.

To make the sauce, melt the butter in a pan, add the flour and cook for 3 minutes without browning. Gradually add the hot chicken stock, white wine and cream and stir until thickened. Stir in the cheese, mustard and tarragon, correct the seasoning and simmer all together for about 20 minutes.

Preheat the oven to 230°C/450°F/Gas 8. Put the chicken in a buttered gratin dish, pour over the sauce and sprinkle with the breadcrumbs and Parmesan cheese. Bake in the preheated oven for 20–25 minutes until the dish is golden brown and bubbling well around the edges. Eat with buttered new potatoes and a crisp green salad.

A small organic chicken, 1.2kg/2½lb or so will feed four or more people, depending on whether the bird or the vegetables have the starring role.

Roasted Chicken and Leeks with Lemon and Tagliatelli

SERVES 4
preheat oven to 200°C/400°F/Gas 6

1 x 1.2kg/2½lb organic chicken
1 onion, peeled and quartered
1 organic lemon, quartered
1 onion, peeled and sliced
85–125g/3–4oz butter
sea salt
black pepper
8 leeks, cleaned and trimmed
olive oil
500g/1lb/ 2oz tagliatelli
juice of a lemon and its finely
    zested rind

Quarter a peeled onion and a whole organic lemon and put alternate hunks inside the chicken. Place the bird on top of a peeled sliced onion in a roasting tin. Rub a generous amount of butter on the breast of the bird, and sprinkle over a good pinch of sea salt and a generous scrunch of black pepper.

Cook for 30 minutes, then baste the bird with the buttery juices and throw in the cleaned, trimmed leeks cut into short batons, roll them in the butter, and add a splosh of olive oil. Season. Return to the oven for a further half-hour. I add the chicken liver to the roasting tin for the final 5 minutes cooking.

Meanwhile, bring a large pan of water to the boil. Test the chicken and leeks with a skewer to check they are cooked through. Transfer the chicken to a carving board to rest and allow for a further rush of fugitive juices to escape.

Cook your tagliatelli, about 125g/4oz per person, none of that silly 60g nonsense. When *al dente*, drain the pasta, leaving a bit of cooking water to lubricate it. Return it to the pot, then add a knob of butter, the meat juices, chicken liver and leeks, the juices from the bird's cavity, everything that has collected in the roasting tray, and the juice of a whole lemon and its zest.

Quickly carve hunks of hot flesh with their crispy salt skin from the bird and throw them into the pot, mixing all the ingredients before you serve.

Tarragon and Garlic Chicken

SERVES 3-4
preheat oven to 200°C/400°F/Gas 6

1 organic chicken
50g/2oz unsalted butter
3 cloves of new season's garlic,
    crushed with the back of a knife
    and finely chopped
a bunch of French tarragon,
    chopped
spritz of lemon juice
sea salt and black pepper
1 lemon, quartered
1 small onion, quartered
olive oil

Push both hands under the skin of the chicken breast, easing it away from the flesh without tearing it, and do the same with the legs. Mash the butter with a fork and amalgamate with the garlic, tarragon, a spritz of lemon juice and the seasoning.

Place a quarter of the herb butter on one breast under the skin, flattening it out with your fingers, then do the same with the other side and the legs. Put the lemon and onion inside the chicken, squeezing a little lemon juice over the breast first.

Pour a little good olive oil over the chicken, which you have placed breast up in a small roasting tin. Season the skin and cook for about 50 minutes, basting with the buttery juices two or three times. Remove from the oven and allow to rest for 10 minutes.

Pour the extra juices from the bird's cavity into the roasting tin, and carve. I served my chicken with Merchant Gourmet's green rice with extra tarragon, and some spinach cooked briefly with no liquid, then turned into a béchamel sauce enriched with some Jersey cream.

Risotto slips easily into the category of food best described as soothing. Comforting as it is in the eating, it is the cooking, with the gradual, gentle application of hot stock and the repetitive, mesmeric stirring of the wooden spoon, that makes it a relaxing ritual which is also simplicity itself – IF you follow the rules. I had rather thought my leek and Vacherin Mont d'Or risotto was the pinnacle of my risotto making, but was overjoyed to be proved wrong when I encountered this recipe from the peerless Italian food writer Anna Del Conte. She, in turn, ascribes it to Giovanni Goria, of the Accademia Italiana della Cucina, via her friend Romana Bosco who runs a cookery school in Turin. Whenever I have empty fridge syndrome, this is one of the few dishes I can still conjure out of the ether for six, eight, ten, even twelve. A house without lemons, good olive oil, Parmesan cheese and risotto rice is an empty house indeed.

Risotto with Lemon

SERVES 4

50g/2oz unsalted butter
1 tbsp olive oil
2 shallots, very finely chopped
1 stick of celery, very finely
 chopped
300g/10oz Italian rice, such as
 arborio
1 litre/1¾ pints homemade light
 meat or vegetable stock
1 organic lemon, zest and juice
5 or 6 fresh sage leaves
a small sprig of fresh rosemary
1 organic egg yolk
4 tbsp freshly grated Parmesan
 cheese
4 tbsp double cream
salt and black pepper

Heat half the butter, the oil, and the finely chopped shallots and celery in a heavy saucepan and cook until the *soffritto* of shallot and celery is done, about 7 minutes. Mix in the rice and continue cooking and stirring until the rice is well coated in the fats and partly translucent.

While this is happening, heat the stock and keep it simmering all through the preparation of the dish. When the rice becomes shiny and partly translucent, pour in about 150ml/5fl oz of the stock. Stir very thoroughly and cook until the rice has absorbed most of the stock. Add another small ladleful of simmering stock and continue in this manner until the rice is ready. You may not need all the stock. Good-quality Italian rice takes about 20 minutes to cook.

Meanwhile, chop the herbs and mix with the lemon zest, adding them to the risotto half way through the cooking. In a small bowl combine the egg yolk, the juice of half the lemon, the Parmesan cheese, cream and a very generous grinding of black pepper. Mix well with a fork.

When the risotto is *al dente* draw the pan off the heat and stir in the egg and cream mixture and the remaining butter. Cover the pan and leave to rest for 2 minutes or so. Check the seasoning, and that there is enough lemon juice, then give the risotto an energetic stir, transfer it to a heated dish or bowl and serve at once with more grated Parmesan in a bowl if you wish.

Anna suggests that this dish is also a good accompaniment to costolette alla milanese or chicken jointed, sautéed in butter and cooked in a casserole in the oven with 200ml/7fl oz of double cream poured over – an old Milanese recipe.

Risottos do not stand around well, but I have found it absolutely fine to get the risotto to the halfway stage up to an hour before you want to serve it, then leave it with a ladleful of hot stock poured over it and a tight lid on it while you have your first course or drinks. Then carry on with another ladleful of stock, cooking the rice for its last 10 minutes. It is as good a first course as it is a main one if you are doing something more than a family lunch or supper.

Continuing with the lemony theme, here is a dish that wouldn't shame your smartest dinner. I take a sort of perverse pride in wowing people with dishes that use the very best ingredients transformed through the alchemy of the stove, yet are almost ludicrously easy in their execution. Remember Carême's dictum, '*faites simple.*' You could offer a bowl of home-made romesco sauce if you feel like it, it works wonderfully well with white fish. The cod – thick, whitely translucent, so tender that it falls away from the skin in giant flakes – is a dish that shuns embellishment, except the best grassy green olive oil. It doesn't even need spritzing with lemon – the Greek potatoes with which you marry the cod bring that, absorbing olive oil, lemon juice and the scent of the herbs and almost braising in their own juice.

Baked Cod with Greek Potatoes

SERVES 4
preheat oven to 200°C/400°F/Gas 6

For the potatoes:
1kg/2¼lb potatoes, cut long and
    thin, rather than chunky, into
    about 4 pieces if they are
    medium sized
225g/8oz onion, peeled and finely
    chopped
6 cloves of garlic
a handful fresh thyme or oregano
salt and black pepper
300ml/10fl oz best olive oil
the juice of 2 lemons

For the fish:
1 thick fillet of really fresh cod,
    about 1 kg/2¼lb, and by thick, I
    mean 2.5–4cm/1–1½ in
olive oil
sea salt and black pepper

Put the peeled and sliced potatoes into a gratin dish or roasting tin so that they fit snugly in one layer. Throw in the onion and garlic and the herbs stripped from their stems, season and add the olive oil and lemon juice. Now add enough water barely to cover. Cook for 45 minutes before turning the potatoes over and cooking for another 45 minutes. An hour and a half should do it. Cook your fish during the last 15 minutes.

Butter a gratin dish thickly and lay your cod to rest in it, skin side down. Dribble some really fine olive oil over the top, Ravida or Seggiano if possible. Season well. Bake for 15 minutes, then test with the point of a sharp knife or skewer. If it goes right through the flesh with ease and no resistance, the fish is done.

This dish works beautifully with upmarket mushy peas. By that, I mean a packet of organic split green peas, which need washing but not soaking, and cooking for about 45 minutes to an hour in water that just covers them by 5mm/¼ in or so. Do not salt until cooked and skim them when they come to the boil, before turning them down to a simmer. When cooked, drain off a bit but not all of the remaining cooking water, add a good lump of unsalted butter, season and serve with a bunch of fresh mint chopped and stirred in once they are off the heat.

The extraordinarily talented Stephen Markwick, chef/proprietor of Bristol's best restaurant Markwick's, and ex-pupil of the great George Perry-Smith, was cooking this dish last time I steamed into his kitchen to watch him at work and write about him. He has quietly been going about his business for several decades, but his dedication to the kitchen and the pursuit of good cooking is as unstale as it is unfaltering. I have never tasted anything less than excellent when dining there, and have always been impressed by the way in which he has ploughed his own furrow. Elizabeth David is an influence without being obtrusively and obviously so, Stephen is too creative for that, and times, after all, have moved on. Stephen serves this lovely dish as a first course with a few croutons of thinly sliced baguette brushed with a little olive oil and crisped in the oven. I think it is as successful as a main course served with plainly cooked rice. Slow braising renders the squid softly succulent, as does cooking it in a flash. Anything in between and you end up with something chewy and rubbery. It will wait around in the pot for you if need be, and it is as delectable warm as it is brought straight from the stove.

Braised Squid
with Leeks, Fennel, Orange, Chilli and Red Wine

SERVES 6 AS A FIRST
COURSE, 4 AS A MAIN
Preheat oven to 140°C/275°F/Gas 1

1 onion, peeled and sliced

4 cloves of garlic, peeled and
 sliced

1 leek, trimmed, sliced and well
 washed

1 small bulb of fennel, sliced

2–3 tbsp olive oil

equal quantities of fennel seeds,
 dill seeds and coriander seeds,
 ground together to make 1 tbsp
 in all

2 small hot chillies, chopped

1 kg/2¼lb cleaned squid, the body
 cut into rings, the wings into
 strips and the tentacles left
 whole

zest and juice of 2 oranges

½ bottle red wine

a small handful of coriander
 leaves, chopped

to finish: a little extra grated
 orange rind and chopped garlic
 mixed together

In a heavy-bottomed casserole, gently fry the onion, garlic, leek and fennel together in the olive oil until softened. Add the ground seed mixture and the chillies, then stir in the squid. Stir around a little until the squid has stiffened and then introduce the zest and juice of 2 oranges and the red wine. Season well – squid absorbs a great deal of salt – and bring everything to a simmer. Cover and braise slowly in the oven for about 2 hours.

Stir in the chopped coriander, sprinkle over the extra orange zest and garlic, and serve directly from the pot in either of the two ways suggested in the introduction opposite.

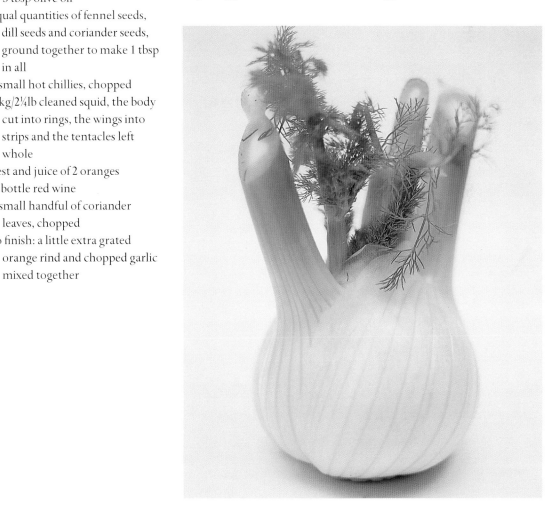

I have been cooking hare, though all too infrequently, since I left university for my first job at Anglia Television in Norwich. There was a fine game shop in Norwich, which had lavish displays of everything of a furred and feathered nature, both in and outside the shop. Shoveller duck, the spoonbill with a shovel-like beak – muddied from its feeding from the bottom of ponds – widgeon, teal, snipe, glorious woodcock, braces of pheasant, pigeon and partridge, hares and the much-spurned meat of the postwar bunny. 'Watership Down' the sign on the shop window read, 'you've read the book, you've seen the film, now try the pie.' And I did. I cooked my way through as much of the winter repertoire as I could afford, learning as I did so from Jane Grigson, Elizabeth David, the shop and the gradual gleamings of intuition my burgeoning experience suggested to me.

I never realized at the time quite how lucky I was to have stumbled on this rarest of shops, where you could order, for a kingly rather than princely sum to me, a newly ex-student, half a dozen saddles of hare with the blood and the innards if the fancy took you, and cook a civet with aillade entirely from this most prized part of the animal. I have to say, since the continuous tenancy of a family of hares in my west of Ireland field, that I have not looked in so gung-ho a fashion on bringing these beautiful creatures to table. Except in March, that is, when the mad March hares cavort with a sort of semi-crazed abandon, often ending up as road kill, begging me to alight from my bike and sling the still warm ginger-faced victims across the handlebars to take home and gut in my shed. Like all good seasonal treats – once a year and honour is satisfied.

Civet of Hare with an Aillade

SERVES 4
preheat oven to 140°C/275°F/Gas 1

1 hare, jointed
flour, salt and pepper
goose fat or olive oil and butter
2 carrots, diced
2 onions, chopped
a few cloves of garlic
3 stalks of celery, strung and
   sliced

For the marinade:
1 bottle robust red wine
1 tbsp Cognac
2 tbsp olive oil
1 onion, thinly sliced
a few cloves of garlic, bruised
a couple of strips of orange rind
a couple of bay leaves
about 12 juniper berries, bruised
   rather than crushed
the same amount of peppercorns

For the aillade:
liver and kidneys of the hare
4 rashers organic green streaky
   bacon, finely snipped
6 or 7 cloves of garlic, chopped
   into tiny dice
4 shallots, chopped into tiny dice
4 tbsp red wine vinegar
a blade of mace
a sprig of thyme
salt and pepper

Marinate the jointed hare for as long as it suits you, anything from one to three days.

Remove the hare from the marinade, drying the pieces thoroughly with kitchen paper, before rolling them in seasoned flour. I find shaking a few tablespoons of flour with some salt and pepper into a Ziploc bag, and sealing the hare inside it while you briefly toss it around is the best way to do the job unmessily, and without a surfeit of flour adhering to the joints.

Heat some goose fat or olive oil and butter in a heavy-bottomed casserole. Brown the two hind legs and the saddle jointed into two portions for a few minutes on each side and then remove them to a plate.

Scrape up any crusty brown bits from the pan, add more fat if you need to and gently sauté together the carrots, onions, garlic and celery. When they have begun to soften, place the hare joints on the vegetables, season well with salt and pepper, strain the marinade over the meat and bring gently to a simmer. Cover with a layer of greaseproof paper and a lid and cook very gently for about two hours, either in the oven or on top of the stove.

Meanwhile, make your aillade. Chop the hare liver and kidneys and put them, with the bacon, garlic and shallots, in a small pan with 4 tablespoons of red wine vinegar, the blood of the hare, mace and thyme and seasoning. Simmer at a whisper for a couple of hours, stirring occasionally to prevent anything from sticking. Pour the contents of the pan over the hare before serving. You may feel like offering a tart jelly as an accompaniment – rowan or crab apple work well.

The following day, you can add the ribs and fore legs to the pot of hare bones and remaining sauce, cover with water, having added the usual stock vegetables, and simmer for a couple of hours until you have the base for a wonderfully gamey hare soup.

I rarely cook boned roast meat. The Chinese have an expression, 'the nearer the bone, the sweeter the meat' and, of course, the better the flavour. But opening out a joint of lamb or pork when the bone has been removed, flavouring it with something quite other, or piling it full of stuffing, is a different thing altogether, and can be a lovely variant to the standard Sunday roast. Pork marries beautifully with the *digestif* of a herb that is fennel seed, and the star anise, dill seed, Pernod and oily orange zest work harmoniously together, particularly if rubbed well into the meat and allowed to penetrate for some time. If you can, buy Middle White or Large Black organic pork, which both lay down a thick coating of ivory fat. The meat is a superb texture if properly hung and the flavour unlike anything you're likely to get from a faster-reared, newer breed.

Roast Boned Leg of Pork
with a Spiced Orange Rub and Orange Sweet Potatoes

SERVES 8
preheat oven to 200°C/400°F/Gas 6

2kg/4¼lb boned leg of pork,
    untied
1 onion, sliced
sweet potatoes, 1 per person
    depending on size

For the marinade:
2 tsp fennel seeds
3 star anise
1 tsp dill seeds
sea salt and black pepper
2 crushed fresh bay leaves
a handful of fresh dill, chopped
zest of 2 organic oranges
olive oil
2 tbsp Pernod

If you can prepare this the night before, do; the maceration will tenderize and flavour more deeply. Crush the fennel seeds coarsely with the star anise, dill seeds, sea salt, black peppercorns and bay in a mortar, then add the fresh dill and orange zest and stir in 2 or 3 tablespoons of olive oil. Rub the paste well into the opened-out pork where the bone has been removed and all over the outside of the meat and into the crevices where the crackling has been slashed. Not easy, but pull it apart and try and push the paste into the gaps. Concentrate on the inside of the joint, the crackling, and the ends. Splosh on a bit of Pernod and leave covered and in the fridge overnight or for as long as you've got.

Bring the meat to room temperature before you roll it up and tie it with string at 2.5cm/1in intervals. Place the joint on top of a sliced onion in a roasting tin. Sprinkle some sea salt over the crackling and put it in the oven. After 40 minutes, baste and turn the oven down to 190°C/375°F/Gas 5. When the joint has been cooking for about an hour, chop each sweet potato, unskinned, into 2 or 3 pieces, roll in the fat surrounding the meat and cook with the joint for 40 minutes, turning them over at half time. The pork will need to rest uncovered for 20 minutes. Do not cover it, or you will jeopardize the brittle, mahogany-coloured crackling.

If you don't already know about this cut of meat, I suggest you become acquainted with it. It is the perfect cut for when you want to lavish on your guests or family something seriously uncheffy, but stunning, for lunch or dinner. You can scythe through the chines with a flourish, giving everyone a springy, juicy, thick white loin chop on the bone. Next to it, sit a whole baked apple, which you have cored and scored around its circumference and stewed in the fatty juices from the meat and some tartly dry cider.

Roast Chined Loin of Pork
with Baked Apples and Cider Gravy

SERVES 6
preheat oven to 200°C/400°F/Gas 6

2kg/4¼lb chined loin of organic pork, preferably from an old breed with a good fat covering, such as Middle White or Large Black
2 large onions
6 sweetly tart cooking apples of the sort that don't collapse, or 6 large Coxes
6 fresh bay leaves
plenty of coarse sea salt and freshly ground black pepper
300–600ml/½–1 pint good dry cider such as Julian Temperley's Kingston Black from the Somerset Cider Brandy Company (see page 282)
cooking water from your vegetables

Peel and slice the onions thinly and place them on the bottom of a roasting tin. Sit the chined loin on the top, then sprinkle a goodly amount of salt over the top and some black pepper, and rub them in with your fingers. The joint will take 1½ hours to cook and a further 15 minutes or so to rest on your carving board, under foil and a tea towel.

Half an hour before the end of cooking time, rigorously core your apples – you do not want to find toenaily bits – and tuck a bay leaf into the top of each hole. Score a line through the skin around the circumference of each apple with the point of a sharp knife, and place them upright in the roasting tin with the meat. Baste them with the meat juices and a good splosh of the cider and cook for the meat's final 30 minutes. The apples may burst, but you are not looking for cosmetic perfection here; the flavour and texture are all.

Keep the apples hot while you slice the crackling horizontally off the joint in one piece, leaving as much of the fat as you can attached to the joint. Place the sheet of crackling under a hot grill and wait until it is molten brittle before returning it to the top of the meat. Do not cover the meat again or the crackling will sog.

Stir the meat juices and caramelized onion together in the roasting tin over a high flame, add the rest of the cider and, when it is bubbling, some water from whatever vegetables you have cooked. Reduce for a few minutes, then strain the gravy through a sieve into a jug standing in the sink, before pouring it into jugs.

Gravy. An emotive word. I remember as a child going to endless Sunday lunches with my parents, and being appalled at the underfilled gravy jugs, the floury taste, the phoney gravy boats, the cooks who thought a teaspoon of bread sauce was an 'ample sufficiency' and didn't understand the concept of a lake of gravy. And the importance of having enough left to make your shepherd's or cottage pie with on Monday. Flour is out of fashion, but is bound to be revived at a later date. Meanwhile, these are my golden rules – making a surfeit should go without saying.

Gravy

onions, peeled and sliced
water from parboiling potatoes
wine
seasoning

Roast your joint on a layer of peeled, sliced onions. The meaty juices will mingle with them, the onions will exude their flavour and juice in turn, and caramelize to a dark, crunchy, almost charred intensity. You have begun.

When you have laid your meat to rest on the carving board, whack the heat up, and put the roasting tin on top of the stove. Add a good splosh of whatever wine you happen to have open and let it seethe for a minute or two to burn off the alcohol. Take the potato water that you saved in a jug when you parboiled your potatoes and parsnips before roasting, and add it a little at a time, including the gorgeous, gluey, starchy bits at the bottom. These will help to thicken the gravy slightly without resorting to cornflour. You can add any other vegetable water as well if you need, as you stir like crazy to release the oniony morsels from their sticking places. They will colour the gravy a rich, burnished mahogany, so forget the horrors of fake browning.

Add more wine and seasoning to taste. Try Madeira or port with beef, really good cider with pork, white wine with chicken or Marsala with veal. Remember to add the blood that has leaked into the carving tray to the gravy before you put it into your jug, or into a French dégraisseur that leaves the fat at the top as you pour. It's as simple as that.

According to legend, Jason returned with the Argonauts from Colchis in the Caucasus, which we now know as Georgia, with rather more than the golden fleece: he brought back the pheasant. Georgian recipes for pheasant include its being braised with walnuts, oranges, grapes and pomegranate juice. The golden rule is to roast the plumper and more tender young birds, remembering that the hens are always better upholstered than the cocks, and braise or stew the oldsters. Geriatric birds should be put in the pot for soup. Sharp, pipped fruits like quince and apple are natural partners, as is the olive with its acetic back notes, and the endive's bitter leaves. But the Georgian way of sweetening and underscoring the flavour is most delectably exotic – a sticky coating of pomegranate molasses is cooked into the dish and it is finished with garnet-like jewels of pomegranate. I favour a bird hung for five to seven days, depending on the ambient temperature. A well-hung pheasant should taste gamey, not merely chickeny, but should not have taken on the greenish hue of incipient decomposition. To my mind, an overripe pleasure is a pleasure despoiled, but then what is taste if not subjective?

Pheasant and Pomegranates with Jewelled Bulgur

SERVES 4

a brace of pheasants
6 pomegranates
butter and olive oil
2 tbsp pure pomegranate
    molasses, good supermarkets
    stock bottles of it now
1 lemon
50g/2oz butter, diced

For the bulgur:
225g/8oz bulgur wheat
1 medium onion, finely chopped
pheasant or game stock or, failing
    that, chicken stock
50g/2oz pine kernels
olive oil
salt and freshly ground pepper
a handful of fresh coriander or
    flat-leaf parsley

Halve five of the pomegranates and squeeze the juice from them. You should end up with about three-quarters of a cupful of juice: about 175ml/6fl oz. Remove the seeds from the last pomegranate, making sure you separate the bitter yellow skin from the jewels.

Brown the pheasant breasts skin-side down first, in a little butter and olive oil, then turn them over and repeat. Finally turn them skin-side down again, and pour over the pomegranate molasses and juice. Bring to a simmer, cover with butter paper and a lid, and cook exceedingly gently until tender and cooked through to pink. This should take about 10 minutes, but test with the point of a skewer that the juices are still running pink rather than clear.

Remove from the heat, pour the juices into a pan, taste for sweetness and add lemon juice to taste. Let the meat relax in the warming oven while you bring the sauce up to boiling point, adding the diced butter bit by bit off the heat, whisking as you go. Season to taste.

FOR THE BULGUR: Soften the onion in a good knob of butter, about 50g/2oz, stir in the bulgur and add enough stock to cover by about 2cm/¾in. Cover with a lid and simmer until the liquid has been absorbed, and the bulgur feels tender when fluffed up with a fork. Roast the pine kernels for a few minutes on a roasting tray in a hot oven, making sure they don't burn. Toss them into the bulgur, and fork them through, adding a good glug of olive oil and some salt and pepper as you do.

Place a hillock of bulgur on a warmed serving plate, then scoop out a hollow in the middle. Scatter pomegranate seeds and fresh coriander or parsley over the bulgur. Place the pheasant breasts in the middle, with the sauce flooded over them. A good, bitter endive or escarole and orange salad is the only accompaniment you will need.

This is how to cook the pheasant legs that you haven't used for the Pheasant and Pomegranates with Bulgur on page 115. Legs lend themselves better to gentle stewing than they do to roasting or frying. Just make sure you use the best glossiest olives, kept in olive oil, not pre-pitted and brined. It is also important to remove the tendons properly, or ask your butcher to do so, when you are plucking and jointing your pheasants. They do not make pleasant chomping.

Pheasant Legs Stewed with Green and Black Olives

SERVES 4

4 pheasant legs
butter and olive oil
salt and freshly ground
   black pepper
2 young leeks, finely shredded
1 small carrot, finely sliced
1 clove of garlic, chopped
1 bay leaf
16 plump black olives, pitted
a glass of red wine
a measure of Cognac or Marc
16 plump green olives, pitted

Melt some butter and olive oil in a heavy-bottomed casserole and very gently brown the pheasant legs all over. Remove them to a plate and season.

Add the vegetables and garlic to the pan and soften gently. Add the bay leaf, stoned black olives and the wine. Place the legs on top, cover with greaseproof paper and a lid, and stew at a murmur on top of the stove or in a moderate oven, 180°C/350°F/Gas 4, until tender. Depending on the age and sex of the birds, this will be anywhere from 20 to 40 minutes, so check with a skewer that the flesh feels soft and yielding right through to the bone. The slower you cook pheasant legs, the more chance you have of them not toughening. Remove the legs to a warmed serving dish, and place them in the warming oven.

Turn the heat up high until the juices in the pot are bubbling, pour over the Cognac, set light to it and let the alcohol burn off. Put the vegetables through the coarse disc of a mouli-légumes, or mash them thoroughly, and return to the pan. Add the pitted green olives, heat through and pour over the pheasant legs.

I think a dish of simple basmati rice, scented with the addition of some whole coriander and fennel seeds, is the best accompaniment, with perhaps a salad of watercress and orange. The orange marries well with the olives and the pheasant.

Chinese Slow-Braised Belly Pork with Butter Beans

SERVES 4
preheat oven to 150°C/300°F/Gas 2

piece of organic belly pork, with
  its rind on, weighing roughly
  750g/1½lb
3 large onions, peeled and sliced
  into thin rings
6 cloves of garlic, peeled and
  bruised with the back of a knife
a thumb of fresh ginger, peeled
  and sliced
225g/8oz butter beans soaked
  overnight in cold water with
  1 tsp bicarbonate of soda
3 star anise
1 heaped tbsp really good honey,
  I use Seggiano's 'Woodland
  Honeydew'
1 tbsp molasses sugar
4–6 tbsp organic tamari sauce
white pepper

Put a layer of onions in the bottom of a heavy casserole and place the belly pork, rind-side up, on top of them. Surround with the soaked, drained beans, rest of the onions, garlic, star anise, honey and molasses sugar, and grind over some white pepper. Cover with cold water, a lot of which the beans will drink up as they cook. Bring slowly to the boil on top of the stove, cover with a layer of greaseproof paper and a lid, and put in the bottom of the oven for 3 hours.

Remove, add the tamari sauce, cover again and cook for another hour or two. I have cooked this for as long as 5 hours. The reason why I don't add the tamari sauce at the beginning of cooking is that it might concentrate the saltiness.

Make some creamy mashed potato or cook some rice. Ladle the vegetables and juices into bowls and place a hunk of collapsed belly pork with its bones on top. You need to remove the rind before serving, but that too will peel off with ease. A thoroughly good dish.

If you, like me, are the kind of person who is put off by a shopping-list-length gallimaufry of ingredients, please think again with this dish. Just reading this recipe should have your taste buds standing to attention. The fresh, raw, zinging nature of the ingredients is everything you could desire when you want substance but lightness in equal measure, and to feel you are eating something that might, for once, be as good for you as it is delicious.

Oriental Noodle Salad

SERVES 4

250g/9oz packet of organic
    spinach or plain egg noodles
3 organic chicken breasts, skin on,
    or chicken thighs; or use large
    raw prawns, 3 or 4 per person
1 clove of garlic, finely chopped
1 red chilli, seeded and diced
a finger of fresh ginger, grated
1 dsrtsp fresh coriander, chopped
4 tbsp organic shoyu sauce
olive oil
the juice of a lime
1 large carrot
a handful of mangetout
a handful of beansprouts
5 or 6 raw chestnut mushrooms
a bunch each of fresh mint and
    fresh coriander

For the dressing:
3 organic lemons
3 organic limes
1 clove of garlic
a finger of fresh ginger, grated
1 dsrtsp runny honey
a piece of stem ginger and 1 tbsp
    of the syrup (optional)
olive oil
salt and pepper

Mix together the garlic, chilli, ginger, coriander, shoyu sauce, olive oil and lime in a bowl, add the chicken or prawns and leave to marinade. Cook the noodles as per instructions for 4 minutes, then coat them lightly with sesame or olive oil so they won't stick.

Peel the carrot, then, with the peeler, ribbon it from top to bottom. Throw the ribbons into the bowl with the noodles. Thinly slice the mangetout into strips, throw them into the bowl and add the bean sprouts and mushrooms.

Remove the chicken or prawns from the marinade. Griddle the chicken for 7 minutes a side or until cooked through; the shelled prawns until pink and cooked through on both sides. Slice the chicken into long strips with the crisped skin and throw them into the bowl; the prawns can go in whole.

To make the dressing, peel the citrus fruits thinly with a potato peeler so that you end up with no pith. Put the slices of peel with the juice of the fruit in a pan with the garlic, fresh ginger and honey. Bring to the boil and reduce by a half until you have a lovely, syrupy sauce. Strain it into a bowl through a sieve, add the olive oil until you have a dressing you like the taste of, then add the finely chopped piece of stem ginger and its syrup and season to taste. Throw half the roughly chopped coriander and mint into the salad, add the dressing and toss with your fingers to amalgamate well. Throw over the rest of the herbs and serve.

Another of Sally's perfect lunchtime salads which you can experiment with, using red peppers, shallots, sweet potatoes, courgettes or any of the good roasting squash such as red onion or butternut.

Roasted Aubergine, Red Onion and Tomato Salad with Chickpeas, Feta and Spinach

SERVES 4
preheat oven to 220°C/425°F/Gas 7

1 aubergine
2 red onions
4 large tomatoes
4 or 5 cloves of garlic
a sprig of fresh thyme
a handful of cooked chickpeas, I always make enough for houmous or soup at the same time
a handful of pousse, the baby spinach leaves
125g/4oz good sheep's milk feta, I buy Mary Holbrook's from The Fine Cheese Company
olive oil
a well-aged balsamic vinegar, you need something mellow and velvety not sharp and rough
sea salt and black pepper

Soak the chickpeas overnight in cold water. Next day, rinse them and just cover with fresh water in a large earthenware casserole. Add an onion stuck with a couple of cloves, a chopped carrot and stick of celery, a sprig of thyme and a couple of fresh bay leaves, bring to the boil, skim, then allow to simmer at a mere burble for 2 hours under cover.

Cube the aubergine, peel the onions and cut them into eighths, and halve the tomatoes. Place them on a roasting tray with the garlic and dribble olive oil over everything. Add the thyme and roast until everything is cooked through, 30–40 minutes. Remove from the oven and add a libation of olive oil and some balsamic vinegar to taste.

Place the roasted vegetables on a pretty, flat plate. Toss in the cooked chickpeas and the raw spinach, which will wilt gently in the warmth, and crumble over the feta. Season and serve.

Something of an annual event in our house, specific to the third week of November to be precise, Gladys's birthday. Gladys looked after my three children, Miranda, Harry and Charissa, for nine years before she was felled by a stroke. She has been a third parent to them all, and is still very much part of our lives. Every year I cook her birthday dinner and this steak and kidney pie is her absolute favourite. So much so, that she is given to asking for it again next year almost before the fork has been returned to the plate at the birthday dinner. I make the steak and kidney a day in advance; as with a good stew, this always improves the flavour. I leave it to cool to a rich, wine-dark meatiness, almost gelled with the nuggets of kidney. The stewing steak I buy from Swaddles Green organic farm is well hung, properly veined with fat and comes with a quarter its weight in kidney – more can be overpowering. This is THE winter dish I would not do without: a traditional, a classic, which tweaking, however subtle or sparing, can neither improve nor embellish. I have, however, sometimes substituted venison steak for the beef steak. Although a leaner meat, the venison makes up for it with its powerful, gamey flavour. I add some crushed juniper berries to the venison version.

Steak and Kidney Pie

SERVES 4
preheat oven to 150°C/300°F/Gas 2

700g/1½lb steak with
    about 175g/6oz kidney
seasoned flour to coat, which you
    can do in a Ziploc bag
butter
3 small onions, chopped
3 large portobello mushrooms,
    or the equivalent weight in
    chestnut mushrooms, wiped
    clean and sliced
2–3 ladles of good chicken
    or game stock
a glass each of Marsala and port,
    or the equivalent in red wine of
    the decent, full-bodied variety
2 bay leaves, a sprig each of
    rosemary, thyme and parsley,
    tied together or wrapped
    in muslin

For the pastry:
preheat the oven to 190°C/375°F/Gas 5

175g/6oz unbleached organic
    plain white flour
85g/3oz good cold unsalted butter
water
beaten egg to glaze

Sauté the floured meat and kidneys in batches in a single layer in some butter in a heavy-bottomed casserole until browned on all sides, a matter of a few minutes. Remove the meat to a plate, scrape the crusty brown bits from the floor of the pan, add a bit more butter and sauté the onion gently until softened and translucent. Cook the mushrooms separately in a small pan in a bit of butter until they start to soften and weep with juice, then return the meat to the pan, add the mushrooms, tuck in the bouquet of herbs, season and add the alcohol, letting it come to a simmer. Add the stock, bring back to a simmer, then cover with a layer of greaseproof and a lid and cook in the oven for 1½ hours. Cool overnight. You can cool the meat and leave it in the fridge for several days before using it.

There are several schools of thought on the pastry. Should it be puff, shortcrust made with butter, or shortcrust made with lard? I use shortcrust most often, but I have been known to veil my meat with a stratospherically light layer of puff pastry leaves – all French flour and L'Escure butter – which you can buy by the kilo from the inimitable Baker and Spice. Commercial pastry you can keep; that is where I draw my purist line anyway.

Make your pastry in the usual way. Spoon the filling into the bottom of the pie dish, placing a china blackbird or egg cup in the middle so that the steam can be released. Brush the edge of the pie dish with water before sticking a thin strip of pastry to it, all the way round. Brush the strip with beaten egg before cloaking the pie with your sheet of pastry and indenting the edges with the tines of a fork to press them together. Use any leftover bits to decorate the top and brush the whole surface with beaten egg just before it goes into the oven. Cook for about 50 minutes. The top should look like golden enamel.

Serve with English mustard, mashed potato and cabbage blanched for 5 minutes then refreshed in cold water and stewed briefly with plenty of butter, salt and pepper. Also some carrots cooked in chicken stock, butter and a teaspoon of molasses sugar at a rolling boil, until the liquid has evaporated and they are caramelized with the butter and sugar mixture.

If the recipe hadn't been Jane Grigson's, I'm pretty sure I wouldn't have stopped, looked and cooked; after all, what is so special about sausages and cabbage? And just how effective can the alchemy of the two be, to transmute them into something so far from what the imagination can conceive of? The answer is, good enough for me to have cooked this dish several times each winter for nearly two decades. The two simple elements transcend their original state and unify so flawlessly that they want for nothing more; no extra can improve them. The long, slow cooking of the cabbage, leaching its intense juices into the finest organic Swaddles Green pork sausages, which in turn exude their fat to coat and intensify the flavour of the cabbage, with only the addition of butter, salt and pepper, is a process of stunning simplicity. The pink and green strata compact almost into a loaf or torte, and the whole, served with its copious juice, wants only for a baked potato, some coarsely bashed carrot and swede, and a trekker's appetite. Never a problem. This is a dish to return to after abandoning it to its own devices for at least a couple of hours. Jane Grigson assigns the recipe to a French neighbour of hers, Madame Glon, who called it chou farci. You may use Savoy or Dutch cabbage.

Stuffed Cabbage in the Troo Style

SERVES 4
preheat oven to 150°C/300°F/Gas 2

1.4–2kg/3–4½lb cabbage
700g/1½lb best organic plain pork
   sausages, Swaddles Green
   make theirs with no nitrites
salt, pepper, butter

Shred the cabbage into thin strips, coring it first, and blanch it in a huge vat of boiling, salted water for 5 minutes. Drain it in a colander and run the cold tap over it to prevent further cooking at this stage. Butter an ovenproof pot.

Slit the sausage skins and push out all the sausage meat onto a plate, discarding the skins. Place a third of the cabbage in the bottom of the pot and season. Press open the sausages and place half the sausage meat in a layer over the cabbage. Continue with a layer of cabbage and sausage, finishing with a layer of cabbage, seasoning each layer as you go, and dotting the top with butter. Cover tightly with a layer of greaseproof and a lid, and cook in the oven for 2–2½ hours. I have served the children at 7 o'clock, then reheated the dish for half an hour later in the evening and it came to absolutely no grief at all.

When I was a child it seemed extraordinarily glamorous to eat salmon fishcakes for breakfast, but that is what my grandfather did, sitting at the head of an immaculately gleaming 18th-century oak refectory table. For a special treat, Rhoda, my grandmother's cook, would make a couple for me too. They are still a treat, and will always remain so. I would not, however, be interested in eating them if they were made with farmed salmon. Salmon fishcakes should be made with the leftovers from a perfectly moist, wild salmon whose flesh has slightly gelled overnight, been flaked but not crushed to a pulp, and bound with some dry, smooth, unbuttery mashed potato and a healthy seasoning of flat-leaf parsley, coarsely ground pepper and sea salt. These fishcakes are one of the small, select band of dishes that one can feel an urge for at any hour, breakfast, lunch or supper, varying their accompaniment to suit the time of day. Even I could not envisage sauce tartare for breakfast.

Salmon Fishcakes with Crème Fraîche Tartare

SERVES 6

about 600g/1lb 4 oz wild salmon, cooked

about 300g/10oz cooked potato, mashed without milk and butter, but even half and half salmon and potato works if that is the quantity of fish you have left

a handful of flat-leaf parsley, chopped

sea salt and freshly ground black pepper

2 eggs, beaten

85g/3oz stale wholemeal bread, baked in small squares in a slow oven to dry out for 15 minutes, then whizzed to crumbs

vegetable or olive oil for frying

Mash the salmon into the potato roughly, so it still has coarse textured flakes and is not a homogenous purée. Season and throw in the parsley, then shape the mixture into 2cm/¾in thick cakes and place them on a large flat plate. Keep covered in the fridge for an hour or two to firm up, or longer if it is convenient.

Whisk the eggs on one large flat plate, and spread the dried breadcrumbs on another. Dip the fishcakes first in the egg on both sides, then turn them in the breadcrumbs, making sure the sides are well crumbed too. Place them on a third large plate. Heat a shallow film of oil, about 50ml/2fl oz, in a frying pan over a medium heat. Put the fishcakes in and fry for 4 minutes or so a side until golden brown. Drain on kitchen paper and serve, two per person, with a dollop of crème fraîche tartare.

This is a lighter tartare than the classic, but every bit as moreish; the sort of thing you have to dip your finger into, or scrape round the plate when you think no one is looking. It works well with white fish as well as fishcakes. Curiously, it appeals to children, too – the usual version does not in my experience.

Crème Fraîche Tartare

MAKES ENOUGH FOR 6

1 organic egg yolk
1 tsp Dijon mustard
sea salt
Tabasco
3–4 heaped dsrtsp crème fraîche,
    d'Isigny is one of the best
2 tsp tarragon vinegar
1 tsp tarragon, chopped
1 heaped tbsp flat-leaf parsley,
    chopped
1 tsp chives, chopped
1 tbsp rinsed capers, chopped
1 tbsp finely chopped cornichons

Beat the egg yolk with the mustard, sea salt, and a few dashes of Tabasco until emulsified. Add the crème fraîche, a dessertspoon at a time, and one teaspoon of the tarragon vinegar, whisking well with a small balloon whisk. Whisk until thick, but pourable. Stir in the other ingredients with the second teaspoon of vinegar. Adjust the seasoning.

A charmoula is a feisty Moroccan spice rub, which lends itself as well to pork, lamb or fish as it does to chicken, so play around accordingly. If you can slash the skin of the fish, flesh or fowl and maximize penetration of the flavours, so much the better, and if you can be bothered to make your own preserved lemons, a simple and satisfying process, do. They will adorn your kitchen beautifully. I have made preserved lemons ever since seeing them grace the shelves of the doyenne of Middle Eastern and Jewish food, Claudia Roden. Seek out their company with turmeric and coriander; you will not be disappointed.

Chicken Charmoula with Preserved Lemons

SERVES 4
preheat oven to 200°C/400°F/Gas 6

For the chicken:
4 organic chicken legs or 8 thighs
a bunch each of flat-leaf parsley
    and coriander
1 onion, peeled and chopped
3 cloves of garlic, peeled and
    chopped
1 tsp paprika
1 tsp cumin seeds
1 tsp coriander seeds
½ tsp dried root ginger
12 glossy black olives, stoned
1 preserved lemon
4 tbsp olive oil
salt, pepper, cayenne

Briefly temper the cumin and coriander seeds in a small frying pan over a medium heat. By that, I mean until you smell toasted spice and they begin to brown, 30–60 seconds. Then pound them together in a mortar. Put the onion and garlic with the herbs, spices and dried ginger in the food processor. Blitz until they look finely chopped. Chop the olives and lemon more coarsely, and stir them into the mixture, then stir in a bit of olive oil to slacken the mixture further to a paste. Season to taste with salt, pepper and cayenne. Slap the paste all over the chicken pieces, down into the slashes, cover with cling film and place in the fridge for at least 2 hours, but overnight if you can.

Remove from the fridge and bring back to room temperature before cooking. Place the chicken in a roasting tin and cook in the preheated oven for about 30 minutes, or until the juices run clear when the meat is pierced to the centre with a fork.

If you like, accompany with a bowl of sheep's or Greek yoghurt thinned with a spoonful of milk, into which you have stirred a teaspoon of tempered cumin seeds and some fresh, finely chopped coriander, salt and pepper.

I serve this dish with couscous steamed in chicken or game stock, then cooled to warm, when you may stir in the following spicy dressing. Feel free to add roasted, skinned red peppers and any other roasted vegetables you like to the couscous.

For the dressing:
1 clove of garlic, crushed to a
   paste with a bit of coarse sea salt
½ tsp ground cinnamon
½ tsp ground allspice
2 tbsp lemon juice
2 tbsp olive oil
sea salt and black pepper

Whisk the garlic, spices and lemon juice together, then stir in the olive oil. Pour into the bottom of the serving bowl, then add the couscous and vegetables and turn them through the oily dressing with your fingers until well amalgamated.

Preserved Lemons

MAKES 1 LARGE JAR

5 organic thin-skinned lemons
about 5 tbsp salt
juice of at least 3 more lemons
1–2 tbsp olive oil

The preserved lemons must be made a month in advance of eating them. Scrub the lemons, then quarter them from the top to within 1cm/½in of the stem end, so that the sections are still attached. Carefully open out each lemon and sprinkle it with about a teaspoon of sea salt. Close up and reshape the fruit. Put a tablespoon of salt in the bottom of a sterilized 450ml/16fl oz jar with a rubber seal. Pack in the lemons, pushing them down well so that they are squashed together and sprinkling a little more salt in between the layers.

Leave the jar to stand in a warm place like a sunny windowsill for 3–4 days, when the juices will have been drawn out of the lemons. Press the lemons down again as much as you can, then pour in enough lemon juice to cover them completely. Before sealing the jar, pour a thin layer of olive oil on top of the juice to act as a protective film. Close the jar and leave to macerate and ripen for a month in a coolish place, when the lemons will be ready to eat. Don't worry if the lemon juice turns a bit cloudy at first as it will clear naturally. There is no need to refrigerate the lemons after opening.

To use preserved lemons, rinse them well under cold running water. Both the pulp and the peel can be used, although in most dishes the peel alone is called for; the juices can be used again to preserve a new batch of lemons, or try a splash in vinaigrettes, marinades and aromatic spiced stews. Keeps for 2 years.

The Indians use yoghurt in very different ways to us in their cooking. There is the famous 'hung' yoghurt that is suspended in muslin or a sieve overnight until it becomes a set curd, and then there is their habit of mixing yoghurt with water in place of buttermilk as a spiced drink. In Jaipur this drink is ubiquitous because of the high temperatures; yoghurt is used as a coolant, as I discovered on my trip there earlier in the year.

Yoghurt is an indigenous part of Rajasthani cuisine, as is the high percentage of protein in the diet, which comes not from meat but from things such as pulses and chickpeas. Desert people are a strong race, with a lot of stamina. They have to be. They are always moving, the terrain is rugged and it's a rough life with the camels, but nature seems to be on their side and provides them with the kind of food the body needs in extremes of temperature. They eat poppadoms at the end of a meal, not as we do at the beginning, to absorb the fat and oil from the rest of the food and to prevent the palate from feeling greasy. They use sugar to bring out salt, and salt to bring out sugar. They try to use the whole of a plant, preserving, drying and pickling, as needs must in the desert. With coriander, for example, the seeds, stems, roots and leaves are all used, each because of their different properties.

As a lifetime hater of milk, thus of milky drinks, a glass of chaas was my ultimate tact test, knowing, as I did, that refusal was not an option. The addition of tempered cumin seeds and asafoetida, tipped crackling from the pan into the glass, were, with the additional spices, the sealant to my resolve. Indeed, one sip and I was converted. A whole glass later, I was begging for more. But this is hot-day food, or, should I say, drink. Then the body does actually crave the heat of the spice and the cool of the yoghurt and that is when to make it.

Chaas, Buttermilk flavoured
with Cumin, Asafoetida and Green Coriander

SERVES 6

500g/1lb 2oz best organic live
   yoghurt, sheep's or cow's
500ml/18fl oz ice-cold water
20g/¾oz salt
½ tsp green chilli, very finely
   chopped
oil
½ tsp finely chopped root ginger
½ tsp cumin seeds
a pinch of asafoetida
½ tsp fresh coriander leaves,
   chopped to tiny flecks

Simply whisk the yoghurt with the ice-cold water, then add salt, chilli, finely chopped root ginger and coriander. Heat a splash of oil in a small frying pan and temper the cumin seeds and asafoetida by throwing them into the oil for 30–60 seconds, when they will give off their characteristic toasty spice smell. Tip the crackling spices into the yogurt drink, and serve at room temperature or chilled.

I have always felt about okra rather how I felt about milk drinks until my conversion. This is another myth that the magic of Jaipur dispelled. It was always the thought of the mucilaginous liquid leaking glueily but irrevocably from the green-taloned okra that put me off, but this trickiest of vegetables just needs a different sort of treatment, one that renders it crisp, dry, gloriously spiced, and with the texture more of a julienned fritto misto than a weeping pile of slime-green fingers. Look no further and serve this with any of your favourite fish or curry dishes, or in a spiced green hillock as a *bonne bouche* with drinks.

Akri Bhindi, or Crisp Okra

SERVES 4

225g/8oz fresh okra
25g/1oz red or green peppers or a
    combination
50g/scant 2oz onion
scant ½ tsp fresh ginger, sliced
    into matchstick strips
½ tsp carom seeds
a pinch of asafoetida
a generous tsp of sea salt
½ tsp chilli powder
20g/¾oz gram (chickpea) flour
20g/¾oz cornflour
½ tsp fresh coriander, chopped
vegetable oil, enough to deep fry

Cut the okra, onions and peppers into thin julienne strips. Add all the ginger, spices and flours and mix well with your fingers to coat the vegetables.

    Heat the oil, then test that it is hot enough by dropping in a tiny bit of the mixture. If it fizzes and starts to brown immediately, get cooking. Fry the okra mixture until crisp and browned, then sprinkle with the coriander and serve.

If anything could turn me vegetarian, the cooking of Rajasthan would be the strongest contender. Pickled, dried, preserved or rehydrated vegetables, shoots, roots, flowers and seeds are all used in the most ingenious assemblies. Pulses are cooked more imaginatively than I believed possible – such unknown delicacies as the sundried cakes of chickpeas that are like rock-hard dumplings until they are braised in liquid. The simplest of ingredients are made fragrant and desirable with a bit of mustard oil here, a *digestif* of fenugreek there, a tempering of turmeric with its musty, fusty power assuaged by onion and clean-scented cumin. And, like this unusual Achari Paneer, many of the dishes can be cooked at home without your being driven frantic by an alien ingredients list. This is a lovely vegetarian dish: tiny quenelles of cottage cheese cooked briefly in pickling spices and the mustard oil that is the standard oil in this part of Rajasthan.

Achari Paneer

SERVES 4

225g/8oz best cottage cheese, sieved and shaped into small walnut-sized balls between two spoons
50g/scant 2oz onion, very finely chopped
100g/3½oz chopped tomatoes
25g/1oz mustard oil
a pinch of mustard seeds
a pinch of fenugreek seeds
a pinch of cumin seeds
½ tsp red chilli
1 tsp coriander powder
lemon juice
salt
sugar
a bunch of fresh coriander, chopped

Heat the mustard oil in a pan and add the whole dry masala - mustard seeds, fenugreek and cumin seeds – to temper. This takes only a minute or so and really brings out the flavour of the spices. Allow the seeds to crackle, then add the onions and sauté until brown. Add the tomatoes, and cook down for 10–15 minutes.

Add the chilli and half the coriander powder, cook for a few more minutes, then drop in the paneer – the little balls of cottage cheese – coating them well in the spice mixture. Add salt, a pinch of sugar and a spritz of lemon juice to taste. Sprinkle over some fresh coriander and serve. You can make the paneer mixture in advance and assemble all the spices and chopped onion and tomato an hour or two before you want to cook them.

Some pilau rice, sweetened and spiced with whole cloves, slices of ginger, sultanas, toasted flaked almonds or pistachios and turmeric, is the only other accompaniment you could want with an assortment of vegetarian dishes. Vegetable *thalis* are an indigenous part of Rajasthan cuisine. They are eaten from a communal plate, intended to reinforce the togetherness of people who either work or play together. *Thalis* are about 'sharing, brotherhood and belonging' I was told by Jitin, the talented chef of the Oberoi's jewel of a hotel, Raj Vilas in Jaipur. 'We eat most food with our hand' he continued, 'that is why Indians never burn their mouths, they burn their hand first!' This dahl is also a dish you could serve if you are cooking a fish or meat curry.

Moong Dahl Tarka, or
Yellow Lentils Tempered with Cumin and Garlic

SERVES 6

200g/7oz split lentils
50g/2oz onion, finely chopped
25g/1oz ghee or clarified butter
½ tsp cumin seeds
½ tsp garlic
25g/1oz chopped tomato
a pinch of turmeric
½ tsp chilli powder
½ tsp cumin powder
salt
a handful of fresh coriander,
  chopped

Wash the lentils, cover with water and bring them to the boil. Remove the scum from the top with a slotted spoon and some kitchen paper, and simmer. Add the turmeric and salt when the dahl have considerably softened and continue to cook until done.

Heat the ghee in a pan, then add the whole cumin and garlic, followed by the onions and tomato. Sauté them with the chilli and cumin powder. When the mixture has softened, add it to the lentils and heat through to boiling. Add a handful of fresh coriander, check the seasoning and serve.

High in the foothills of the Himalayas at Simla, where the climate is more temperate than Jaipur, the wisdom is not dissimilar. I watch Rajiv, another talented chef, scorching whole tomatoes on the barbecue, mulching them into an instant chutney with pungent mustard oil, onion, ginger, Kashmiri chilli powder, cumin, coriander and a splash of sugar, a chunky sunset of an accompaniment for the powerfully spiced gravy that swamps his 'Chaa Meat', slow-cooked goat, annealed by curd cheese and fresh coriander leaves. Indians understand the effects of foods on the body. Excessive warmth is thought to be the cause of many maladies, so 'heating' and 'cooling' foods are balanced in an Indian meal. Yoghurt, rice and ghee are cooling to the body; meat and cashew nuts are heat inducing and consumed in moderation.

This dish of goat represents the Himachulis belief in a balanced meal. Black cardamom is used for savoury dishes here, Rajiv is insistent that green cardamom is only used in desserts. I am trusted to roll out and stuff the 'keema aur matter kulcha', leavened bread that we roll to Lycra stretchiness and stuff with black-cardamom-spiked lamb mince, or fresh peas with a suspicion of asafoetida. A typical lunch carried by the women to their husbands in the fields and eaten simply with a dollop of fiery mango pickle. You can make the Chaa Meat with lamb or mutton instead of goat.

Chaa Meat

SERVES 5

1kg/2¼lb shoulder of lamb,
  mutton or goat, cubed
1 tsp salt
1 tsp paste made with crushed
  garlic and grated root ginger
85g/3oz of ricotta, a substitute for
  Indian curd cheese,
a couple of bay leaves.
125ml/4fl oz mustard oil
1 tsp green chilli, chopped
85g/3oz onions, sliced
2 bay leaves
½ tsp coriander seeds, crushed
a pinch of turmeric powder
a pinch of coriander powder
a pinch of cumin powder
85g/3oz gram (chickpea) flour
salt
500g/1lb 2oz whisked yoghurt
coriander leaves, chopped

Mix the salt, garlic-ginger paste, ricotta and bay leaves to make the marinade. Add the cubes of lamb and leave for at least an hour.

When the lamb has marinated, put it in a heavy-bottomed pot, cover it with water and bring it slowly to the boil. Simmer it at a blip until tender, 1–1½ hours.

Heat the mustard oil, add the sliced onions and chopped chilli and sauté. Add the whole spices and the meat and cook for a few minutes. Then add the spice powders and salt and simmer. Add the gram flour and cook briefly, then blend in the yogurt and continue cooking over a slow flame until the gravy is thick. Serve piping hot sprinkled with chopped coriander leaves.

This is the simplest chutney in the world to prepare – up-front exotic, unusual and highly versatile. Its sweet sharpness is a foil for any rich or fatty meats, and I think it takes the place of our own green gooseberry sauce with a humble herring or mackerel. Fillet the fish and grill skin side uppermost until charred and bubbling black. Do not cook the flesh side, its oiliness should not dry out, but you could slather and scorch it briefly with a spoonful of chutney on the flesh side if you prefer an integral dish to having your chutney on the side. Cape gooseberries are always for sale at Christmas time, so try this chutney with your cold goose or turkey, in or out of a sandwich.

Cape Gooseberry Chutney

MAKES A GOOD BOWLFUL

400g/14oz Cape gooseberries, hulled
30ml/1fl oz vegetable oil
¼ tsp mustard seeds
¼ tsp cumin seeds
50g/2oz chopped onion
1 tsp fresh ginger, chopped
1 tsp green chilli, chopped
salt
¼ tsp red chilli powder
¼ tsp cumin powder
¼ tsp coriander powder
½ tsp unrefined sugar

Heat the oil, then add the mustard and cumin seeds. After the mustard seeds have started to splutter, add the chopped onions. Cook until translucent, then add the other chopped ingredients. Cook for 2–3 minutes, add the powdered spices and salt, cook over a low flame, then add the gooseberries and sugar. Gently sauté over a low flame for a few minutes, making sure the gooseberries retain their shape and do not collapse. Cool.

A patrician, exquisite dish of marinaded quail, which are submerged in a gravy sharpened and freshened with pastes of coriander and mint leaves and the seeds of black cardamom. Rajiv was given the recipe for this dish by 80-year-old Madan Ram, who was the chef to the Ranas of Rampur Bushair. It has been eaten by rajahs and kings. Traditionally, the hunters brought back quail, boar and partridge, and Madan got to work immediately with his cleaver and his spice box. I get my organic quail from The Ark Chicken Company, but I think the recipe would work as well with any small game bird such as partridge, pigeon, snipe or woodcock.

Bateyr Hara Masala

SERVES 4

8 quail
125g/4oz paste of fresh coriander
25g/1oz paste of fresh mint leaves
1 tsp pomegranate seeds
lemon juice

For the marinade:
30ml/1fl oz wine vinegar
35g/1½oz ginger-garlic paste
1 tsp red chilli paste (just crush a
    seeded red chilli with a bit of
    salt in a mortar)
salt

For the gravy:
125ml/4fl oz ghee or clarified
    butter
a pinch black of cardamom seeds
2–3 cloves and a bay leaf
2 tsp ginger-garlic paste
175g/6oz chopped onion
a pinch of red chilli powder
1 tsp cumin powder
1 tsp coriander powder
⅓ tsp garam masala powder
200g/7oz chopped tomato

Mix together the marinade ingredients, making the ginger-garlic paste with crushed garlic and grated root ginger. Add a bit of salt and marinate the whole birds for at least an hour.

To make the gravy, heat the ghee in a pan, add the whole spices and then the ginger-garlic paste. Add the chopped onion and cook on a medium heat until softened and translucent. Add the spice powders and some more salt, and cook gently until the oil separates from the masala. Add the tomatoes.

Grill the quail on all sides on a barbecue, or under a grill, until they're still a bit bloody, then add them to the gravy with the mint and coriander paste, and finish cooking. Pierce with a skewer, or insert a fine-bladed sharp knife; the flesh should be pink but not look raw or feel tough. Finish the dish with the crushed pomegranate seeds and a squeeze of lemon juice. Eat with your fingers, you cannot do otherwise with quail.

Another lovely vegetarian side dish that you might prefer to serve with drinks. They are really little more than spiced potato and pea cakes. Garam masala and chat masala are both mixtures of spices. Garam masala contains cumin, cardamom, coriander and other spices; chat masala is a mix of coriander, cumin, chillies and dry mango powder.

Mater Tikki

SERVES 1

200g/7oz potatoes, boiled and
   mashed
½ tsp fresh mint
½ tsp fresh coriander
½ tsp fresh root ginger
1 medium green chilli
25g/1oz fresh or frozen peas,
   blanched
½ tsp garam masala
½ tsp chat masala
salt
½ tsp cumin seeds
lemon juice
300ml/10fl oz vegetable oil

Mix together the chopped mint, coriander, ginger and chilli and add to the mashed potato with both masalas and some salt. Heat a little oil in a small pan then crackle the cumin seeds for a few seconds till they exude their toasty scent, before adding the peas and cooking gently until soft. Mash the cumin and peas together a little with a fork, adding the lemon juice and salt.

To make the tikkis, take lumps of the potato mixture and flatten them with the palm of one hand. Pop a bit of pea mixture into the centre and enclose it in the potato until you have a small potato cake. Use a little flour if the mixture is a bit damp and coat the palms of your hand with the flour so that you can work the mixture with the heel of your palm. Heat the vegetable oil until a tiny bit of the mixture thrown in fizzes and begins to brown instantly. Drop in the tikkis and cook them for about 3 minutes a side. Drain and serve with minted yoghurt and a few thinly sliced mild onion rings.

Prepare the tikkis an hour or two in advance if you like, spreading them out on a plate ready to fry.

A simple vegetarian dish of spiced potato and spinach which you can serve as part of a vegetarian *thali* or with fish or meat. If you have left-over cooked spinach and potato, or can contrive to cook extra and keep some back, you are on your way. Also very good to spruce up cold meat, turkey or goose at Christmas, or roast pork or chicken on a Monday night. After the rich excesses of Christmas, a spiced lentil and spinach soup or vegetable dish fresh and warming with chilli, cumin, coriander and ginger is something I seem to crave.

Palak Aloo

SERVES 1

vegetable oil, a thin film
½ tsp cumin seeds
½ tsp garlic, finely chopped
70g/2½ oz onion
70g/2½ oz tomato passata
300g/10oz spinach, briefly cooked
    and coarsely puréed
½ tsp cumin powder
½ tsp coriander powder
½ tsp garam masala
¼–½ tsp red chilli powder,
    use at your discretion
1 heaped tsp fresh coriander,
    chopped
½ tsp root ginger in
    matchstick strips
150g/5oz boiled potato cut
    into large chunks
salt

Heat the oil in a pan, then add the cumin seeds until they crackle, 30 seconds or so, before adding the finely chopped garlic. Add the chopped onion and cook until softened, then add the tomato passata and continue to cook. Add the spinach, then mix the powdered spices, masala, chilli and coriander with a couple of tablespoons of water, a brilliant trick to avoid the subtle spices burning while frying them. Add them with the ginger to the spinach mix and fry briefly. Add the potatoes and heat through, carefully stirring so they don't break up.

Do not be put off by the ingredients list, the process is simplicity itself, the spices all things you will keep in your store cupboard if you are a keen cook. The result, a coolly elegant, subtly spiced, yoghurt-based dish, is a perfect contrast to the sweet starchy potato dish opposite. Just remember to hang the yoghurt the night before. I find a J-cloth or nylon sieve as effective as muslin, which I don't always have when it's not the jam-making season.

Tadkeywala Dahi

SERVES 1

150g/5oz hung yoghurt
50g/2oz onion, finely chopped
50g/2oz tomatoes, finely chopped
½ tsp cumin seeds
½ tsp coriander seeds
¼ tsp mustard seeds
1 whole red chilli
5ml/1 level tsp vegetable oil
tip of a tsp of turmeric, grate some root if you can get it
tip of a tsp of red chilli powder
½ tsp garlic, crushed to a paste with a little salt
½ tsp fresh coriander, chopped
½ tsp fresh mint, chopped
½ tsp fresh root ginger in matchstick strips
salt

Put the turmeric and chilli in a bowl with a couple of spoons of water to prevent their burning. Heat the oil, add the mustard seeds, coriander and cumin seeds and the whole red chilli. Then add the turmeric and chilli in water and the garlic paste and stir together. Add the onions, stir them in and cook gently until they have softened. Add the tomatoes, continue cooking for a few minutes, then add the chopped fresh coriander, mint, ginger and salt.

Take the mixture off the heat, mix in the hung yoghurt, and serve warm. You could also serve this alongside any plainly cooked white fish or chicken, alone with rice, or with a peshwari naan or a paratha to dip into the juices.

Three days in Bangkok recently taught me just how little I know about Thai food and its subtle variations in heat and style from the north to the south of the country. Watching fresh green coconuts being grated in the market, by women up to their elbows in the white, woody shavings, also made me realize that whatever I cooked on my return could only be an approximation. Chilli, lemongrass, galanga and coconut, fish sauce, shrimp paste, kaffir limes, coriander and garlic – the heat of Thai food is always ameliorated by the harmony procured by the addition of the salt, bitter, sweet and citrus sharpness of the other ingredients. I didn't have galanga, kaffir limes, fresh coconut, lemongrass or fish sauce when I made this, but fresh ginger, limes, a splosh of sherry and creamed coconut in a block defied authenticity with bravura. Just what is cooking all about if you can't think substitution when faced with the inadequacies or shortfall of the depths of your fridge and store cupboard?

My Thai Chicken

SERVES 4

4 large organic chicken breasts
   without their skin, or any cut
   of chicken you happen to have
vegetable oil, something
   unobtrusive such as groundnut
   or grapeseed
2 onions, finely chopped
5 cloves of garlic, finely sliced
2–3 red chillies of whatever
   strength you are comfortable
   with
2 fingers of fresh ginger sliced into
   matchstick strips
a splosh of dry sherry or fish
   sauce
grated zest of 2 limes, kaffir if you
   can find them, and the juice of
   both
300ml/10fl oz chicken or game
   stock, I used pheasant
225g/8oz mangetout, topped and
   tailed
2–3 handfuls of frozen peas
a third of a packet of organic
   creamed coconut, it comes in a
   block
a large bunch of fresh coriander
sea salt and black pepper

Heat the oil in a heavy-bottomed frying pan, then put in the chicken breasts and fry them for about 2 minutes a side until they are beginning to brown. Remove to a plate, add a bit more oil and gently fry the onion, garlic, chilli and ginger together until softened and translucent. Return the chicken breasts to the pan, add a splosh of sherry or fish sauce and allow it to bubble up briefly before you grate the lime zest over the chicken and squeeze on the juice. Season and simmer gently, turning the chicken over after about 7 minutes.

Meanwhile, throw the mangetout into the boiling stock and cook for a couple of minutes. Reserve the stock and refresh the mangetout under cold running water in a colander so that they don't cook any further at this stage.

Reheat the stock to boiling point, throw in the frozen peas and cook them for 5 minutes. Remove the peas from the stock and put them in a bowl. Pour the hot stock on to the lump of creamed coconut and stir to help it dissolve completely, then pour it over the chicken. Cook gently for another 7 minutes or until the chicken is cooked right through with the juices running clear when you pierce the flesh with a skewer. It is important that the liquid does not boil at this stage or the coconut will separate. Finally toss in the mangetout, peas and half the fresh coriander.

Turn out on to a large warmed plate, and scatter on the rest of the fresh coriander. I served my chicken with some plainly boiled green rice, a deliciously smoky Chinese variety, with a firm, slightly chewy texture.

My love affair with Spain is a recent one, nothing too exclusive, but something I am slowly cultivating, albeit in an *ad hoc* sort of way. What I do know, is that each trip I make there – filming the Labeque sisters, French pianists, in Barcelona; visiting the bodegas of Jerez, Sanlucar de Barrameda and Santa Maria with Sam Clark, from the lovely restaurant Moro, whose recipe this is; looking at a fruit-growing estate in Seville in the hazy heat of picking time, when velvet-fuzzed bright apricots and sweetly acidic-scented, white nectarines are in abundance – has been a miniature of perfection, wonderful food, wine, music and hosts. This dish is very Spanish in taste; complex, comforting, substantial, it needs no accompaniment other than a good glass of Rioja and a tomato salad.

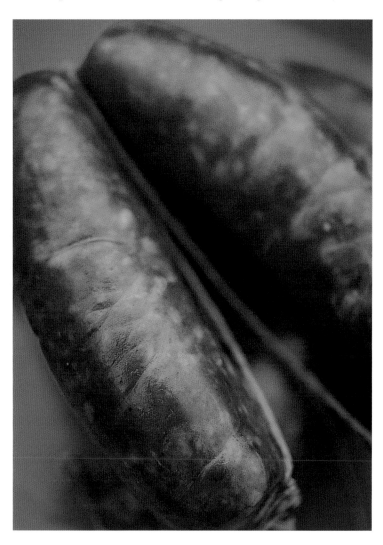

Paella de Cerdo con Chorizo y Espinaca

SERVES 4

7 tbsp olive oil

350g/12oz organic pork fillet, halved lengthways, then sliced into 5mm/¼in strips

125g/4oz mild chorizo, cut into little pieces

2 large Spanish onions, finely chopped

1 large green pepper, halved, seeded and finely chopped

4 cloves of garlic, finely chopped

225g/8oz paella rice, Calasparra is the one, you can buy it in good supermarkets now

1 tsp sweet smoked Spanish paprika

2 ñora peppers or dried peppers, not too hot

900ml/1½ pints hot chicken stock or water

500g/1lb 2 oz spinach, washed and drained

1 lemon, cut in wedges

sea salt and black pepper

In a 30–40cm/12–16in paella pan or frying pan, heat the olive oil over a high heat. Stir fry the pork for a few seconds so it is still a little undercooked. Season with salt and pepper. Remove from the pan with a slotted spoon and put to one side.

Turn down the heat to low and fry the chorizo for a minute. Add the chopped onion and green pepper and cook for 20 minutes, stirring occasionally. Add the garlic and continue cooking for a further 5–10 minutes. At this point the mixture should have caramelized and taste sweet. Stir the rice into the pan for a minute to coat it in the mixture. Up to this point everything can be cooked in advance.

The next stage requires about 20 minutes more cooking time. Add salt and pepper, for this is the time to season the rice perfectly. Add the paprika and ñora peppers, drained of their water, followed by the hot stock, and simmer for 15 minutes or until there is just a thin layer of liquid around the rice.

Meanwhile, in a large saucepan briefly wilt the spinach with a little salt and put it to one side with the pork fillet. Evenly scatter the pork over the rice, followed by the spinach. With the back of a spoon gently push the pork and spinach partially into the oily liquid that remains at the bottom of the pan. Tuck in the lemon wedges, cover the paella tightly with foil and let it sit for 5 minutes before serving.

I have eaten a 'white' daube several times at Lindsay House, the Soho restaurant of my favourite chef, Richard Corrigan. He understands the cheaper cuts of meat better anyone else I know, potting, curing, brining from snout to tail the cuts that many people reject nowadays, mostly out of the combined qualities of shameful ignorance and a feeling that anything that requires longer, slower cooking requires, absurdly, longer, slower preparation. Total myth. Pork shoulder, like shoulder of lamb, wins for taste over leg every day in my book, and lends itself perfectly to the gentle braise that should be at the heart of winter cooking. The sharpness of the apricots – I use unsulphured sticky dark ones, Richard doesn't, he goes for colour – is an inspired touch over the more traditional use of prunes, a sweeter cousin. My interpretation of Richard's dish is just that, a bit of guesswork and poetic licence. If you want to eat the real thing, go to the restaurant.

Daube of Pork with Apricots

SERVES 8
preheat oven to 170°C/325°F/Gas 3

1 shoulder of pork, about 1.5 kg/
   3lb 5oz
3 organic unsulphured apricots
   per person

Marinade:
1 tbsp cumin seeds
½ tbsp fennel seeds
85g/3oz runny honey
100ml/3½fl oz red wine vinegar
8 cloves of garlic
4 sprigs of thyme, the leaves
   pulled from the stems
500ml/18fl oz red wine
5 sprigs of mint, finely chopped
the zest of an organic orange
sea salt and black pepper
2.5 litres/4½ pints of veal stock,
   failing that beef stock

Soak the apricots in an equal amount of freshly squozen orange juice and sweet white wine to cover.

Remove the rind of the pork and cut the meat into 125g/4oz pieces. Mix the marinade ingredients together in a large bowl, add the meat, mixing everything together well with your fingers, cover the bowl and put it in the fridge for 24 hours. Remove the meat and pat it dry with kitchen paper, then brown it in batches in olive oil on all sides in a large heavy-bottomed casserole. Remove it to a plate.

Pour the marinade and meat juices into the casserole and reduce over a high heat to about half their original volume. Return the meat to the pot, cover it with the veal stock, a sheet of greaseproof paper and a lid and cook for 2 hours in the oven.

Meanwhile, gently cook the apricots in their marinade until soft but still holding their shape, and add them to the pork at the end of cooking.

Mashed potato, briefly cooked and refreshed buttered cabbage, perhaps a baked onion, what more could you want?

My cousin Deborah is as much of a culinary conjuror as I am when it comes to magicking up something of a feast from the peasant end of the spectrum of ingredients. Breast is one of the utterly undervalued and underused cuts of meat, be it lamb or veal. The tender, sweet delicacy of this cut of veal, with its gorgeous glueiness, defines the word comfort.

Stuffed Braised Breast of Veal

SERVES 8
preheat oven to 170°C/325°F/Gas 3

1.2kg/2½lb boned breast of veal
2 sticks of celery, roughly
   chopped
2 carrots, roughly chopped
2 onions, roughly chopped
50g/2oz butter
splash of olive oil
150ml/5fl oz vermouth or white
   wine
1 lemon
600ml/1 pint chicken stock
1 sprig each of thyme, rosemary,
   parsley and a bay leaf
1 tbsp crème fraîche
salt and pepper

Stuffing:
50g/2oz butter
1 onion finely chopped
50g/2oz pancetta, chopped
250g/9oz cooked spinach, chopped
50g/2oz boiled rice
50g/2oz Parmesan cheese, grated
1 large egg, beaten
a pinch of grated nutmeg
black pepper to taste

First make the stuffing. Melt the butter and cook the onion until soft and transparent. Add the pancetta and cook through. In a bowl mix the onions and pancetta with the spinach, add the rice, Parmesan cheese, egg, nutmeg and black pepper and mix them together thoroughly.

Open up the breast of veal, sprinkle lightly with salt and black pepper. Spread the stuffing in the middle of the meat. Roll up the breast and tie with string along its length.

Melt the butter and olive oil in a casserole large enough to take the veal and vegetables. Brown the veal all over in the butter and oil mixture. Remove the veal from the casserole and brown the vegetables. Add the herbs, the juice of the lemon and the skins of the lemon halves after they have been squeezed, the vermouth or white wine and stock. Bring to a simmer. Add the veal, cover with a lid and put in the middle of the oven. Baste and turn the meat two or three times during the cooking.

Check the veal after two hours. If it is tender when it is pierced with a fork, it will be cooked, if not leave for the extra half hour.

When it's done, remove the veal to a warm dish to rest while you make the sauce. Skim any fat off the pan juices and reduce if necessary over a high heat until you have about 425ml/15fl oz. Strain into a clean saucepan, check the seasoning and whisk in a tablespoon of crème fraîche. Serve with the veal.

I always cook more pulses than I need. Mindful of their expansion I may be, but I am singularly incapable of emptying less than a packet into the bowl to soak or, in the case of lentils, straight into the pan. It is probably because they so easily have two incarnations – and keep extremely well in the fridge as long as you remember to bring them back to room temperature before serving them. This dish is perfect for a summer lunch, supper or picnic and can be prepared in advance before being left to marinate for a couple of hours. Or you can eat it warm as soon as you have made the dressing.

Puy Lentil, Feta, Roast Tomato and Onion Salad Marinated in a Coriander, Red Chilli and Ginger Dressing

SERVES 6
preheat oven to 200°C/400°F/Gas 6

350g/12oz Puy lentils
4 large organic tomatoes
2 onions, peeled and cut into 6 pieces
olive oil
3 handfuls of pousse, the baby spinach whose stalks are tender enough to eat
175g/6oz best sheep's milk feta, I use Mary Holbrook's, available by mail order from The Fine Cheese Company. Rinse the feta in cold water when you take it out of its brine.
3 cloves of garlic
4cm/1½in finger of fresh ginger
1 red chilli, seeded
a large bunch of fresh coriander
a generous tsp of Dijon mustard
olive oil
juice of 1½ lemons
sea salt and black pepper

Put the lentils in an enamel pot and just cover with water. Bring them to the boil, take any scum off the surface, then simmer them until cooked, about 40 minutes. They do not need to be pre-soaked.

Meanwhile, halve the tomatoes and place them on a baking tray with the onions. Pour over a generous libation of olive oil and put the tray of vegetables in the oven to roast for about 30 minutes. The tomatoes should be weeping juice and soft, and the onions should have caramelly bits and also be soft. Drain the lentils and place them in a bowl with a splosh of good olive oil and the spinach, which will begin to wilt in their heat. Stir until it has. Crumble the feta over the top.

Now make the dressing. Chop the garlic, ginger and chilli and put them in a food processor with the coriander. Add the juices from the roasted tomatoes and onions, the mustard, then some more olive oil, about 5 tablespoons, and the lemon juice. Season and blitz. Taste and adjust anything that needs it. Place the warm tomatoes and onions in the salad and pour over the dressing, turning the whole salad when you have done so with your fingers. Serve or leave to marinate for a couple of hours and eat at room temperature.

Buy the thickest fillet of cod you can find. The Puy lentils need no soaking, so the whole dish can be made in 50 minutes. The marriage of lentils and bacon, pancetta, smoked ham or prosciutto is as well known as it is delicious. The equation can be complicated and enhanced with cod, which parties well with both lentils and bacon, be they wrapped, over, under or beside it. In fact, the cod is all the better for the smoky strength of the pig, which does nothing to undermine the fish's more subtle flavour but everything to cod it up.

Roast Cod with Braised Puy Lentils and Roasted Vegetables

SERVES 2
preheat oven to 220°C/425°F/Gas 7

200g/7oz Puy lentils
1 bulb of fennel
1 onion
olive oil
a small sprig of fresh thyme
12 cherry tomatoes
450g/1lb or so thick cod fillet
3 or 4 rashers streaky bacon
2 heaped tbsp crème fraîche

Just cover the lentils with water in a large, heavy-bottomed pot. Bring them to the boil, then cover and turn down to a simmer. They will take about 40 minutes to cook.

Meanwhile, chop the fennel bulb in half and each half into thirds, cut the peeled onion into large chunks, and place both in a small roasting tin. Pour a slug of olive oil over the top, season, add the sprig of thyme and put in the oven to roast.

After 20 minutes, add the tomatoes. All the vegetables should be soft after a further 20 minutes, but pierce with a skewer to test. Put the cod in a gratin dish, pour a good couple of tablespoons of olive oil over the top, season well and cook in the hot oven for 12 minutes before piercing with a skewer. The flesh should be unresistant right the way through.

While the fish is cooking, snip the bacon into tiny strips and fry them in a little pan until well browned on both sides. Drain the lentils, then add the bacon. Tip in the roasted vegetables with their juice, and the crème fraîche. Serve the cod alongside or on top of the lentils. You may wish to serve some creamy mashed potato, too.

Baked Turbot with Sauce Bretonne

SERVES 6
preheat oven to 200°C/400°F/Gas 6

1 x 2.25–3kg/5–6lb turbot
50g/2oz unsalted butter
150ml/5fl oz white wine
a small bunch of chervil
    and flat-leaf parsley, chopped
sea salt and black pepper

For the sauce:
4 organic egg yolks
2 tsp Dijon mustard
a few drops of tarragon vinegar,
    if you don't have any, use white
    wine vinegar with a teaspoon
    of fresh tarragon
2 tbsp watercress, chopped
2 tbsp chopped chervil, chopped
125g/4oz melted unsalted butter,
    the creamy solids removed
sea salt and pepper

Stuff the fish with the herbs. Grease a large roasting tin with butter, and place the fish in it. Pour over the white wine, dot the fish with butter and season. Cover the fish with a sheet of greaseproof paper and cook it for about 25 minutes before testing it with a skewer right the way through. How long it will take depends on the thickness of the fish, so if it is only a tiny bit resistant at its thickest point, check it again in 5 minutes. It is not difficult – fish are not temperamental or more difficult to master than meat, but there is less leeway between being cooked and overcooked. Roughly 10 minutes before you are going to test the fish, start making your sauce.

Stir together the egg yolks, salt and pepper with the Dijon mustard. Add a few drops of the tarragon vinegar, then add the watercress and chervil and slowly stir in the melted butter, a few drops at a time to start with, as you would for mayonnaise. The sauce will hold if you place it over a bowl of hot water, but do not make it in advance – you want the herbs to be green and fresh tasting. You can experiment with other herbs like chives, flat-leaf parsley and dill, the best herb if you want to try the sauce with a piece of poached wild salmon or sea trout.

A perfectly beautiful pale salad, lightly bound with a herb mayonnaise. Each ingredient adds a different texture and flavour; the whole is a dish of gentle subtlety requiring absolutely nothing else. When I first made it, my youngest daughter Charissa and I ate the whole bowlful.

Jersey Royal, Chicken, Green Bean, Egg and Avocado Salad in a Herb Mayonnaise

SERVES 2

2 handfuls of green beans
350–400g/12–14oz small Jersey Royal new potatoes, scraped, boiled and still warm
1 organic Hass avocado
2 organic eggs, or free-range Clarence Court's Cotswold Legbar eggs
125g/4oz or so of left-over chicken, without the skin, pulled along the grain into 5mm/¼in strips
home-made mayonnaise made with an egg yolk, half olive oil, half sunflower oil, lemon juice and salt, with a handful of snipped chives, finely chopped flat-leaf parsley and 6 finely chopped lovage leaves if you have them, stirred in

Soak the green beans in cold water for an hour to invigorate them. Top and tail and throw them, a handful at a time, into a large pan of rapidly boiling, well-salted water. Do not put a lid on the pan or throw all the beans in at once, so lowering the temperature of the water to below boiling. If you do, the beans will turn out khaki rather than sparkling green. Cook until they have just lost their bite. Resistant green beans are horrid, the French never fell for the bizarre *al dente* bean habit we seemed to embrace 10 years ago. Plunge the beans immediately into cold water to arrest the cooking, drain them and chop into thirds.

Meanwhile, softly hard boil the eggs, halve them and cut each half into three. Slice the larger cooked potatoes in half, leave the pebble-sized ones whole. Cut the avocado into slices.

Place everything in a roomy, pretty bowl. Pour over the herbed mayonnaise, and turn the salad lightly so that nothing gets broken up. Serve while the beans and potatoes still have a memory of warmth about them.

You can use loin of venison for this dish if you prefer, taking it off the bone and marinating it in red wine for a couple of days. Wild roe deer does have an incomparable flavour, but it is not always possible to lay your hands on it. The best unintensively reared venison I can get comes from Graeme Wallace out on the Blackdown Hills. I find that keeping his medallions of venison in the packet in my fridge for two to three weeks improves both the flavour and texture. I want game, not beef. The sweet-sour, aniseedy-earthy, creamy-perfumed elements of the subtext are powerful foils to the venison.

Medallions of Venison with Spiced Beetroot, Cornichons, Tarragon and Sour Cream

SERVES 4

700g/1½ lb or so of medallions, at
   least 1cm/½in thick
2 shallots
butter
6 juniper berries, crushed
1 heaped tsp redcurrant jelly
50ml/2fl oz port
125ml/4fl oz red wine
300ml/½ pint game or chicken
   stock
4 or 5 cornichons
fresh tarragon, finely chopped
50ml/2fl oz sour cream
2 or 3 medium beetroot,
   scrubbed, whiskers still
   attached, wrapped in foil and
   baked in a medium oven
25g/1oz unsalted butter
well-aged balsamic vinegar

Chop the shallots finely and sweat them in a little butter with the crushed juniper berries until softened, before adding the redcurrant jelly, port and red wine. Reduce them by about a half, then add the stock and again reduce by a half.

While this is happening, cook the medallions in a pan with a little melted butter, turning them frequently and making absolutely sure that you don't overcook them. Dried-out venison is not one of the great pleasures of life; tender, pink, stickily oozing venison is. Check with the point of a skewer – you want a little blood, but the meat should feel soft right through, after about 3 minutes a side. Season.

When the stock has reduced, finish it with a generous tablespoon of sour cream, some finely sliced cornichons and a little finely chopped tarragon. The beetroot you can cook in advance, peel when it is not too hot, and grate. Then all you need to do is heat it through in a bit of butter, salt and pepper and a little aged balsamic vinegar.

Roe deer produces the best-flavoured venison, in a different league from red. It needs to be well hung and then marinated, before being covered in a protective coating of fat. It has so little fat of its own that it dries out disastrously without it. I think roast venison works much better with mashed potatoes than roast, and a coarse mash of carrot and swede. You can then serve roasted parsnips for texture. A great dish for a party of eight or more. The streaky bacon is not worth eating. Don't be tempted to use smoked — its flavour is too pervasive.

Roast Haunch of Venison

SERVES 8

a haunch of venison
1 bottle good red wine
2 tbsp olive oil
brandy
1 tsp juniper berries, bruised
1 tsp black peppercorns
organic, unsmoked streaky bacon
3 onions, sliced
1 tbsp elder and blackberry jelly
    or any sharp jelly

My haunch weighed more than 2.25kg/5lb. I kept it in the fridge for four days — longer would have been fine — before putting it on a large, shallow plate in a coolish place for two days, with a marinade of the wine, olive oil, a measure of brandy and some juniper berries and black peppercorns. Again, a few days longer would have been fine. I basted or turned it over from time to time, and kept it under clingfilm.

When you're ready to cook the venison, preheat the oven to 200°C/400°F/Gas 6. Season and cover the whole of the top of the haunch with slices of organic, unsmoked, streaky bacon, place it on a bed of sliced onions in a roasting tin, and cook it for two hours.

Transfer the meat to a carving dish, cover it with foil and leave it to rest for 25 minutes, allowing the juices to work their way back through to the edge of the meat from the middle. I made a ruby red gravy from the marinade stirred into the caramelized onions with a tablespoon of elder and blackberry jelly.

I am not suggesting Christmas Eve is the only time you eat this dish, it is too good for that, but I always cook a special fish dish then in both anticipation and dread of the monstrous meat fest that ensues. This Christmas Eve we had lightly smoked eel fillets from Brown and Forrest for lunch with a home-made horseradish cream and granary toast. With them, I served shot glasses of the first of my late bottled damson and mulberry gin. In the evening I roasted enormously thick hake steaks on the bone, hence the charnel house oven temperature, and cooked Poor Man's Potatoes, the Spanish patatas a lo pobre. The latter is a oily, garlicky potato dish that I make with both red and green peppers, decanting the excess deliciously scented olive oil into a jar to use for cooking stewing meat, onions, fish or any dish that can carry the robust flavours.

Roast Hake Steaks with Poor Man's Potatoes

SERVES 4
preheat oven to 230°C/450°F/Gas 8

4 extra-thick hake steaks on the
    bone, mine were about 4cm/
    1½ in thick
sea salt and black pepper

For the potatoes:
about 15 tbsp best extra virgin
    olive oil
3 large onions, sliced thinly
5–6 cloves garlic, sliced thickly
3 peppers, red and green, I usually
    use two red to one green, the
    red are more digestible
3 or 4 fresh bay leaves
1kg/2¼lb firm waxy-fleshed
    potatoes
a couple of handfuls of cherry
    tomatoes (optional)
sea salt and black pepper

In a large heavy-bottomed pot, heat 5 tablespoons of the olive oil, then add the finely sliced onion and some salt to help release the juice. Cook gently for about 20 minutes, stirring occasionally, until softened and translucent. Add the sliced garlic, roughly chopped peppers and the bay leaves, which you can break a bit to release their flavour, and cook for a further 15 minutes.

Cut the potatoes lengthwise, then cut each slice into two or three chunks and salt them lightly. Add the rest of the olive oil to the pan and when it has heated up, throw in the potatoes and the tomatoes if you are using them. Leave everything to simmer for 40–50 minutes, by which time the potatoes will have cooked through completely when you pierce them with a skewer. Drain the oil through a sieve into a jug, enough will have adhered to coat the vegetables without them swimming, and all the flavours will have married most pleasingly.

About 15–20 minutes before the potatoes are ready, brush the hake steaks on both sides with olive oil, put them in a gratin dish and season. Put the fish in the oven, and test it after 15 minutes with the point of a skewer through its thickest part. The flesh should not resist you at all and be flaky, translucent and juicy without having softened to a pulp. The potatoes will keep warm in the warming oven if there is any discrepancy over timing. If you use cherry tomatoes, you will have no need of a further vegetable.

I am so easily led, but I suspect that is the fate or the temperament of many a keen cook. This is the third book I have written to include a recipe for Irish stew, and just in case anyone has even noticed and feels short-changed, they have all been different. This latest is my under-the-influence version of how Richard Corrigan, the divine Irish chef of Lindsay House, and I cooked it when he came down to appear in my recent television series for U.K. Food. We managed what amounted to a four-course thesis on the merits and demerits of everything from scrag to middle neck of lamb; whether barley should or shouldn't be used (and, I might say, another major influence, Simon Hopkinson, to whom I gossiped subsequently on the subject of Richard's theory, disagreed totally); stock versus water; and which vegetables and herbs.

I am now convinced that Richard is right, although I don't know whether I'll always be bothered to bring the meat to the boil first and discard the water, and plunge the potatoes into the stew 40 minutes or so before the dish is ready, rather than burying them at the outset as I have always done. But Richard has managed to shame me into not using barley any more, as he thinks it's a starch too far with the potato. Simon differs, but then he's not Irish, although Richard's reasons are textural rather than to do with authenticity. And I actually taught him something, a first and probably a last! He took one look at my Swaddles Green organic scrag, cut into thick, bony, fatty chunks, and said that he'd been trying to get meat that looked as good as mine but had never succeeded.

Irish Stew

SERVES 6

1.5kg/3lb 5oz organic scrag of
    lamb
4 onions, sliced
450g/1lb carrots, cut into thick
    discs
3 strung stalks of celery, cut into
    short lengths
a bouquet of fresh herbs
1kg/2¼lb floury winter potatoes
sea salt and black pepper

Cover the meat with water in a large, heavy-bottomed pot and bring it slowly to the boil. Remove the meat to a plate, throw out the scummy water and start again – put the vegetables at the bottom of the pot, tuck in the bouquet, place the meat on top of the vegetables, and just cover with water, or tuck in the potatoes before covering with water. I think I will continue to cook the potatoes in the pot from the start, since they help the water to become thickened and starchy. Season, bring to the boil, cover with a lid and cook at a gentle blip for a couple of hours.

Then, Richard's thickening trick: remove a good couple of ladles of potato, vegetable and juice, mash to a coarse pulp with a potato masher and return to the pot. Consume in large quantities, perhaps with some colcannon. Even better the next day if you allow the dish to cool, skim off the congealed meat fat, and reheat when you want it.

Colcannon

SERVES 6—8

1kg/2¼lb green cabbage, finely
    chopped
2 small leeks, finely chopped
150–300ml/5–10fl oz milk
1kg/2¼lb potatoes, roughly
    chopped
salt and pepper
a pinch of grated nutmeg
125g/4oz butter

Simmer the cabbage and leeks in just enough milk to cover, until soft. Boil the potatoes until tender, drain and mash them, then season to taste with salt, pepper and nutmeg. Add the cabbage, leek and milk mixture. Place in a deep, warmed serving dish, make a well in the centre and pour in the melted butter. Serve the vegetables with spoonfuls of the butter.

This is for an older leg, a hogget rather than a tasteless and underage youth, or indeed for a real oldster – a ruby red leg of mutton which Somerset Lamb Direct rear and will send to you in the post. See page 282 for details.

Leg of Lamb Braised slowly with Haricot Beans

SERVES 8
preheat oven to 230°C/450°F/Gas 8

500g/1lb 2oz haricot or flageolet
   beans, soaked overnight
butter and olive oil
1 leg of lamb
a small ladleful of brandy
225g/8oz unsmoked streaky
   bacon, snipped into strips,
   rind removed
2 carrots, peeled and diced
2 stalks of celery, peeled and sliced
2 onions, peeled and chopped
3 leeks, cleaned and sliced
12 whole cloves of garlic, peeled
a bunch of fresh rosemary, thyme
   and bay tied together
½ bottle white wine
1–1.5 litres/1¾–3 pints chicken
   stock
sea salt and black pepper

Drain the beans, just cover them with fresh water and bring them to the boil. Remove any scum with a slotted spoon and kitchen paper, then simmer for an hour. They will be undercooked. Drain them but keep their liquor.

Heat a knob of butter and a good slug of olive oil in a large, heavy-bottomed pot. Season, then gently brown the joint on all sides. Pour the brandy into the pot, warm it, then set light to it with a taper, letting it flame and crackle until the alcohol has burnt off.

Put the joint and all the juices into a roasting tin. Add a bit more fat and oil to the pot and brown the bacon, adding the vegetables and garlic when the fat begins to run. When the vegetables have began to soften, scrape the contents of the pot into the roasting tin, add the bouquet of herbs, beans, and enough wine and stock, which you have heated together, to cover the vegetables but not the meat. Add some of the bean liquor if you need to.

Cover the tin with foil and cook in the oven for 3½ to 4 hours, turning every 40 minutes or so. Adjust the seasoning and cut the lamb into thick slices, heaping each plate with mashed potato, vegetables, beans and juices as you go.

Every year I feel impelled to come up with a different solution for the remains of our lovely organic Bronze turkey; pies, risottos and fricassés have all had their year, as have pulled and devilled turkey, and turkey curry. This year I made the most successful dish yet, spurred on by the thought that the friends we were having over to supper would consider cold turkey, if not exactly an insult, perhaps something unexpected in the originality and expectation department. This is something to do when you really want to finish the bird, since I do not believe in removing the meat from the carcass until the point you are going to eat it: it dries out more quickly away from the bone. So, remove all the meat you can and make a huge pot or two of turkey stock the afternoon of the gratin supper. The sauce you are going to swathe the bird in is unctuously creamy, but made less so with equal quantities of hot stock. You can prepare the dish, right up to the heating up and blasting under the grill, a bit earlier in the afternoon. White and dark meat should be used in as equal quantities as possible. I fed seven people, with second helpings for those who wanted them.

A Gratin of Turkey… or Chicken, Guinea Fowl, Pheasant

SERVES 7

about 1kg/2¼lb turkey meat,
   pulled along the grain into
   roughly equal-sized pieces
50g/2oz butter
2 heaped tbsp plain flour
300ml/½ pint or so of rich
   Channel Islands milk
10–12 tbsp double cream
12–14 tbsp turkey stock, but you
   may need more of all three:
   milk, cream and stock
nutmeg, sea salt and pepper
4 tbsp Parmesan cheese, coarsely
   grated
2–3 handfuls of breadcrumbs
a further tbsp or two of Parmesan
   cheese, coarsely grated

Melt the butter, then stir in the flour off the heat. Return to the stove, add half the hot milk and whisk it in. Add the rest of the milk, continuing to whisk until you have a satin-smooth, but far too thick, blanket of sauce, about 5 minutes. Add the cream and the hot turkey stock, half of each at a time, and continue to whisk. Season, being sparing with the salt at this stage as the Parmesan is salty, and cook very, very gently for about 20 minutes on a heat diffuser if you have one. You should no longer be able to smell flour when it has been cooking long enough. You want a thick, velvety pouring consistency, so if the sauce still looks too solid, add some more cream and stock, and whisk them in. Off the heat, whisk in the Parmesan and adjust the seasoning.

Pour a layer of sauce into a large gratin dish, just to coat the bottom of the dish. Add the turkey, pour over the rest of the sauce, sprinkle with breadcrumbs and grated Parmesan and cook in a hot oven for 15 minutes. Finish under the grill until bubbling and golden. If you are making it in advance, allow the dish to cool down before you sprinkle it with breadcrumbs and cheese.

A traditional Provençal bourride is a rich fish stew enlivened and enriched with dollops of aïoli, a pungent with-garlic-and-green-olive-oil mayonnaise that is stirred into it at the last minute. I think this dish lends itself equally well to being made with chicken. The bird is jointed and braised in strong herbs and saffron, the juices acidic with tomato and white wine. The acid balance is then rescued and somehow brought back from the brink at the last moment by the emulsification of the garlic, egg yolk and oil .

A Bourride of Chicken

SERVES 6

For the chicken:
1 decent-sized organic chicken, skinned and jointed, each leg cut into 2 pieces. Leave the wings on the carcass for stock
350g/12oz leeks, the whites only, well washed, trimmed and sliced
6 or 7 carrots, thinly sliced
2 medium onions, thinly sliced
400g/14oz tin of whole organic tomatoes
3 cloves of garlic, finely chopped
olive oil
3 strips of orange peel
a good pinch of saffron filaments
a few sprigs of fresh thyme, bay leaves and marjoram or oregano
150ml/5fl oz dry white wine
sea salt and fresh black pepper

Heat some olive oil in a heavy-bottomed casserole, then add the leeks, carrots and onions and sweat them gently for 10 minutes. Add the garlic and tin of tomatoes, chopping them down into the pan as you go. Stir everything together, then add the pieces of chicken, orange peel, saffron, a couple of sprigs each of the herbs, stripped from their stems, and a couple of bay leaves.

Simmer very gently for another 10 minutes, then add the wine and bring back to boiling point. Cover with a layer of greaseproof paper and a lid and cook on top of the stove until the chicken is tender and the juice runs clear when the flesh is pierced with a skewer, about 20–25 minutes.

You can get the dish to this point an hour or so in advance, then just warm it through when you're ready to eat. You can also make the aïoli in advance and merely effect the heating through and their ultimate marriage when you are ready to do so.

For the aïoli:

4 large cloves of garlic, peeled

sea salt

1 organic egg yolk

150–300ml/5–10fl oz best extra
    virgin, cold-pressed green olive
    oil, you need this intensity and
    fruitiness for *le vrai aïoli*

lemon juice

Pound the garlic in a mortar with a little bit of sea salt, add the egg yolk and stir it in with a wooden spoon. Start pouring the olive oil in a drop at a time, stirring continuously until the liquid begins to emulsify to yellow ointment. Then you can pour in a slow, steady stream, making sure that your stirring incorporates the oil as quickly as it descends into the bowl. Add lemon juice to taste at the end.

If you are going to keep the aïoli for an hour or two before using, pour a thin film of olive oil over its surface to prevent a crust forming. You can stir this oil back into the aïoli when you are ready to drop it into the bourride.

To add the aïoli to the dish, put a couple of ladles of the hot sauce into a bowl. Whisk in the aïoli quickly with a balloon whisk, then put it back into the pot off the heat, and whisk it in further before you serve it. A few plain boiled potatoes are all you need to crush into the bourride, followed by a green salad.

This dish is a true classic. It is perfect at an al fresco summer lunch, with a huge white spoon planted into the thickly sticky ointment of aïoli.

It is not the ingredients that are sufficiently different for me to have the nerve to give you this recipe, it is the technique. Or techniques, since I am also giving you a completely unorthodox version, given to me by the talented chef of The Fat Duck at Bray, Heston Blumenthal. Heston's is as scientifically unimpeachable as a recipe can be and, since he is in cahoots with Peter Barham, a physics professor at Bristol University, he is in something of an unparallel universe to my own. I first met Heston and Peter at a hifalutin' sounding conference on molecular gastronomy at Erice in Sicily earlier in the year. What I learned, in a reductionist nutshell, was to question the methodology of everything I had ever cooked, because there was probably a better way of doing it scientifically speaking. And that I should never have ignored the huge part that science plays in the cooking of good food in such a comprehensive way. You do not have to be a scientist to understand the reasons and methods behind the processes. Scientists, food technologists, food writers and chefs all gathered together for three days to try to understand better what happens to food when we subject it to the alchemy of cooking, to try to define taste and texture and what we mean by them; and to cast aside some of our insular prejudices.

Mashed Potato – My Mash

SERVES 3

one large or two medium
    potatoes per person. Choose a
    floury textured, absorbent
    variety rather than a firm, waxy
    one
150ml/5fl oz full-cream milk
85g/3oz unsalted butter
seasoning

My favourite potato for mash is the 'salad blue' grown organically by my friend Peter Whiteman in Devon. Not only does it have the right floury texture, it is a deep violet colour, making, after the paling effects of the milk and butter, a thrillingly exotic parma violet-coloured mash. Quantity is down to the individual, but my Irish blood is clearly dominant in the amount I and my family seem to get through.

Mash is both vehicle, background and food in its own right. It should be cooked as carefully and with as much attention as whatever else is going to grace your plate, which it often isn't. There is absolutely no excuse in my book for watery, lumpy, slack or under-seasoned mash, even less for butter-free mash, unless you are being ersatz Provençal and pouring in a glug of olive oil. Low-fat spreads and skimmed milk are not what mash is all about. And if you are worried about the butter quota, just eat less mash, ergo you eat less butter.

Peel the potatoes, cut them into large chunks and cover them with water in a saucepan. Sprinkle in some salt, and bring them to the boil with the lid on, then turn down the temperature to a leisurely simmer and cook until you can pierce them right through with a skewer without resistance. No hard edges but not so cooked that they are beginning to collapse. Drain the potatoes, then put a clean tea towel over the top of the pan, and force the lid down as hard as you can for 5 minutes, just as you would to absorb the steam when you have been cooking rice.

Turn the potatoes into your mouli-légumes with the coarse disc in place, and gently heat about 150ml/5fl oz of full cream milk or Channel Islands milk with a good lump of unsalted butter, about 85g/3oz for 3 people, in the pan in which you cooked the potatoes. Mouli the potatoes into the pan as the milk heats and the butter melts, then season to taste. Over gentle heat, stir the potato, milk and butter well together with a wooden spoon, altering the texture and flavour if it is not quite right with the addition of more butter and/or milk and seasoning.

You will realize when you begin to stir, just how smooth this precious kitchen gadget renders your potatoes. If you do not have a mouli, may I suggest they are invaluable? Soups have more texture and body mouliedd than if you swirl them to oblivion in a liquidizer, and your mashed potato will be peerless. Enough said.

Well not quite. Richard Corrigan passes his potatoes through a potato ricer twice, and probably uses half the amount of butter to potato. Sublime and sublimely rich. It is brought to the table in little copper saucepans. I always ask for more, despite the butter content; I just can't help myself, it is the best.

Heston's Mashed Potato

potatoes, Belle de Fontenay, Bintje or Charlottes are particularly good for mash, but Desireé can work well, too
butter, a third the weight of your potatoes or less

Peel and slice the potatoes into 2.5cm/1in chunks. Soak them in hot water, around 65°C/150°F, for 30 minutes, keeping the water at as constant a temperature as you can. Presoaking fixes the starch molecules, making an even network of gelatinized starch surrounded by water. In effect, you've stopped free starch molecules running around.

After 30 minutes, put the potatoes in cold running water until cold – they will look opaque – then put them into a pan of barely simmering salted water. Cook them at a blip – if the water boils too much they will break up – for about 30 minutes, until the point of a knife goes in without resistance. Drain the potatoes, put them back in the pan with a cloth under the lid and shake them while they dry out.

Then put them through a potato ricer or the finest disc of a mouli on to diced cold butter in a bowl. Heston uses a third the weight of butter to potato, you may wish to use less. He then pushes them through a drum sieve twice; you can use the mouli. Forcing the potato down rather than from side to side, stops it from going gluey. By this method, you have gelatinized the starch and made an emulsion, rather like mayonnaise.

To finish, put the mash in a pan and warm some milk in another pan. Pour the milk over your potato base a bit at a time, over a gentle heat, whisking it as you go, until you achieve the desired texture. Add freshly ground white pepper at the end.

You can keep this base in the fridge until you need it. Never before have I come across a scientific way of making mash that means you can keep it in the fridge for up to four days without its being beyond redemption. I never put mash in the fridge full stop, but having gelatinized the starch, it will not come to grief, as long as you bring it back to room temperature before heating it through gently as above.

Another utterly unorthodox yet scientifically proven way of cooking this classic dish to perfection. You may cook this version the day before and merely heat it through when you want it, without it separating into an oily, unappetizing mass. First buy your mandolin, preferably of the strong plastic Japanese variety, from Hansen's, the cookery shop (0207 351 6933).

Heston's Pommes Dauphinoise

SERVES 2
preheat oven to 110°C/225°F/Gas ¼

450g/1lb potatoes
150ml/5fl oz milk
1 sliced clove of garlic
a sprig of thyme and a bay leaf
some nutmeg, cayenne and salt
100ml/3½fl oz cream
85–150g/3–5oz unsalted butter

Slice the potatoes on your mandolin straight into a gratin dish containing the milk, which should cover the potatoes, so you may need another 150ml/5 fl oz. Add the garlic, herbs, spices and salt, err on the generous side with the salt as the potatoes draw it in, and bring it up to a simmer. Simmer for 5 minutes, making sure the potatoes do not stick to the bottom of the pan, then remove the thyme and bay leaf. The potato starch thickens the milk, so you can use less cream.

Then add the cream and unsalted butter, depending on your taste, and place the gratin dish on a baking tray in the oven for 4 hours under a tightly wrapped foil lid. After each hour, if you can remember, remove the foil lid and press down the potatoes with a spatula to bring the liquid back up to the surface. When you remove the dish from the oven, there will be liquid covering the top of the potatoes. Leave the dish overnight in the fridge with the foil cover on, and a couple of weights on top of it, and the potatoes will reabsorb the liquid.

When you want to use the potatoes, remove the gratin dish from the fridge in time to bring them up to room temperature, preheat the oven again, heat the dish through for 20 minutes, then place it under the grill until it is golden and bubbling.

Ingredients ready for a jambon
persillé, a stunning party dish
which can be prepared ahead
of time and kept in the fridge.
Try it — you won't regret it.

the advance party

3

Some dishes are made for parties and the best of them, if you are the party giver, are the ones that simply demand to be prepared in advance. Jambon persillé, a beautiful pink and green mosaic, Jackson Pollock of a dish, is one of them. When my first attempt plopped out of its glass bowl on to a plate, glistening rosy-pink chunks and grassy green seams glued with the transparently binding jelly from the trotters, I did stop for a brief minute to marvel. It tasted as stunning as it looked. Make the dish the day before you need it.

Jambon Persillé

SERVES 12
it really isn't worth making less, but it keeps well in the fridge

1 x 2.5kg/5½lb unsmoked
   shoulder joint of organic
   bacon, tied
4 organic pig's trotters, split
a bunch each of tarragon, thyme
   and parsley
12 black peppercorns
6 juniper berries, bruised
1 bottle of dry white wine
6 tbsp flat-leaf parsley, chopped
2 cloves of garlic, crushed
2 tbsp tarragon vinegar
grated nutmeg
pepper

Cut the bacon into three large chunks, still tied, and place in a heavy-bottomed pot with the trotters, herbs, spices and wine. Top up with water if you need, just to cover the meat completely. Bring to the boil slowly, scum rigorously and continue cooking at a mere blip for 2 hours. Remove the bacon to a plate and leave it to cool. Remove the herbs, then continue to boil the liquid and trotters for a further 30 minutes. Strain into a large bowl and cool quickly. Once the liquid is cool, skim off as much of the white fat as possible.

Don't cut the meat until the stock has completely cooled, or it will dry out. Leaving some but not all of the fat on it, cut the meat into 1cm/½in squares. Place them in the bottom of a large, glass bowl. Some people use a terrine, but I think a great circular domed mosaic is more breathtaking. Add the parsley, crushed garlic and tarragon vinegar to the cooled liquid, then the nutmeg and pepper, and tip the contents over the bacon. Stir to allow the parsley to mix in with the bacon. The bacon should be completely covered. Keep any extra liquid to use as jellied stock. Cover the bowl with clingfilm and put it in the fridge overnight.

When it has set, spoon off the white fat down to the darker jelly. Remove the bowl from the fridge 30 minutes before you want to serve the jambon. Immediately before serving, dunk the bowl into boiling water for about 15 seconds. Turn the jambon persillé out on to a plain white dish. Serve it with mustard, cornichons, buttered new potatoes and a plain cos lettuce salad, or with home-made bread and best butter.

When, last summer, the nearest bakery to me that makes anything faintly resembling a decent loaf erased three-quarters of its loaves from its repertoire, it was clearly time to take action. Hobbs House bakery at Chipping Sodbury doesn't deliver its wondrous bread this far south of Bristol. And my infrequent trips to Baker and Spice in London are utterly spoiling when they happen, but make the thought of being despoiled the rest of the time with inferior supermarket pap – for which you are paying for air and water rather than flour and time – distinctly unappealing.

Bread, a work in progress

The world falls into two camps at this point: those who make their own bread and those, like me, who don't. Or didn't. As I write this, I realize my early weeks as a bread-making novice have now turned into months. Seven months. And bar the odd loaf bought hungrily from the two impeccable sources mentioned above, I have kept up this new pursuit as doggedly as the running I started nearly two years ago. In fact, the two are not altogether unallied. Training for my first marathon earlier in the year gave me a prodigious appetite for carbohydrates, and turned me into a breakfaster. Home-made bread, toasted, with home-made crab apple or bramble jelly in the autumn and early winter, later followed by Seville orange marmalade – my other new-found skill – is now a habit it would be difficult to break.

Literature on the subject of bread making is so extensive as to be seriously off-putting to the beginner, even a relatively experienced cook like myself. What you want is a simple, crusted loaf that has a fine texture and flavour, and is not gluey, taut-grained, crumbly, spongy or leaden. You want it to work the first and every subsequent time, instilling confidence, a sense of achievement and the feeling that finally, finally, one has the sort of kitchen that smells how a kitchen should. There is no better scent than that of a fresh, yeasted loaf rising, cooking and cooling before you eat it – still warm, nutty, crusty, with a just-too-large-to-be-decent slab of deliquescent unsalted butter.

The last few months have taught me many things. First, it is perfectly possible to fit bread making into the most hectic of schedules, and without being a martyr to the cause. It does not demand the sort of attention that many supposedly simpler dishes do. I can leave it to rise and go out running AM or make and eat dinner as it rises PM. If you bake three loaves at a time and freeze one or two, depending on the size of your family, bread making does not become a chore, it stays a delight. Every bag of flour you buy, albeit the same make as the last one you bought, is different, so you need to feel what you're doing, not just follow instructions. That takes experience, but all the bread I've baked has been better than supermarket bread, and most of it has been REALLY good. The ambient temperature makes a difference.

Fresh yeast bought at the supermarket bakery counter isn't always fresh. I have been sold dead yeast on a number of occasions. Always inspect the packet before you walk away. If it is pale and crumbly rather than rubbery, and in a homogenous, springy block, do not accept it. Some recipes say 30g of yeast per 450g loaf, some say 45g per three 450g loaves. I have made both. My son Harry was complaining at the over-yeasty taste of the bread with the larger concentration, when I found the second recipe on another packet of flour, which, incidentally, reversed the kneading and knocking-back processes from my original recipe. Less yeast, and kneading after the first mixing rather than the second, work much better, both for texture and taste.

As for the kneading, four or five minutes is not enough. You have to knead vigorously for eight to ten minutes and only then, in my experience, will your loaf not turn into a compressed breezeblock. It is the only hard work throughout the process, and its rigours are both comforting and enjoyable if you are prepared to find them so, which I decidedly am. No bread-making machine or dough hook I've used has done it for me so far, and the dried yeast you use in machines does not make bread of the taste or texture that you are making homemade bread for in the first place. Circular loaves baked in a low-sided tin work the best as you get the highest surface area of crisp crust, but don't make a loaf in too big a tin, since the loaf will spread sideways during the rise as well as upwards.

Experiment. Once you have cracked the making of a basic loaf, change it. I have made the following over the last seven months: wholewheat and rye bread; a spelt loaf with handfuls of millet thrown into it – spelt is an early Egyptian flour made of a durum-type wheat; granary bread with two-thirds malted grain granary flour, either Dove's or Shipton Mill, both organic, and one-third white or wholemeal flour added; 100 per cent wholemeal bread with a handful of sunflower seeds, poppy seeds or sesame seeds – or all of them – the tops brushed with milk just before baking, and one of each of the above seeds scattered on each of the three loaves; white bread made with strong, unbleached organic flour, with and without the addition of any or all of the three seeds.

I find producing a home-made loaf at any meal brings about a quite extraordinary reaction. It is not nostalgia exactly, because most of us were not lucky enough to be brought up on home-made bread. But it is nostalgia for what might have been and could obviously be, when the beholder sees the apparent ease with which the warm, yeasted offering is brought to the table as though it were just an ordinary part of the proceedings and of keeping a good table. It sort of makes it seem possible, which I now know it is, without being a slave to it.

Malted Grain Loaf

MAKES THREE LOAVES

*I leave it to you to vary the flavour with the
different flours and seeds*

1kg/2¼lb Shipton Mill or Dove's
    Farm organic malted grain
    flour
500g/lb 2oz strong organic
    wholemeal flour, again Shipton
    Mill or Dove's Farm
3 heaped tsp sea salt
45g/1½oz fresh yeast
3 heaped tsp molasses sugar
900ml/1½ pints hand-hot water; it
    should neither feel boiling, nor
    tepid
3 tbsp extra virgin olive oil
sesame, sunflower or poppy seeds
    and a little milk for the top of
    the loaves

Tip the flours out into a very large mixing bowl and add the salt. Boil a kettle, and put about 200ml/7fl oz of boiling water in a measuring jug, topping up to the 425ml/15fl oz mark with water from the cold tap. The water should now feel hand hot. Drop in the molasses sugar and fresh yeast and stir vigorously for a few seconds until the liquid looks creamy. Leave it for 15 minutes to rise. I still find this as absorbing as I did when I baked my first loaf, the living organism fizzing, popping, bubbling, and the sudden rush and rise in volume like a geyser with a will of its own inhabiting the jug.

Pour the contents of the jug into the flour, and then another 425ml/15fl oz of hand-hot water immediately afterwards, then pour in the three tablespoons of olive oil. With one hand, start working the wet dough together until it coheres completely into a ball, then remove it from the bowl on to the work surface and start kneading it. Sometimes the dough will appear too dry to work, sometimes too wet and claggy. Simply add a little more water for the former, and sprinkle with a little more flour for the latter, the dough should not feel sticky. After you have started working the dough vigorously with both hands on the work surface, you will, from time to time, probably need to shake a little more flour on to the work surface. The dough will elongate into a sausage each time you work it, which you need to furl back into a ball shape each time before repeating the process.

After 10 minutes, place the ball back in the bowl and cover the top with a clean linen tea towel, which you have wetted under the hot tap and wrung out. Leave at the side of the stove for about an hour, or until it has swollen to about twice its original volume and appears light and spongy. Turn the oven to 230°C/450°F/Gas 8 to warm up. Brush the insides of your bread tins with olive oil. Turn the dough out on to the work surface, and divide it into 3 pieces with a sharp knife. Knock the air out of each loaf for 3 or 4 minutes, without kneading it, and place each loaf in its tin.

Re-cover with a hot, damp cloth, and leave in the warmth close by or on top of the oven for 20–25 minutes. Brush the top of each loaf with a little milk, and sprinkle over a handful of seeds. Put two loaves together on a higher shelf and one on a lower. Set the timer for 35 minutes, but it could take 40. You want a distinctive hollow sound when you tap the base of the bread while turning it

out on to a rack with a palate knife. Allow it to cool for at least 40 minutes; bread is steamy, doughy and indigestible if you eat it too soon. These principles apply to all the other types of loaves I listed, and to rolls, which naturally take less long to cook. When you are using a plain flour and wish to add seeds to the actual bread mix, throwing in a handful of all three types of seeds – sunflower, sesame and poppy – seems to work beautifully.

Progress...

Since writing the above beginners' treatise, my baking technique has advanced dramatically after a highly informative day with master miller John Lister of Shipton Mill in Gloucestershire. It appears that the rise of the commercial loaf, in both senses, is the result of two things. Post-19th century, came the discovery that brewer's yeast could enable the baker to prove the loaf quicker and quicker, using more and more yeast. Then, in the 1950s, came the Chorleywood bread process. They discovered that one of the key elements of good bread is putting in energy. 'Kneading is not for fun, it is to condition the dough,' John told me. 'Then came the discovery that there are chemicals which can achieve this in a very short time, you can do the mix in 20 seconds, and that 20 seconds is the equivalent to 11 kilowatt hours of energy. It will prove in minutes, but high-speed bread is totally different to the hand-baked loaf. You are trading time for the mechanical input of energy and chemicals. You can make things bread shaped but they are not bread. The fermentation process is the most important part of bread making. If you remove this process, how can you still call it bread? Imagine if the French took fermentation out of wine making and still called it wine. Fermentation is the critical part, it transforms wheat flours from inedible to edible. If you allow time for the fermentation to happen properly, the bread starts to digest the proteins in the wheat and transform them from indigestible to digestible. People might be put off by having to leave their bread to rise for 24 hours, but you just leave it alone in a warm place and it's ready. Bread NEEDS fermentation, it is the crucial element that changes it from raw to cooked. A long fermentation means the yeast produces sugars, and converts the carbohydrates into sugars so that they can multiply faster, then the sugars caramelize and you get a beautiful coloured crust that you can recognize immediately.'

Not only beautiful to look at, this bread has the texture that no instantly made loaf has, and a crust that you really have to chew – crisp, crusty and almost cracks like an egg shell when you cut it. Good bread is also about the wheat the miller buys, the art of blending it, how it comes out slightly toasted from between the millstones in a process that, again, you cannot speed up. 'Every time I try to make things more complex I come back to the simple best four loaves and change the process. Look at Monsieur Poilâne, he only makes one loaf. It's about best wheats, the simplest process and really understanding fermentation. It's a lifetime's work, just focusing on those aspects,' John told me. So don't expect to achieve instant perfection. Just enjoy, as I do, the mysterious part of the process that is responsible for every batch you bake being wholly unlike the one you last baked. It is eternally fascinating to me how ambient temperature, the amount and age of yeast and flour, the warmth of your hands and the strength you exert that particular day during the kneading, as well as many other things that I am only just beginning to learn to analyse, can affect the finished loaf.

Here is a sensationally good white loaf made with Shipton Mill's strong white flour, a handful of their newly toasted, deliciously oily wheatgerm and an overnight or overday rise to maximize the fermentation. I now make bread on a terracotta stone. It should be a thick one according to John, but my pizza stone does two loaves beautifully. It radiates the heat evenly and there are no tin sides to give you a less crusty crust. Heat transfer is critical during baking and stones radiate heat in a totally different way to a metal tin. I also throw in a splash of water or squirt it into the oven with my iron spray – the steam helps to caramelize the surface of the loaf. I think it works best after the loaf has been in the oven for 10 minutes, but see what you think. Order flour from Shipton Mill (see page 282 for details). They sell more than 20 different kinds.

White Loaf

MAKES TWO LOAVES

1kg/2¼lb Shipton Mill traditional organic strong white flour
3 tsp fine sea salt
35g/1½oz fresh yeast (you can buy it at the bread counter of your supermarket IF they have an instore bakery)
600ml/1 pint warm water at 30°C in summer, 40°C in winter. To guess it, it needs to be hand-hot, not boiling

Allow approximately 14½ hours from the time you start the dough to cooking your bread. Dissolve a piece of yeast the size of a pea in 120ml/4fl oz of warm water. I stir the yeast in with a tiny whisk in a jug. Leave it for 10 minutes, then add it to 200g/7oz of the flour to which you have added half a teaspoonful of fine sea salt. Mix the dough a little with your fingers until it just coheres, then cover it with a tea towel soaked in cold water and wrung out – this prevents a skin forming. Leave it for 12 hours at room temperature in the kitchen. I have left it a couple of hours longer when convenient and it has not come to any harm.

Twelve hours later, dissolve the remaining yeast in 120ml/4fl oz of warm water, whisking it as before. Leave it for 10–15 minutes in the warmth of the kitchen. It won't froth up as it does with a quick-rise bread when you add sugar to the yeast and water at this stage.

Mix the rest of the bag of flour with the remaining salt and throw in a handful of wheatgerm. Add the starter dough, which will be spongy, to the mixture, then the yeasty liquid followed by the remaining 350ml/12fl oz of warm water. Work it in the bowl with your fingers until it coheres, then remove it to the work surface and knead energetically for 8–10 minutes.

Put it back in the large bowl, cover with the damp cloth again, and leave it for an hour to rise; it will double in volume. Put the dough back on the work surface, seize it, and bash the air out of it, then leave it uncovered for 15 minutes.

Preheat the oven to 220°C/425°F/Gas 7 and put the baking stone on the middle shelf to heat up. Divide the dough into two pieces with a knife and bash out the air again. Form each piece into a ball and cover with a damp cloth for 50 minutes. It will double in size again. Snip a little decorative hole or two in the middle of the top, scatter a tiny bit of flour over and, with a flat spatula, plop the loaves on to the hot stone. After 10 minutes, spray or throw a little water into the oven until the steam hisses. The loaves will need 35–40 minutes, check that the bottoms sound hollow before leaving them to cool for an hour on a rack.

Below: *White loaf*

Eric Treuille and his wife Rosie Kindersley are the new owner-managers of my favourite playing-truant shop, Books for Cooks in Notting Hill, London. Eric has a lovely version of focaccia with thyme, Gruyère and crème fraîche, the centrepiece of a light lunch that needs no more than a Provençal tomato salad or roasted tomato soup. Eric suggests making and kneading the dough and leaving it to rise in the fridge all day or all night, for 8–12 hours, before letting it stand at room temperature, knocking it back and shaping it.

Focaccia with Potato, Thyme, Gruyère and Crème Fraîche

MAKES I LARGE LOAF
preheat oven to 220°C/400°F/Gas 6

For the dough:
500g/1lb 2oz strong white all-
   purpose flour
2 tsp sea salt
325ml/11fl oz tepid water
2 tsp dried yeast

For the topping;
500g/1lb 2oz baby potatoes
125g/4oz grated Gruyère
2 tsp fresh thyme leaves
sea salt and black pepper
4 tbsp crème fraîche
coarse salt to sprinkle

Put the flour in a bowl, make a well in the middle and put the salt on the raised ridge of flour around the sides. Pour the water into the well and sprinkle over the yeast. Leave for 5 minutes to soften, then stir to dissolve. Draw in enough of the flour to make a soft paste. Cover with a cloth and leave to sponge for 20 minutes until bubbly and slightly puffed up. Draw in the rest of the flour to make a rough, sticky dough. Turn out on to a lightly floured surface and knead for 10 minutes until smooth, light and elastic. Put back into the bowl, cover with a cloth and leave until doubled in size, about 1½ hours.

Cut the potatoes into 5mm/¼in slices. Bring a pan of salted water to the boil, add the potatoes and bring back to the boil. Cook until the centres are just tender when pricked with the tip of a knife, about 5 minutes. Drain well and cool. Deflate the dough by pressing down with the palm of your hand. Roll out into a flat round, about 23cm/9in across, and place on an oiled baking sheet. Spread about half the cheese evenly on top of the bread dough, arrange the potatoes on top, scatter with thyme and sprinkle with a little salt and pepper. Cover with a cloth and leave until risen, about 30 minutes. Dot teaspoons of crème fraîche over the potatoes and scatter on the remaining cheese.

Bake for about 30 minutes or until the potato topping is crisp and golden and the bread sounds hollow when tapped underneath. Cool on a wire rack. Serve warm or at room temperature, sprinkled with coarse salt and cut into wedges.

Falafel are one of the national dishes of Egypt, where they are made with dried white broad beans and chickpeas. I make mine with chickpeas alone, and have long pondered the curious fact that deep-fried foods accompanied by cooling yoghurt or tahini sauce are perfect in the heat. I often serve falafel at large gatherings, winter and summer – they are the perfect food to eat in your fingers while you drink. Remember to soak the chickpeas overnight and you can then keep the ready-made mixture for up to 24 hours in the fridge before you use it. On the subject of tinned chickpeas, I'm afraid the answer is no. It is hardly a bother to soak your own, which in this recipe are whizzed to a gritty rawness in the Magimix. You could not emulate the texture with the tinned kind; they are mushy and the taste is not so good. Falafel also make a perfect outdoor lunch or picnic food, clutched inside a pitta bread with some salad and a yoghurty, minted, cucumber-studded dressing.

Falafel

MAKES ABOUT 30

350g/12oz organic chickpeas, soaked overnight
a medium onion, chopped, nothing bigger, or the juice from the onion prevents the falafel from adhering when they are cooking
4 cloves of garlic, chopped
2 green chillies, seeded and finely chopped
a handful of flat-leaf parsley, chopped
a handful of fresh coriander, chopped
2 tsp cumin seeds
2 tsp coriander seeds, ground with the cumin in a mortar
sea salt and black pepper
an unobtrusive oil for frying, ground nut or grape seed

Drain the soaked chickpeas and dry them. Put them in a food processor with the onion, garlic, chilli, chopped herbs, ground spices and seasoning. Blitz to a pulp, but don't expect the mixture to be smooth, the chickpeas will give it a grainy texture. Take walnut-sized quantities of the mixture and shape it into patties. You can use the falafel immediately, or put them on plates and keep them in the fridge.

Heat the oil. About 500ml/18fl oz will be enough if you decide to fry the falafel waist deep before turning them over and cooking on the other side. I did this very successfully. Otherwise, use double the quantity of oil and deep fry. Either way, drop in a bit of the mixture to test whether it's hot enough. It will resurface bubbling furiously if the oil is to temperature. Don't cook too many patties in one go, you will reduce the temperature of the oil. Cook until a deep golden brown, about two minutes a side if you are turning them over, then remove them to a plate and drain them well with kitchen paper, top and bottom.

Serve with some tahini sauce or a bowl of Greek yoghurt. Thin the yoghurt with a little milk and stir in a teaspoon of tempered, ground cumin, a clove of crushed garlic and some salt and pepper.

A gloriously Mediterranean-coloured mosaic of a dish that you can prepare up to the point of cooking in advance if you are going to serve it hot, and finish completely if you are going to serve it cold. I love the meatiness of monkfish, which lends itself so well to roasting, and the fact that the copious juices the fish exudes are tantamount to self-basting; most convenient. The saffron, scarlet and emerald green colours are set off brilliantly by the fish's white background, and the fish juices are suffused with the scent of lemons, thyme and cracked black peppercorns. The joy of this dish, too, is that the fish, stuffed with roasted red peppers and anchovies and tied like a parcel with string, takes no more than five minutes to prepare for the oven. Ask your fishmonger to skin and take out the backbone of the monkfish for you, leaving the fillets on either side still attached.

Above and below: Roast Stuffed Monkfish

Roast Stuffed Monkfish with a Lemon and Caper Sauce

SERVES 10
preheat oven to 200°C/400°F/Gas 6

2.25 kg/5lb monkfish, a single tail if possible. Ask your fishmonger to remove the bone, leaving the fillets on either side still attached

1 tbsp each of thyme, black peppercorns and sea salt

a pinch of saffron threads, soaked in a tablespoon or two of warm water for 10 minutes

50g/2oz tin of anchovies in olive oil, drained, or 50g/2oz salted anchovies washed and de-spined under the cold tap

2 roasted, seeded and peeled red peppers, or buy the wood-roasted piquillo peppers that Brindisa import if you can get them

3–4 tbsp best olive oil

50g/2oz unsalted butter

1 lemon

a handful of flat-leaf parsley, chopped

2 tbsp capers, drained then rinsed in a slotted spoon under the cold tap

Put the thyme, peppercorns and salt in a mortar and crush until coarsely ground. Open the fish out like a book and spread the anchovies and red peppers evenly over both surfaces. Pour over the saffrony liquor, then half the olive oil. Close the fish together, and hold it while a friend or child ties string around it at 2.5cm/1in intervals, to make 10 portions.

Scatter the seasoning mixture in a roasting tin, roll the fish in it to coat, then pour on the rest of the olive oil. Put the fish in the middle of the oven for about 35 minutes to roast. Check with the point of a skewer that it has cooked right through and is not resistant in the middle. Remove it to a hot serving dish if you are going to serve it hot and rest it, shrouded in foil, while you make the sauce.

Boil the remaining liquor in the roasting tin down to about half the quantity you started with. Meanwhile, peel the lemon, removing all the pith with the blade of a sharp knife, and divide the fruit into segments. In a small frying pan, melt the butter gently until it begins to turn brown and nutty, add the pieces of lemon, then throw in the drained capers. Add the fish liquor and stir it in, then pour it over the fish and strew over the parsley before you carve the fish into tranches 2.5cm/1in thick. Remember to remove the string before serving.

If you are serving the fish cold, do not offer the butter sauce. You may make the sauce with olive oil instead or omit it, merely pouring over the reduced liquor while the fish is cooling.

The English fishcake, alone and palely loitering in its mild, parsleyed, potatoey way, has always lent itself to a good spicing. Children demand ketchup, though in my youth there was the horror of anchovy essence that came in a dismal yukky pink bottle and was shaken with abandon into what I imagine was a béchamel sauce. And then along came people like the wonderful Kiwi chef Peter Gordon, grilling scallops and dressing them with crème fraîche, sweet chilli, lime and coriander, or painting them with his scrumptious tomato chilli jam, with its anchovied undertones of fish sauce. I make and keep a permanent home for this condiment in my fridge since discovering it. The jam works as well with pork, white fish and vegetables as it does slathered on Montgomery Cheddar or an oozing goat cheese bruschetta, made with Golden Cross or Ragstone.

I've always been of the opinion that a good kedgeree deserves a generous spicing of garam masala, and that a salmon fishcake is never better than when it is accompanied by almost its own weight, or at least size, of crème fraîche tartare. Hardly sacrilegious, then, to apply heat, citrusy spice and musky sweet-sharp undertones to cod, which is capable of absorbing them to great and good effect. You may make the codcake mixture well in advance and keep it covered in the fridge until frying time. The dipping sauce keeps equally well and should be served cold. These codcakes also make a sensational first course, in which case they will feed four.

Codcakes with Kaffir Lime Leaves and Thai Dipping Sauce

SERVES 2 AS A MAIN DISH

1 shallot
2 cloves of garlic
2 small hot red chillies, seeded
    and chopped
a handful of fresh coriander
    leaves, coarsely chopped
8 kaffir lime leaves, cut into strips
1 tbsp Thai fish sauce, *(nam pla)*
sea salt
450lb/1lb cod fillet

Peel and chop the shallot and peel and crush the garlic cloves. Place the shallot, garlic, chillies and coriander in a food processor with the lime leaves and fish sauce and blitz. Scrape into a bowl and season with sea salt. Throw the cod in chunks into the processor and blitz to a paste, but not to a sludge. Tip the fish into the spice bowl and mix everything together thoroughly.

Form the mixture into eight flat patties – you can flour your palms a little to prevent sticking – and put them covered in the fridge until an hour before you want to use them.

For the dipping sauce:

6 tbsp rice vinegar

4 tbsp light muscovado sugar

1 tbsp organic shoyu sauce

1 small red and 1 small green
   chilli, seeded and finely
   chopped

1 tbsp coriander leaves, very finely
   chopped

juice of 2 kaffir limes or 1 lime

groundnut or grape seed oil for
   frying

Heat the vinegar and sugar in a small pan until the sugar has dissolved and the mixture is syrupy, then stir in the shoyu sauce. Leave it to cool before adding the chillies, coriander and lime juice. Chill.

Heat about 6 tablespoons of oil in a frying pan. Fry the fishcakes, a few at a time, until golden on each side, about 4 minutes. Drain them on kitchen paper and serve them with the dipping sauce. I have made much smaller patties for a starter and cooked them for a little less time. They are just as successful and good for serving with drinks when you need something easy to pick up in your fingers.

Ketchup equals Heinz, but this is the real McCoy and well worth the effort, if only to do justice to a particularly fine sausage or fish cake. It is different, rather in the way that home-baked beans are an entirely different dish to the tinned version and instant coffee is quite unlike fresh.

Home-made Ketchup

MAKES SEVERAL BOTTLES

2 cloves

1 bay leaf

a small piece of cinnamon bark

250ml/9fl oz cider vinegar

8 tbsp light muscovado sugar

1 tsp celery seeds

½ tsp ground mace

¼ tsp ground coriander

1.5 kg/3lb 5oz ripe tomatoes

½ tsp sea salt

1 tsp English mustard powder

1 clove of garlic

Tabasco sauce

1 tbsp tomato purée

Tie the cloves, bay leaf and cinnamon together in a bit of muslin. Put the vinegar and sugar in a heavy-bottomed enamel pan and bring to a simmer. Add all the other ingredients and bring to the boil, stirring to prevent anything from sticking to the bottom of the pan. Reduce to a simmer and let the mixture blip away for about 40 minutes, stirring occasionally.

Remove the spice bag, liquidize the sauce and sieve into a bowl. Cool, then pour through a funnel into sterilized bottles. The ketchup will keep for up to a month in the fridge. Something to do at the tomato glut time of year, particularly if you have quantities of your own to pick.

Now those two fabulous salt beef bars in Soho's Great Windmill Street are no more, and Bloom's in the Whitechapel Road has gone the same way, access to a warm, ruby-red, salt beef sandwich, with its marrow-soft yellow fat, sharp gherkin and rye bread, is strictly limited, unless you decide to make your own. This you can do quite simply, knowing that if you have the urge, it will take five to ten days between making the salt beef and tasting the first satisfying slice that you cut from the joint. Some things are as enjoyable in the anticipation as they are in the immediate consumption.

Salt Beef

SERVES 10 OR MORE

a 2–3kg/4½–6½lb piece of organic beef, brisket, silverside foreflank or shin

1 bouquet garni

1 of each of the following, chopped: carrot, onion, celery stick, leek

1 garlic bulb cut in half across the middle

For the brine:

5 litres/9 pints of water

500g/1lb 2oz demerara or light muscovado sugar

1kg/2¼lb coarse salt

1 tsp black peppercorns

1 tsp juniper berries

5 cloves

2 bay leaves

a sprig of thyme

a bunch of parsley stalks

150g/5oz saltpetre (optional)
  Leave it out if you want to stay organic, but the meat will be greyer as a result, without the through and through pink that saltpetre assures

Put all the ingredients for the brine in a large saucepan and stir well over a low heat until the sugar and salt have dissolved. Bring to the boil, allow to bubble for 1–2 minutes, then remove from the heat and leave until absolutely cool. Cover your piece of beef completely with the cold brine, weighting it down if necessary. Leave the meat in the brine for 5–10 days in a cold place. If the joint weighs under 3 kg/6½lb, do not leave it in the brine for more than a week, or it will be too pickled.

Before cooking, remove the meat from the brine and soak it in cold water for 24 hours, changing the water a couple of times. Put it in a pan with the bouquet garni, vegetables and garlic, cover it with cold water and bring to the boil. Poach at a gentle simmer – a 3kg/6½lb piece will take about 2½ hours.

Serve the salt beef hot, with plenty of mashed potato and cabbage, horseradish and English mustard, or eat it warm or cold in a sandwich made with strong, freshly made English mustard, cornichons and rye bread.

When Simon Hopkinson alerted me to Elizabeth David's Grillade des Mariniers du Rhône, made with lean beef, in her magical book *An Omelette and a Glass of Wine*, I got thinking. The sharp wine vinegar and salt anchovies would surely work spectacularly well with lamb, using a cut like the breast that can tolerate hours of gentle stewing before cooling overnight and skimming off its thick crust of snowy fat. It did indeed suit this notoriously fat, gluey, almost gelatinous cut of lamb to perfection, the affinity between lamb and anchovy being one I'm sure you know about. I usually push fillets of anchovy into the nicked fat of shoulder of lamb, with garlic and rosemary before roasting it. The result is not fishy, but lends a miraculous depth of flavour to the meat. My children are pretty vociferous in their hatred of this small, silver, salt-of-the-sea fish, but they have yet to guess and raise hell.

Don't be shy of serving a cheap cut of meat at a party. I served this at one of my publisher's dinners, at which the Michelin-starred chef Richard Corrigan was a guest. I had been determined not to serve him food that smacked of a restaurant kitchen, it is not my style; and I fear it has induced much of the sense of inadequacy that seems, at present, to stalk the home kitchen. Anyway, it is just the sort of cut that Richard has helped put back on the carnassial map. He adored the dish, and the organic lamb breast from Swaddles Green Farm to feed 12 people came to £8. Honour and satisfaction in one.

Another dish to make a day before you need it. You can double the quantity and make two giant pots with the minimum of extra effort if you are feeding a large party.

Grillade of Lamb Breast

SERVES 6

preheat oven to 140°C/275°F/Gas 1

2 organic lamb breasts, boned
450g/1lb onions, peeled and finely
    sliced
25g/1oz unsalted butter
1 heaped tsp flour
2 tbsp flat-leaf parsley, chopped
a clove of garlic, chopped
3 tbsp olive oil
1 tbsp red wine vinegar
4 anchovy fillets
sea salt and freshly ground black
    pepper

Put half the onions in a layer in the bottom of a heavy-bottomed, but not too deep, earthenware casserole. Place the breasts, laid out flat, in a single layer on top of them and season. Put the rest of the sliced onions in a layer on top of the meat. Work the butter and flour together in a small bowl, divide it into tiny knobs and dot the mixture over the top of the onions. Cover with a layer of buttered greaseproof paper and a lid and cook for 2–2½ hours. The meat should be utterly tender when pierced with a skewer. Leave to cool overnight.

With a slotted spoon and copious amounts of kitchen paper, pick and scoop out every bit of solidified white fat you can. Mix the chopped parsley, finely chopped garlic, olive oil, chopped anchovies and vinegar together into a vinaigrette. Pour it over the casserole 1½ hours before you want to serve it, replace the greaseproof and the lid, and cook for a further 1½ hours.

This grillade can be reheated as successfully as any stew. I would be hard pressed to think of a fuller-bodied, better-flavoured winter dish.

This Polish recipe comes from my friend Ewa, whose restaurant in London's Shepherd's Bush is one of my favourite haunts and a place where you go to celebrate. When you walk through the doors, you are no longer in England, you are in an eastern European salon. People play the piano and sing; there is a spirit of true generosity, bounty, plentifulness; the tables have bottles of Bison Grass vodka awaiting you; and there is matchless borscht, blinis and soft crescents of pierogis. There is barley soup, veal paprikarz studded with red peppers and shredded pickled cabbage, great pork knuckles marinaded, smoked and roasted, and the mighty Bigos, a hunters' stew that defines the word hearty. With hunks of meat and smoked sausage, dried fungi and sweet shreds of sauerkraut, this is a dish of deep-down earthiness and strength.

Bigos, or Hunters' Stew

SERVES 10—12

1kg/2¼lb cabbage
1kg/2¼lb sauerkraut
10 dried boletus or other fungi, or
    fresh mushrooms if you prefer
2 onions
2 cooking apples
2 tbsp lard or speck, available
    from many supermarkets
500g/1lb 2oz each of cold roast
    pork and cold roast beef,
    but any left-over joint will do,
    duck, venison, lamb
600g/1¼lb sausage, Polish if
    possible
400g/14oz boiled ham cut into
    small cubes
10 prunes, stoned
10 juniper berries, crushed
10 peppercorns
2 bay leaves
150ml/5fl oz dry red wine
1 tsp honey, salt and pepper

Drain the juice from the sauerkraut and chop it finely. Chop the cabbage finely. Pour boiling water over the cabbage and drain. Rinse the dried mushrooms, cover with a little warm water and leave to soak for 15 minutes. Then cook them gently in their liquid in a pan for 30 minutes, drain, and cut into strips, keeping the juice. Peel the onions and chop them. Peel the apples and cube them, then fry with the onions in a tablespoon of lard or speck.

Put the cabbage and sauerkraut into a large saucepan. Add the onions, apples, mushrooms, mushroom liquor, prunes, juniper berries, bay leaves and pepper. Add 800ml/1¼ pints of boiling water, cover, and cook over a gentle heat for an hour.

Cut the meat into cubes. Slice the sausage and fry it lightly in the rest of the lard or speck. Add all the meats to the saucepan, pour in the wine and the honey and cook for a further 40 minutes. Stir frequently, taking care not to let it burn.

Ewa says this dish tastes best on the third day, but it will keep for up to a week in the fridge. It is eaten in Poland in the cold months, between September and April. Serve with some kasha if you like.

Buckwheat Kasha

1 cup of toasted buckwheat
50g/2oz lard or speck
salted water

This is the most valued kasha in Poland, with a taste and aroma full of character. It is an indispensable addition, instead of potatoes, to all kinds of Polish beef dishes, and very good with Bigos. Ewa 'dry roasts' it by pouring 1 cup of toasted buckwheat into a small pan in which the lard or speck has been heated. It is much tastier cooked in lard than in butter. Stir until the grain has absorbed the fat and is slightly browned. Pour a cup of boiling salted water over the kasha, and cook over a very gentle heat. When the kasha has absorbed the water, cover it and place in a warm oven for 45 minutes.

A dish which comes from traditional Slavic cuisine and has acquired long-lasting popularity in Polish kitchens in both cities and villages.

Pierogi

For the dough:
400g/14oz flour
a pinch of salt
1 egg

For the pork filling:
about 225g/8oz cooked pork
1 onion, chopped
1 clove garlic, chopped
lard or speck
salt and pepper

For the cream cheese filling:
175g/6oz cream cheese
1 cooked potato
1 onion, chopped
1 clove of garlic, chopped
lard or speck
salt and pepper
1 raw egg

Mix the flour, salt and egg and add some lukewarm water to make quite a slack dough, which does not stick to the hands or pastry board when well kneaded. Divide the kneaded dough into 4 parts, then roll each one out very thinly. Using a tea cup or wine glass, cut out circles 5–6cm/2–2½in in diameter. Place a heaped teaspoon of filling in the centre of each circle , fold over, and press the edges together firmly so that they cannot open during cooking.

The most popular fillings are cream cheese, and potato or pork. For the meat filling, gently soften the onion and garlic in some speck or lard and season. Mouli it with the cooked meat. For the cream cheese filling, mouli a cooked potato with the cream cheese, adding an onion cooked as above and seasoned, then add a raw egg to the mixture.

Drop the filled pierogi into a wide pot of boiling, salted water and bring it back to a simmer. When they rise to the surface, keep the pierogi in the water for a further 4–5 minutes, then take them out with a slotted spoon and drain well.

You can sprinkle a few tiny cubes of pork crackling over the pierogi, serve them with thick soured cream, or place two or three of them in your borscht.

Prunes and beef, lamb and apricots, pork and either — it is curious how meat and dried fruits form an alliance. This recipe, with obvious Arabic influence, is a classic Moroccan tagine. By all means substitute lamb and apricots if you would rather, and cook the dish at least a day before you want to serve it.

Beef and Prune Tagine

SERVES 4

350g/12oz Agen prunes, soaked in
  ½ fresh orange juice, ½ water
  overnight
1kg/2¼lb shin of beef or chuck
  steak, cut into 5cm/2in cubes
olive oil
2–3 tbsp flour
4 medium onions, finely sliced
3 fat cloves of garlic, finely sliced
3 stalks of celery from the heart,
  strung with a potato peeler and
  finely sliced
1 tsp coriander seeds
1 tsp cumin seeds
1 tsp cinnamon bark
1 tsp ground dried ginger root
½–1 tsp cayenne
2 fresh bay leaves
2 pieces of orange peel, without
  pith
beef or chicken stock or water
sea salt and black pepper
a handful of fresh coriander,
  chopped

Soak the prunes in the orange juice and water the night before you want to cook this dish.

While you warm 2–3 tablespoons of olive oil in a heavy-bottomed casserole, dry the meat with a piece of kitchen paper and put it into a Ziploc bag with the flour, sea salt and black pepper. Shake the bag until all the meat is lightly covered with flour but not clogged. Put the meat straight into the pan, in a single layer, while it is still dry. Brown on all sides for a few minutes, then lift the meat out of the pan with a slotted spoon and put it on a plate.

Add a little more oil to the pan, throw in the vegetables and sweat them gently. Temper the coriander and cumin seeds in a small frying pan for a minute or so, until they exude their toasted spice smell, then crush them in a mortar with the cinnamon bark. Add them with the other spices to the vegetables when they have softened, after about 10 minutes, then add the bay leaves, orange peel and prunes, without their soaking liquid, a couple of minutes later. Return the beef to the pan, and just cover with stock or water. Bring to the boil, cover, then simmer at a mere blip for about 1½ hours until really tender. Check the seasoning and, if possible, cool and refrigerate ready to heat and serve a day or two later. Sprinkle with chopped fresh coriander before serving.

I serve my tagines, be they fish, flesh or fowl, with couscous and some harissa, home-made or from a squeezy tube, which people can dollop into the meat juices as their taste buds dictate.

This will keep contentedly in the fridge for two or three weeks. Rather like preserved lemons, it is something that once you have, you will make use of, even *ad hoc* for things like pepping up a Bloody Mary. If you can't be bothered to make your own, the squeezy tubes, a Moroccan equivalent of tomato paste, are extremely good, and will spice up everything from tagine to mayonnaise.

Harissa

MAKES 1 JAR

3 red peppers, blistered on all
    sides under the grill, seeded,
    cored and skinned
2–3 red chillies, seeded
1 tsp tomato purée
1 tsp ground coriander
1 tsp ground cumin
4 tbsp best olive oil

Blend all the ingredients to a paste in a mortar or a blender. Put the harissa in a bowl to use immediately, or scrape it into a jar, cover with a thin film of olive oil and put the lid on before keeping it in the fridge.

Harissa is not just for cranking up the heat of a meat, fish or vegetable tagine; it is infinitely more versatile than that. Try it with some barbecued lamb shoulder, the pieces rolled in crushed coriander and black pepper before being suitably charred. Or spread it on some good crusty ciabatta or Pugliese bread and add roasted vegetables and feta cheese. It is even good with a strong cheddar, Mrs Kirkham's Lancashire or a mature goat cheese.

This is perfect for a summer lunch you want to prepare the day before. All you have to do on the day is make the sauce, an easy five-minute job, and pour it over the chicken breasts removed from their overnight cold bath. Then leave them to languish in this most delectable black velvety liquor for three hours before lunch. It is a dish which, for me, conjures up an almost medieval world of food, the sweetness of the muscovado sugar and the lemon zest creating a Moorish feel. My friend George Morley wrote out the recipe for me three summers ago, and I have gazed at it hungrily ever since, waiting for the right occasion. This summer finally gave me one, with George as a guest, of course. It was only on reading the collected works of the most brilliant Italian food writer of them all, Anna Del Conte, that the origins of the dish became clear: it was one she, a historian by training, had unearthed. It is brilliant for when you have a lot of people, but you can adjust it for fewer. The one thing I have done is increase the sauce quantity from the original. And significantly. It needs it.

A 17th-century Mantuan Chicken Dish

SERVES 12

10 large organic chicken breasts, in fact mine were so large that 8 would still have been generous
1 litre/1¾ pints chicken stock
300ml/½ pint dry white wine

For the sauce:
5 flat tbsp light muscovado sugar
125ml/4fl oz dry white wine
85g/3oz sultanas
grated zest of 2½ lemons
5 tbsp best balsamic vinegar, a well-aged, velvety 4-star vinegar; you want rich, mellow velvet not sharp, thin acid
2 tsp sea salt
freshly ground black pepper
125ml/4fl oz best olive oil

Put the breasts in a single layer in as many heavy-bottomed pans as you need, I used three, and cover each with the stock and white wine mixture. Poach at a mere burble, turning every 5 minutes, until cooked through with a faint pink in the liquid when pierced with a skewer; 20–25 minutes should do large chicken breasts and they will continue to cook as the liquid cools. When cool, transfer to one pan with their liquid, cover and keep in the fridge overnight.

Just over 3 hours before you want to eat, take the chicken out of the fridge and make the sauce. Put the sugar and wine in a small pan and bring it very slowly to the boil, stirring to dissolve the sugar completely. Draw off the heat, and add the sultanas and lemon rind to infuse. Leave to cool, while you cut each breast into 1cm/½in slices, downwards, reassembling them on a large serving dish. Strain the sauce, reserving the zest and sultanas in the sieve. Add the vinegar to the sauce, and the salt and pepper, then start adding the oil in a trickle, whisking as you go to form an emulsion. Return the zest and sultanas to the sauce, taste, adjust the seasoning, and pour over the centre of the breasts. Cover with clingfilm and keep at room temperature for 3 hours. Serve with new potatoes or plain rice and some cold white wands of leeks.

When I make fresh tomato sauce, I make huge quantities of it, particularly in the autumn with my own tomatoes, and serve it with cod, spiced with chilli, with pasta, moulied into soup, in gratins and tians, with courgettes and aubergines and anything I can think of. This recipe is the kind of assembly job that lasagne is, a layer-by-layer dish, but it has the advantage that you can make the tomato sauce and the pancakes a day or two in advance, before building, stratum by stratum, this savoury cake. You sprinkle mozzarella and fresh Parmesan cheese between the layers before baking the dish like a pasta gratin. Only it isn't pasta, it is layers of soft pancakes bubbling with tomatoey, oily juices and oozing fresh mozzarella. My children were as impressed as I was the first time I made it, and I then went on to experiment further with a creamy pesto sauce. A substantial and unusual dish, beautiful enough for a party.

Pancakes Layered with Mozzarella di Bufala and Tomato Sauce

SERVES 4

For the pancakes:
125g/4oz flour
salt
2 eggs
300ml/½ pint of milk
a tiny knob of butter

PANCAKES:
This recipe makes thicker pancakes than you would normally have, but you may add a bit more milk if the batter feels really thick. Leave the batter to rest for 30 minutes and then whisk again. Heat a tiny knob of butter in a heavy pan, pour in a small ladle of batter, wait until it begins to bronze and bubble before flipping and repeating, then place on a plate with a palate knife and repeat. For some inexplicable reason, the first pancake doesn't usually work. You should end up with 8 good-sized pancakes from this amount of mixture.

For the tomato sauce:

about 1kg/2¼lb tomatoes, peeled
    seeded and chopped

1 onion, chopped

2 sticks of celery, chopped

2 cloves of garlic, chopped

1 bay leaf

1 teaspoon each of molasses sugar
    and tomato purée

a splosh of red wine (optional)

For the béchamel sauce:

425ml/15fl oz full cream milk

35g/1½oz butter

35g/1½oz flour

grated nutmeg

salt and pepper

For the assembly:

2 fresh mozzarella di bufala,
    chopped into small dice

4 tbsp fresh Parmesan cheese,
    grated

a handful of fresh basil, chopped

Tomato Sauce

Sweat the chopped onion in some olive oil. Add the skinned, seeded and chopped tomatoes, celery, chopped garlic and bay leaf, stir in the molasses sugar and tomato purée and cook the whole lot down for at least 30 minutes until reduced, thickened and jammy. You can add a splosh of red wine when you add the tomatoes if you like. Pass your tomato sauce through the coarse disc of the mouli if you prefer your sauce less textured. Use tinned tomatoes if it is not the time of year for good fresh tomatoes.

Béchamel Sauce

Heat the milk. Melt the butter in a saucepan. Add the plain flour, cook for a few minutes, then stir in the hot milk. Cook the béchamel for at least 20 minutes so that it no longer smells floury. Season with grated nutmeg, salt and pepper.

Assembling the dish

Once you have made the tomato and béchamel sauces and the pancakes, you are ready to assemble the dish.

Preheat the oven to 180°C/350°F/Gas 4. Stir the tomato sauce into the béchamel. Butter a gratin dish, place a pancake on the bottom and spread a thin layer of the tomato and béchamel sauces over the top. Sprinkle with mozzarella, Parmesan, basil, salt and pepper and cover with another pancake. Continue layering the pancakes until you have a sort of leaning tower of Pisa, 8 pancake-storeys high. The top must be sauce, Parmesan, basil, salt and pepper, not mozzarella, which would turn to goo.

Cover the dish with a sheet of greased greaseproof paper and bake for about 20 minutes. Remove the greaseproof and continue to cook for a further 10 minutes until bubbling and gorgeous. Leave it to stand outside the oven before you cut into it just like a cake in triangular wedges. Serve with a plain green salad. This is substantial with a capital S!

I am an inveterate tinkerer, and I loved the idea of a baked pesto and béchamel gratin. It worked like a dream. Quantities for the pancakes and béchamel as for the tomato sauce version on pages 196–97.

Pancakes Layered with Pesto and Mozzarella di Bufala

SERVES 4

preheat oven to 180°C/350°/Gas 4

Ingredients for the pancakes and
    béchamel

For the pesto:
2 handfuls of fresh basil leaves
25g/1oz pine nuts
1 clove of garlic, crushed
125ml/4fl oz olive oil
1 tsp sea salt
25g/1oz Parmesan cheese, grated

There are three things you need to remember for this recipe. First, use fresh pesto. Second, don't add more than 3 tablespoons of it to the béchamel for this quantity of ingredients and people – it is extremely rich and olive oily. Third, if you add the pesto to the béchamel when the sauce has already begun to cool down, it will keep its magical brilliant green hue and not turn muddy khaki. I am not sure why, since once it goes into the oven it is going to be cooked. I can only imagine the layers of sauce and pancake somehow protect it.

You can make the pesto by grinding the basil, pine nuts, garlic, salt and olive oil in a pestle and mortar, or whizz everything to a paste in a food processor. Either way, stir in the Parmesan afterwards.

This is a great vegetarian party dish. You can, of course, make your fresh pesto in advance and keep it in the fridge under a layer of olive oil that you then stir back into it when you are ready to use it. This time, try a tomato salad as a side dish, rather than an all green feast.

Left: *Pancakes layered
with Mozzarella di Bufala
and Tomato Sauce*

In Sicily this is called Pasta 'Ncasciata, the pie being encased — 'ncasciata — in the fried aubergines. The Sicilians add salami to theirs, but I keep mine vegetarian. I feel the meat is not necessary since the dish already has a rich flavour and succulent texture. This is a stunning dish worthy of a celebration, and another thing to make when you have been cooking vats of tomato sauce. The huge dragons' tongues of the aubergines that arrive in my organic vegetable box turn the dish into a beautiful parcel.

Sicilian Pasta Pie

SERVES 6
preheat oven to 190°C/375°F/Gas 5

700g/1½lb aubergines, about 2
   large specimens
salt
900ml/1½ pints fresh tomato
   sauce, made with 1.2kg/2½ lb
   tomatoes as in the recipe on
   page 197
400g/14oz penne or rigatoni
50g/2oz freshly grated Parmesan
   cheese
1 tbsp dried oregano
freshly ground black pepper
2 hard-boiled eggs, sliced
150g/5oz Italian salami, thickly
   sliced and cut into strips
   (optional)
200g/7oz fresh mozzarella di
   bufala, sliced
50g/2oz caciocavallo cheese, sliced
2 tbsp brown breadcrumbs
2 tbsp extra virgin olive oil

Cut the aubergines lengthways into thin slices and place them in a colander, sprinkling salt between the layers. Leave to drain for an hour. Rinse the aubergines thoroughly, pat each slice dry, and fry them a few at a time in plenty of hot vegetable oil. They shouldn't absorb a lot of oil and turn greasy if the oil is hot enough and you don't fry too many at a time. When they are golden on both sides, remove the slices and dry them well on kitchen paper.

Cook the pasta, drain it when *al dente*, and immediately dress it with the tomato sauce. Add the Parmesan and oregano, mix well, taste and check the seasoning.

Line the bottom and sides of an oiled 20cm/8in springform tin with the aubergine slices. Cover the bottom with a layer of pasta then add sliced egg, salami if you are using it, more aubergine and mozzarella and caciocavallo slices. Repeat these layers until all the ingredients are used, finishing with a layer of pasta. Sprinkle with the breadcrumbs and drizzle over the olive oil. Put in the oven to bake for 30–40 minutes, or until the dish is heated right through.

Remove from the oven and run a spatula between the pie and the inside of the tin. Place a round serving dish upside down over the pan and invert the pan onto it. Leave the pie to stand for a few minutes, then unclip the tin and carefully remove it. Remove the base of the tin and serve immediately. If the pie collapses, it hardly matters, the flavour should overwhelm everyone.

Risoni with Seafood and Roasted Vegetables

SERVES 4
preheat oven to 220°C/425°F/Gas 7

350g/12oz risoni (rice-shaped
pasta)

1 small aubergine, cut into
2.5cm/1in cubes

1 onion, cut into thin wedges

1 red pepper, cut into 2.5cm/1in
pieces

1 large plum tomato, cut into
thin wedges

2 cloves of garlic, finely chopped

85ml/3fl oz olive oil

½ tsp coarse sea salt

125g/4oz prepared squid, cut into
thin rings

225g/8oz raw tiger prawns, peeled
and fried in olive oil until pink

3 sundried tomatoes in olive oil,
sliced small

1 red chilli, seeded and chopped
small

1 tbsp white wine vinegar

5 tbsp flat-leaf parsley, chopped

salt and freshly ground pepper

50g/2oz rocket (optional)

Cook the pasta until *al dente*, drain and leave to cool. A little slug of olive oil splashed over after draining prevents it from sticking unpleasantly. Put the aubergine, onion, red pepper and fresh tomato in a bowl with the garlic, 2 tablespoons of olive oil and the sea salt, and mix well. Roast, spread out in a small tin, for about 30 minutes until well coloured around the edges. Leave to cool.

Heat 1 tablespoon of olive oil in a frying pan, add the squid, and fry over a high heat for 2½ minutes until lightly browned. Season with salt and pepper and leave to cool.

When the pasta, vegetables and squid are barely warm, put them in a large bowl with the remaining oil, prawns, sundried tomato, chilli, vinegar, 4 tablespoons of parsley, 1 teaspoon of salt and a few good scrunches of black pepper. Toss together lightly, then fold in the rocket if you've decided to use it.

Spoon everything on to a large plate, and sprinkle with the remaining parsley.

When I went to lunch in Dorset with the incomparable Italian food writer Anna Del Conte, she had cooked the nearest equivalent to Italian pumpkin gnocchi she can make in England, using a combination of butternut squash and orange-fleshed sweet potato. These come close, she informed me, to the spicy sweetness and moist texture of a northern Italian pumpkin and are a traditional speciality of the Veneto and southern Lombardy. The first dressing is the classic dressing from Veneto, while the second one from Lombardy is the one that is generally used everywhere else.

Gnocchi di Zucca, or Butternut Squash Gnocchi

SERVES 4—5
preheat oven to 180°C/350°F/Gas 4

500g/1lb 2oz butternut squash
500g/11lb 2oz orange-fleshed
    sweet potatoes
1 tbsp vegetable oil
200g/7oz flour, preferably
    Italian 00
2 tsp baking powder
salt
2 large organic eggs
4 tbsp freshly grated Parmesan
    cheese
a generous grating of nutmeg

For the first dressing:
70g/2½oz unsalted butter
25g/1oz Parmesan cheese, grated
1 tbsp sugar
1 tsp ground cinnamon

For the second dressing:
70g/2½oz unsalted butter
6 fresh sage leaves, snipped into
    pieces
50g/2oz Parmesan cheese, grated

Line a baking tray with foil and brush it with oil. Cut the squash in half, scoop out and discard the seeds and fibres, and place the squash, cut side down, on the foil. Pierce the sweet potatoes with a skewer and place them on the foil. Bake for about an hour, until both vegetables can be pierced easily with a fork.

Peel the sweet potatoes and scoop the flesh out of the skin of the squash. Purée both vegetables through a food mill or potato ricer into a bowl. Mix in the flour and baking powder and then break in the eggs. Mix very well to incorporate, then add the Parmesan and season with nutmeg and salt to taste.

Bring a large saucepan of salted water to boil. Anna finds it easiest to make the gnocchi with a piping bag and a large, plain nozzle, but you may prefer to make them by shaping them into small balls with floured hands. To pipe the gnocchi, fill the bag with the squash mixture and hold it over the saucepan, squeezing it with one hand and cutting the mixture as it comes out of the nozzle with the other. Cut short shapes about 2 cm/¾ in long, letting them drop straight into simmering water. Don't cook all the gnocchi together, do it in three batches. Cook them for a minute or two after they have come to the surface of the water. Lift out each batch with a slotted spoon and place in a shallow, large ovenproof dish. Dress each batch separately and keep the dish in a low oven.

FOR THE FIRST DRESSING:
Melt the unsalted butter and then pour it over each batch of gnocchi. Sprinkle with the Parmesan, sugar and ground cinnamon

FOR THE SECOND DRESSING:
Put the unsalted butter and the snipped sage leaves in a small pan and let the butter melt and begin to foam. Spoon over each batch of gnocchi and sprinkle with the freshly grated Parmesan.

It is funny how the inspiration of someone else's lunch, in this case Anna's gnocchi, should inspire and osmose into something intimately connected, yet utterly different. It may be linked by flavours, a method here, a texture there, but be a completely different dish in its own right. I often find, too, that an ingredient or combination of ingredients get stuck on a sort of loop tape of consciousness, and I go on using them and experimenting over days, or occasionally weeks if they are in season. The roasted squash is great with roast pork or veal, or a pork chop. The skins of the red onion squash soften palpably into an edible texture that is brilliant with the mealy sweetness of the innards, so try them. The penne opposite was an utterly and unexpectedly delicious dish, made from some onion squash remaining unroasted from the previous night.

Spice-roasted Red Onion or Butternut Squash

SERVES 2
preheat oven to 200°C/400°F/Gas 6

⅔ of a red onion squash
    or ½ a butternut squash
sprigs of rosemary and thyme,
    exceedingly finely chopped
1 clove of garlic, finely chopped
good olive oil
1 red chilli, seeded and finely
    chopped
sea salt and black pepper

Scoop the seeds out of the squash and cut it in melon-like slices. Put the finely chopped rosemary, thyme, garlic and chilli into a little bowl of good olive oil, sea salt and pepper to macerate, before spooning a little into the boat of each squash.

Bake the squash until cooked through, about 30–40 minutes, basting them a couple of times. You can add a knob of butter at the end if you feel like it.

Penne with Roasted Squash, Prosciutto, Sage and Parmesan

SERVES 2
preheat oven to 200°C/400°F/Gas 6

⅓ a red onion squash
    or ½ a butternut squash
olive oil
1 red chilli, split down
    the middle and seeded
225g/8oz penne
butter

4 slices of prosciutto
a good handful of
    fresh sage leaves
fresh Parmesan cheese
sea salt and black pepper

For this recipe, I think it is better to remove the skin of the squash before cooking. Cut the squash into small cubes. Roll them in about 4 tablespoons of good olive oil in a roasting tray, season and add the split chilli. Roast until the squash is tender, about 20 minutes. Remove the chilli, which will have exuded enough warmth into the olive oil for this dish.

Cook the penne in plenty of boiling salted water. I favour the extra-large Carluccio variety, which has apertures large enough to contain, as well as to be coated by the sauce. Make sure when you drain the penne that you return a little of the cooking water to the pan with it, then slather on a bit of butter.

Meanwhile, tear the prosciutto into bits and cook it separately in a couple of tablespoons of olive oil for a couple of minutes until crisp. Remove the prosciutto with a slotted spoon and throw in the sage, cooking until deliciously frizzled and browned.

Throw the squash, prosciutto and sage into the pot with the penne, stir in a tablespoon or two of Parmesan, adjust the seasoning and serve. Pass round some more Parmesan at the table. There is great contrast between the salt cheese, sweet, yielding, mealy-fleshed squash, crisp, salt prosciutto and astringent sage.

Please see this dish as a suggestion rather than law. A couple of nights later I raided the fridge and cooked something not dissimilar, roasting more squash with red onion chunks and half a remaining cauliflower. Cauliflower? Weird, but it worked, browning and intensifying in flavour as I turned it during the roasting. I had no meat, but added a tablespoon of crème fraîche and 125g/4oz cubed Roquefort with the roasted vegetables to the final assembly. No Parmesan.

Since we are on the subject of sage, and it is something to which I seem to turn instinctively at the beginning of winter, the following gratin was a natural. Sage is the herb that has the greatest affinity with cheese; hard cheese that is – think of Sage Derby. In the days when a lot of Welsh farms made their own Caerphilly, they often used to add sage to it. The following is a dish that I cooked entirely with the contents that I found lurking in my fridge, but really any well-matured hard cheese would work equally well. This is the sort of comfort food that you will eat a lot more of than you think you will, but then what comfort food isn't?

Potato, Leek, Bacon, Sage and Cheese Gratin

SERVES 2
preheat oven to 200°C/400°F/Gas 6

700g/1½lb potatoes
3 or 4 fat leeks, well washed, trimmed of their dark green leaves and thinly sliced
6 rashers of oak-smoked streaky bacon, I use Swaddles Green Farm's organic bacon which is not cured with nitrites
a generous handful of fresh sage leaves
125g/4oz mature hard cheese, I used Mrs Kirkham's Lancashire, grated thickly
600–900ml/1–1½ pints chicken stock
butter
1 tbsp seeded mustard
about 4 tbsp crème fraîche
sea salt and black pepper

Slice the peeled potatoes on a mandolin or on the slicer disc of a Magimix. Place them in a colander, wash to rid them of their starch, and pat them dry in a cloth. Butter a gratin dish and put in half the potatoes, then add all the chopped leeks in a layer. Snip the bacon into strips, removing the rind, and fry until crisply frazzled in its own fat. Remove it with a slotted spoon and dot it over the leeks. Frazzle the snipped sage leaves briefly in the bacon fat until browned and crisp, then dot them over the leeks with the bacon fat. Sprinkle over the grated cheese and add the rest of the potatoes. Pour the hot chicken stock over the potatoes, until it just reaches the top layer, but does not submerge them. Add seasoning, dot with butter and place a layer of greased greaseproof paper over the top of the dish.

Cook for 45 minutes. Remove from the oven, check with a skewer that the potatoes are nearly cooked through and pour over the mustard and crème fraîche that you have stirred together. Smooth over the top with a rubber spatula. Place the dish back in the oven, without the greaseproof paper, for a further 15 minutes, when it should be golden, bubbling and cooked right through. A complete supper dish.

This, this like many dishes permanently in my repertoire, is one I constantly play around with, each time thinking I have cracked the code and come up with the ultimate answer. But then I think of another twist, something to tempt the children with that is not going to be the self-same way they remember it from last time. So here is the most recent version of kedgeree I made, with Merchant Gourmet's red, wild and white rice that all cooks miraculously at the same time.

Spiced Kedgeree

SERVES 2

200g/7oz natural smoked haddock
2 large onions, peeled and sliced into thin rings
olive oil and butter
1 tsp cumin seeds
a pinch each of cayenne, fenugreek and turmeric
1 sachet of Merchant Gourmet's red, wild and white rice or 125g/4oz of organic basmati rice
4 eggs
a cup of frozen peas
2 tbsp crème fraîche
a handful of flat-leaf parsley, chopped
sea salt and black pepper

Place the smoked haddock in a gratin dish. Pour boiling water over to cover – the only cooking the haddock needs as it is already smoked. Leave for 10 minutes before draining off the water and gently pushing the flesh away from the skin with a spoon and fork into large translucent flakes.

Throw the onions into a little heated olive oil and butter in a large heavy-bottomed frying pan, along with the cumin seeds and some salt to draw the moisture from the onions. After a couple of minutes, add the other spices – the tip of a spoon end should be enough because you want warmth and spice rather than real heat. Stir into the onions and cook gently for a few more minutes, before turning the heat down and covering with a lid to simmer for 20 minutes.

Cook the rice. Boil the eggs for 6 minutes and then run them under cold water until you can pick them up to peel them. Cook the frozen peas in boiling water for 3-4 minutes, drain and add a little butter.

Check the onions are softened before adding the rice, fish and peas to them in the frying pan. Stir gently to amalgamate and to prevent the rice from sticking. Add the crème fraîche. Transfer the kedgeree to a warmed shallow bowl, or serve it straight from the pan. Halve the eggs and place them around the edge and add a good scattering of parsley. This is a complete supper dish.

Another of those recipes that my friend George Morley lobbed my way one day, as she is prone, and highly encouraged, to do. She said she'd just done it for a party and it was sensational. I seem to have built up a deep-litter system of recipes that way, which I fully intend to keep until the occasion where the people suit the recipe, no small consideration, and then either it's the wrong season, I can't find the recipe or an ingredient, or something newer has risen to the surface of one of my Vesuvial agglomerations of things to be tried and tested.

The recipe came from Anna Del Conte's book *Entertaining all' Italiana* – George was the editor of the book, giving it a doubly immaculate pedigree. That autumn I went to interview Anna about the reissue of her *Gastronomy of Italy*. On my return home, I thought, that's it – party or no, I'm going to cook this dish. I made one slight change: I added a little lemon rind and juice to the torta. And I think an extra couple of hours soaking of the rice in the mixture helps; you know how firm good risotto rice grains like arborio or carnaroli are in the centre. I corralled two friends to come and eat the torta with my family – Brigid and Georgina, who is studying in Bologna, so steeped in good Italian food at the moment. Both pronounced it a triumph. I am promising myself that come the porcini season, I will attempt a Torta di Porcini. You will have to wait for that. The Torta di Porri is best served warm, but Anna also makes it a day in advance and serves it at room temperature, having kept it out of the fridge.

La Torta di Porri, or Leek and Rice Pie

SERVES 6

preheat oven to 180°C/350°F/Gas 4

700g/1½lb leeks, washed thoroughly, green parts cut away and white parts cut into very thin discs, 3mm/⅛in

4 large organic eggs

150g/5oz arborio or other risotto rice

200ml/7fl oz extra virgin olive oil

sea salt and freshly ground black pepper

7 tbsp freshly grated Parmesan cheese

lemon zest and juice

225–250g/8–9 oz frozen filo pastry, thawed, you will not need the whole box. There are two lengths of filo in the supermarkets, I buy the longest

Lightly beat the eggs and put them in a bowl with the leeks, rice, half the oil, two teaspoons of salt, plenty of pepper and the Parmesan. Add the grated zest of an organic lemon and the juice of half of it. Mix very thoroughly with your hands. Set the bowl aside for 3 or 4 hours, mixing it whenever you remember to keep everything equally well lubricated.

Oil a 25cm/10in springform tin. Pour the rest of the oil into a small bowl. Carefully unfold the filo pastry leaves, one at a time, taking care to leave the other leaves covered, since filo pastry dries out and cracks very easily. Lift out and lay one leaf over the bottom and up the sides of the prepared tin, allowing the ends to hang down over the outside of the tin. It will tear a little, but don't worry. Using a pastry brush, brush the leaf all over with a little of the oil and then cover with another leaf of the pastry. Lay it across the previous one so that the sides of the tin are covered all round. Brush with oil and lay two more leaves the same way.

Now fill the tin with the leek mixture. Fold the overhanging pieces of filo back over the top, one at a time, to make a lid. If the filo is not long enough, lay four more leaves over the top, brushing each sheet with oil. Cut them to fit inside the tin and fold the overlap over to form a ridge around the edge. Brush each one with oil before you place the next. Bake for 45–50 minutes on a preheated baking tray, otherwise the base filo will not cook through and crisp. Let the pie cool for 10 minutes and then remove the side of the tin and turn it over on to an oven tray. Put the pie back in the oven, upside down, for 5 minutes to dry the bottom. Turn on to a pretty round serving dish.

I've since remade this dish, with a larger amount of ingredients, so the torta was deeper, and I soaked the rice with the egg, oil, Parmesan and leeks for 4 hours. The consistency was perfect. I used the whites of 1.2kg/2½lb leeks, 200ml/7fl oz olive oil to soak and more to brush with, 9 heaped tablespoons of Parmesan and 6 eggs. Also, the zest and juice of a whole organic lemon, which I am convinced improves the dish. The same amount of arborio rice as above. Cooking time the same, but I allowed 10 minutes to crisp up the underside of the torta after I had turned it over and returned it to the oven. I served it with wedges of red onion squash baked in the oven with chopped red chilli and garlic, splashed with olive oil and seasoned with salt and pepper.

I think crab is at its best served chilled, but not icy cold. It is rich though, and you do not need a huge amount of it. The crab that I picked for this dish yielded 350g/12oz of brown meat and a little less of white, enough for four.

Chilled Crab, Cucumber and Avocado Salad

SERVES 4

1.5kg/3 and a bit lb crab, cooked
2 ripe Hass avocados
a cucumber
2 limes
a mixed bag of herbs, ideally a
    tbsp of each of the following:
    chervil, dill and chives
a few bunches of watercress and
    some rocket or the heart of a
    cos lettuce

Make a dressing with a dessertspoon of home-made mayonnaise, a teaspoon of seeded mustard, a tablespoon of cider vinegar and about 4 to 5 tablespoons of your best olive oil. Then sieve a couple of tablespoons of the brown crab meat into it and season to taste. You might like to add a tiny pinch of cayenne instead of black pepper.

Put the white crab meat on to a plate with the salad leaves. Add long slivers of avocado and chunks of peeled, seeded cucumber, the finely chopped herbs, and a few quarters of lime to squeeze on. Pour over the dressing, and serve the salad with a loaf of good country bread.

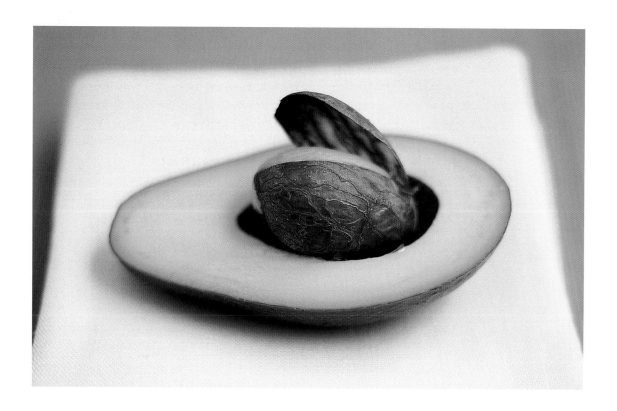

The following jellies and jams are a few of the things I make seasonally to be consumed in future weeks or months. A pot of crab apple jelly, with its sparklingly brilliant, clear amber-red complexion and a squirl of lemon peel at its summit, is a lovely autumn or Christmas present, as is a little bottle of damson and mulberry gin, made in September and matured by Christmas. The cakes and biscuits can be made a day or two ahead for puddings, birthdays, teas or late-night kitchen raids.

These biscuits are great with drinks, particularly a Sunday lunchtime Bloody Mary, see my home-made one on page 34.

Sesame and Roquefort Biscuits

MAKES 20
preheat oven to 180°C/350°F/Gas 4

125g/4oz unsalted butter
125g/4oz self-raising flour
125g/4oz Roquefort, Troupeau or
  Papillon are the best
50g/2oz sesame seeds

Blend the butter and flour together in a food processor until they resemble crumbs. Crumble the cheese into the mixture and blitz for a second or two. Remove from the bowl and knead briefly by hand to distribute the ingredients evenly. Roll the dough into a sausage shape, wrap in clingfilm and refrigerate until 20 minutes before you want to bake them, up to a couple of days is fine.

When you are ready to bake the biscuits, cut the dough into thin slices, coat with sesame seeds on both sides and place on a greased baking tray, a little distance away from each other. Bake for 10 minutes or so. Do not remove the biscuits to a rack to cool until you have let them firm up for a few minutes.

Quite simply, your kitchen should never be without this jam, and it keeps in the fridge for weeks if it is allowed the chance to do so. Great with a Montgomery Cheddar sandwich, in a toasted sandwich, or slicked onto bruschetta under a row of slices of Ragstone or Golden Cross goat cheese. Serve it with cold pork, on griddled scallops, or come up with your own idea. Versatile it is. I have upped the quantity from Peter Gordon's original recipe and this quantity of ingredients make enough for two outsize jars. Mine took double the cooking time he suggested, nearly an hour and a half, so don't panic if nothing seems to be happening after an hour.

Tomato Chilli Jam

MAKES TWO LARGE JARS

750g/1lb 10 oz very ripe organic
    tomatoes
4 red chillies, with their seeds
6 fat cloves of garlic, peeled
3 thumbs of fresh ginger, peeled
    and roughly chopped
40 ml/1½fl oz Thai fish sauce,
    (nam pla)
450g/1lb unrefined golden caster
    sugar
150ml/5fl oz red wine vinegar

Blend half the tomatoes, the chillies, garlic, ginger and fish sauce to a fine purée in a blender. You need the chilli seeds for the heat, which is not intense, and the tomato seeds for the pectin that will make the jam set.

Put the purée, sugar and vinegar into a deep pan and bring to the boil slowly, stirring all the time. When it reaches the boil, turn down to a gentle simmer and add the remaining tomatoes cut into tiny dice, about 5mm/¼in, skin and all. Skim off the foam and cook gently for about an hour and a quarter to an hour and a half, stirring every so often to release the solids that settle on the bottom and prevent them from burning. Be sure to scrape the sides of the pot too, so the entire mass cooks evenly.

When the jam is done, pour it into warmed glass jars. Allow it to cool to room temperature before storing in the fridge or a cold larder for later use.

I came to marmalade making late in life, after the odd abortive sojourn resulting in burnt, caramelized offerings, or something that was over or under sweet, too runny or set like a stone. After a whole day's instruction from my friend Gale last year, I can now face the annual boiling, when the kitchen is shrouded in steam and the tangiest, sharpest, most citrussy of aromas for a whole day. Batten down the hatches and demand room service if you possibly can – after all your family and friends will benefit for the rest of the year. This method is infallible, and sharp enough for me, which no shop-bought marmalade ever is. And shreds should be shreds, not lumps of peel. Unrefined sugar is as much of a must as Seville and organic oranges. Refined sugar seems to leave a toxic froth on the surface, which can only be the result of the 14 or so chemical processes to which it is subjected I assume. And unrefined tastes better.

Organic Seville Orange Marmalade

ENOUGH FOR 17 POTS OF VARYING SIZES

2kg/4½lb organic Seville oranges
3 organic lemons
3.2 kg /7lb organic unrefined granulated sugar
4.5 litres/9 pints water

Wash the oranges and lemons, halve and squeeze them, reserving the juice and the pips from the squeezing separately. Extract the remains of the pulp, pith and pips from the orange halves with your fingers and put them into a muslin bag with the other pips. Halve the halves, and pile the quarters into a tight stack that you can feed down the feeder tube of the Magimix through the slicer disc. Trim any bits of peel that have not been properly shredded.

Put the sliced peel into a large preserving pan, with the squeezed juice, water and the muslin bag tied to the side, and bring gently to the boil. Cover with a lid and put into the simmering oven of an Aga, or continue to simmer very gently on top of the stove. It will take about 2½ hours inside the Aga or rather less, about 2 hours, on top of the stove, for the peel to have absolutely no bite to it right the way through.

Remove the jelly bag and suspend it over a bowl for the juice to drain through for about 30 minutes, then add the juice to the liquid in the pan. Now divide the mixture accurately into three batches for the next stage, because it sets better in small quantities. Put one-third of the mixture back into the preserving pan, with one-third of the sugar, and heat gently, stirring to dissolve the sugar completely. The mixture mustn't boil until the sugar has completely dissolved. Now boil hard until you reach setting point;

ours took about 15 minutes, but start testing after 10. Put a small saucer in the fridge to cool, then place a teaspoon of boiling juice on the saucer, and put it in the freezer for a couple of minutes. While you do this, remove the marmalade from the heat so that it doesn't cook any further. If the liquid on the saucer wrinkles when you push it with a finger, it has reached setting point.

Now leave the pan off the heat for 30 minutes before you ladle the marmalade into warm clean jars, otherwise the shreds will rise up the jar to the top, and you'll have half over-shredded, half gel marmalade. Don't fall at the last fence. Be patient, the waiting is all. Repeat with the remaining two-thirds of ingredients.

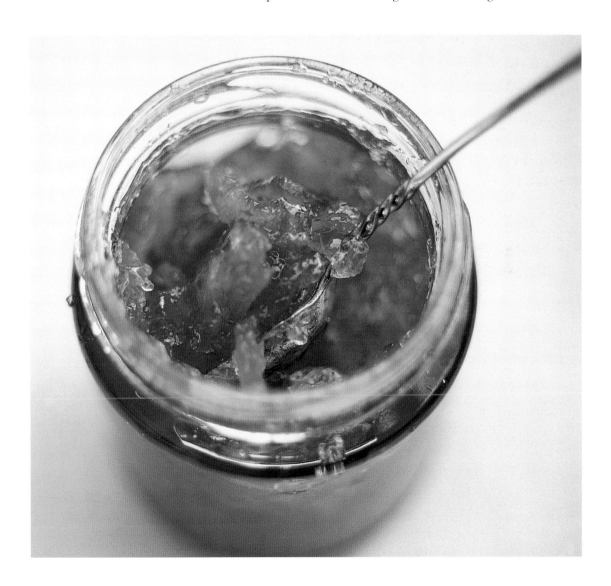

This recipe makes three puddings. Be generous, give a couple away. If you don't, I can guarantee they'll still be sitting in your kitchen reproachfully in June and you won't feel at all like cooking or eating them then. Try to force yourself to make them a couple of months in advance. I didn't this year, I made them only two weeks before Christmas. It was a new recipe, stuffed full of Agen prunes – a real plum pudding this – dried apricots and fresh dates. I wanted more fruit than vine fruit. I gave one to my friend Nick Welsh, Harry's erstwhile tutor at Eton and a mighty keen cook. He doesn't make a Christmas pudding because although he loves them, his wife Sal and children don't. When they arrived to spend New Year's Eve with us – the first I haven't spent in Ireland for a decade, so the food HAD to be good to compensate – Nick declared that it was the best pudding he'd ever tasted, that Sal now loved Christmas pudding, and perhaps I should make a tradition of it and give them one every year. I guess I better had. Everything in this pudding was organic, except the Guinness and Cognac.

Christmas Pudding

200g/7oz plain flour
1 tsp ground cinnamon bark
1 tsp ground mace blade
1 tsp ground cloves
1 tsp ground dried ginger root
1 tsp allspice
200g/7oz each of sultanas, raisins
    and currants
225g/8oz each of Agen prunes,
    unsulphured dried apricots and
    stoned dates
450g/1lb molasses sugar
125g/4oz each of Brazil nuts and
    blanched almonds, chopped
200g/7oz brown breadcrumbs
125g/4oz butter, chopped into
    tiny bits from a cold packet, I do
    not use suet in the pudding,
    but use 175g/6oz of beef or
    vegetarian suet if you want to
3 sharp eating apples such as
    Coxes, grated with their skin
    into the mixture
1 large carrot, peeled and grated
6 eggs
300ml/10fl oz Guinness
50ml/2fl oz Cognac
juice and grated zest of an orange
 a bit of milk to mix

Grease three 600ml/1 pint pudding basins. Sift the flour into an exceptionally large bowl, add the spices and dried fruits, then the sugar, nuts, breadcrumbs, other fruits and carrot, the chopped butter or suet, followed by the eggs, Guinness, Cognac and orange zest and juice that you have beaten together with a whisk. Stir the liquid well into the dry ingredients. Add a little milk if you need to, to make a soft dropping consistency.

Fill the pudding basins just over three-quarters full. Cover with a layer of greaseproof and a layer of foil on top of it, both pleated in the middle to allow for the pudding to rise. Tie securely with string, making a handle as you go, and place in large casseroles on a trivet or layer of foil. Fill half way up the sides of the puddings with boiling water, put a lid over each pan, and bring to the boil. Then allow to cook at a gentle blip of a simmer for 6–7 hours, topping up with water every couple of hours.

Take the puddings out of the water, remove the foil and greaseproof and allow to cool. Re-cover with foil and greaseproof in the same way, ready for blast-off on Christmas Day, when they will need 2–3 hours further cooking.

This year I used Julian Temperley's wonderful 10-year-old Somerset Cider Brandy (see page 282 for details) for my brandy butter. It may not be allowed to call itself Calvados, but it is up there with the best of them. I also used it to ignite the pudding.

Somerset Cider Brandy, Brandy or Rum Butter

MAKES A GOOD BOWLFUL

225g/8oz packet of best unsalted butter
125g/4oz unrefined icing sugar for brandy butter, or half unrefined icing sugar, half light muscovado sugar for rum butter
2–3 tbsp Somerset Cider Brandy, Cognac or dark rum
grated zest of an orange
a small grating of nutmeg
a squeeze of lemon juice

Start with soft butter, which you can cream further in a bowl with a wooden spoon, before adding the sifted sugar and all the other ingredients. Now work the butter, sugar and alcohol with your fingers, the aim being to incorporate all the liquid and end up with a slushy alcoholic mixture. It will firm up in the fridge. A suspicion of nutmeg only. Good with the pud and the mince pies.

Enough for two enormous jars, or about four dozen mince pies. This, too, should be made weeks in advance, but yet again, I made mine three days before I used the first of it this Christmas. I nearly relented and bought some I was so busy, then I thought guiltily of how the children would never forgive me. It takes longer to buy the ingredients than it does to make if you need a spur. With Miranda and Charissa weighing and stirring, chopping and bottling, it was done in minutes. There is something tremendously satisfying about using the largest wooden spoon you possess to stir the largest tonnage of ingredients you are ever likely to fill a bowl with.

Home-made Mincemeat

MAKES TWO BIG JARS

About 350g/12oz each of organic
    sultanas, raisins and currants
175g/6oz blanched almonds,
    finely chopped
3 Coxes apples, cut into dolls' size
    dice
400g/14oz dark muscovado sugar
200g/7oz organic mixed peel,
    finely chopped
grated zest and juice of 1½ organic
    lemons, and the zest of an
    organic orange
1 tsp nutmeg, finely grated
¼ tsp ground cloves and
    cinnamon
⅛ tsp ground mace and dried root
    ginger
175g/6oz beef or vegetarian suet
4 tbsp dark rum
125ml/4fl oz Cognac or Somerset
    Cider Brandy

Simply mix all the ingredients together really well in a colossal bowl. Decant into sterilized jars, cover and keep. Turn the jars upside down every so often so that the liquid permeates the mixture constantly.

When Sally Edwards used to bake this cake at her River Café in Taunton, the strongest-willed non-puddinger would have weakened. She gave me the recipe to cook on camera, about three minutes before I had to make it, when she joined me to cook on *Tamasin's Weekends*, which I made for UK Food recently. I've never made a cake faster in my life, and thank God the result was every bit as good as hers. The crew hoovered it up instantly. It is really a pudding cake, and should be eaten with a memory of warmth to it, alongside some spiced plums, apricots or pears. The top should be both crunchy and gooey at the same time.
A cross between macaroon and meringue was the production team's verdict.

Almond Macaroon Cake

SERVES 6—8
preheat oven to 180°C/350°F/Gas 4

175g/6oz unsalted butter
150g/5oz unrefined
   vanilla caster sugar
a pinch of salt
zest of an organic lemon
2 organic eggs
4–5 tbsp crème fraîche
150g/5oz unbleached
   self-raising flour
85g/3oz freshly ground almonds

For the topping:
2 egg whites
125g/4oz unrefined
   vanilla caster sugar
85g/3oz ground almonds

Grease a 15cm/6in cake tin, then place a circle of greased greaseproof paper in the bottom of it. Cream the softened butter and sugar together thoroughly. Add a pinch of salt, the lemon zest and the eggs, one by one, beating as you go. Fold in four tablespoons of crème fraîche, the sifted flour and the almonds. If the mixture is a little heavy, slacken it with another tablespoon of crème fraîche. Bake in the centre of the oven for 30 minutes.

Five minutes before you are due to take the cake out, whisk the whites stiffly, incorporate half the sugar and whisk again until stiff. Fold in the almonds and the rest of the sugar lightly and quickly. Take the cake out of the oven and gently but swiftly pile the macaroon mixture on top and spread it across. Return the cake to the oven for about 20 minutes. The top should be biscuit coloured and crisp to the touch. Cool for 10 minutes, turn out and serve warm with crème fraîche. You can also leave the cake to cool completely, and warm it gently a few hours later when you want to eat it.

This wonderfully old-fashioned cake is best made a couple of days before you want to eat it, cut into squares, rather like treacly-black, molasses-laden gingerbread. Curiously, it is as good eaten with a good fruity slice of Montgomery Cheddar as it is served for tea or pudding, with a moreish butterscotch sauce. Any which way you please.

Parkin

MAKES 12—16 SQUARES
preheat oven to 180°C/350°F/Gas 4

125g/4oz butter
85g/3oz light muscovado sugar
350g/12oz organic blackstrap
   molasses
225g/8oz plain or wholemeal
   flour
2 tsp baking powder
1 tsp ground root ginger
1 tsp mixed spice
salt
4 tbsp milk
flaked almonds (optional)

Melt the butter, sugar and molasses together in a pan over a gentle heat. Remove from the heat and add to the remaining ingredients in a bowl, beating them together lightly until well amalgamated. Grease and line a roasting tin with greaseproof paper, pour in the mixture and bake for about 40 minutes, until just firm to the touch. You can add flaked almonds to the top about 15 minutes into the cooking time if you like.

Cool on a wire rack with the greaseproof still attached, then wrap in greaseproof and foil and keep for a couple of days before cutting into squares. You can always go down the clotted cream route if you prefer it to the idea of butterscotch sauce, and you are going to eat the parkin warm.

Butterscotch Sauce

SERVES 6

250ml/8fl oz single cream,
175g/6oz light muscovado sugar
125g/4oz butter

I find single cream, light muscovado sugar and butter melted together in a pan and whisked until well amalgamated and hot, makes the kind of sauce that is irresistible to the toothed and toothless of all ages.

Citrus works wonderfully with cardamom. This is a light, sticky pudding of a cake, perfect with crème fraîche or orange ice cream.

Lemon and Cardamom Cake

MAKES A 23CM/9IN CAKE
preheat oven to 180°C/350°F/Gas 4

2 heaped tsp cardamom pods
175g/6oz unsalted butter
125g/4oz light muscovado sugar
3 eggs, the Clarence Court
    Cotswold Legbar eggs make a
    very light cake (Sainsbury's and
    Waitrose sell them)
200g/7oz plain flour
1½ tsp baking powder
½ tsp bicarbonate of soda
50g/2oz fine maize meal
10 tsp Greek yoghurt
grated zest and juice of 2 large
    organic lemons
demerara sugar to sprinkle

Grease and line a 23cm/9in springform cake tin. Crush the cardamom pods with a pestle and mortar to split them, remove the husks and crush the seeds.

Cream the butter and sugar until light and fluffy, then beat in the eggs one by one, adding a little sifted flour if the mixture begins to curdle. Sift the flour, baking powder and bicarb into the mixture, then add the cardamom seeds. Fold in the maize meal and Greek yoghurt, add the lemon zest and juice, and plop the mixture into the tin, smoothing the top. Bake for 35 minutes, then gingerly open the oven door, pull the cake towards you, and throw a handful of demerara over the top of it. Carry on baking for a further 15 minutes, then test with a skewer. Almost clean means that it is cooked – you want a slightly damp centre with a crust of crunchy sugar on top.

Cool for 10–15 minutes, then finish cooling on a rack. Eat it, if your timing is impeccable, with a memory of warmth to it.

This is my take on the classic lemon cake, whose top you attack with deep skewer holes and trickle down a sticky, tangy lemon syrup. This is the same with ginger and lemon, but the ginger's heat and strength does not overwhelm the citrus. The top ends up looking rather like a glossy, caramel-coloured brandy snap.

Drenched Ginger and Lemon Cake

SERVES 6—8
preheat oven to 180°C/350°F/Gas 4

175g/6oz unsalted butter
175g/6 oz light muscovado sugar
2 large eggs
grated zest and juice of 2 lemons
1 tsp baking powder
a pinch of salt
175g/6oz self raising flour,
    I used ½ Shipton Mill's
    wholemeal, ½ Dove's Farm
    organic plain white
3–5 tbsp milk
4 pieces of ginger from a jar
    of stem ginger in syrup
35g/1½oz demerara sugar
2 tbsp ginger syrup

Butter a 15–18cm/6–7in cake tin and line the base with a circle of buttered greaseproof paper. Cream the butter and muscovado sugar until light and fluffy, then beat in the eggs one at a time. Grate the lemon zest into the mixture, then sift over the baking powder, salt and flour and fold them in lightly with a metal spoon. Stir in enough milk to give a dropping consistency, then add the finely chopped ginger and fold in lightly. Plop into the tin, smooth the top, and bake in the centre of the oven for about 40–50 minutes, until springy to the touch in the centre.

Remove from the oven, and leave for 15 minutes before turning out on to a rack. When still warm, place on a plate, and with a long skewer, pierce holes all over the cake from the top through to the bottom. Put the demerara sugar, lemon juice and ginger syrup in a pan, stir as it heats to dissolve the sugar, then bubble it up fiercely for a minute or so. Pour it as slowly as you can over the top of the cake, allowing it to seep down the holes. Serve warm or cold with crème fraîche.

This is a delicious, densely fruited moist loaf, which needs no more than spreading with a thick slice of unsalted butter.

Malt and Apple Loaf

MAKES A 450G/1LB LOAF
preheat oven to 170°C/325°F/Gas 3

50g/2oz sultanas
50g/2oz raisins
50g/2oz unsalted butter
50g/2 oz malt extract
a sharp eating apple like a Cox,
    peeled and diced and spritzed
    with fresh lemon juice
300ml/½ pint of hot water
2 tbsp apple juice concentrate
300g/10oz plain or wholemeal
    flour
½ tsp bicarbonate of soda
1 tsp ground mixed spice
½ tsp ground cloves

Soak the sultanas and raisins in the apple juice concentrate mixed with the hot water for 30 minutes. Then place them in a saucepan with the butter and malt extract, and heat through until the butter and malt has all melted and dissolved.

Combine the dry ingredients and the diced apple in a bowl, then pour on the hot ones and stir together thoroughly. Plop the mixture into a greased 450g/1lb loaf tin and bake for 1–1½ hours, when a skewer will come out clean. Turn out after 15 minutes and cool on a wire rack.

I have always found redcurrant jelly just too sweet for lamb, equally so for venison and hare, but add some spice and cider vinegar, and you have something with the sharpening effect of mint sauce, but with the fruity strength and acidity of the redcurrant. Redcurrants set blissfully easily, so this is a very satisfying jelly to make.

Spiced Redcurrant Jelly

MAKES 3 OR 4 JARS

1.5kg/3lb 5oz redcurrants
900ml/1½ pints water
3 cloves
a short length of cinnamon bark
250ml/9fl oz cider vinegar
1.5kg/3lb 5oz unrefined
   granulated sugar

Throw the redcurrants into a large preserving or enamel pan as they are, with their stalks. Add the water and spices, bring to the boil and simmer until the redcurrants are soft. Strain the juice through a muslin or jelly bag into a bowl, suspending it above the bowl and leaving it to drip overnight. You do not want to squeeze or hurry any of the juice through; this will make your jelly cloudy instead of sparkling.

Add the vinegar and sugar to the liquid in the pan, and boil until it reaches setting point. To test for the setting point, put a small saucer in the fridge to cool, then place a teaspoon of boiling juice on the saucer, and put it in the freezer for a couple of minutes. If the liquid on the saucer wrinkles when you push it with a finger, you have reached the setting point.

Pour into clean warm jam jars and cover while they are still very hot.

This was my father's favourite breakfast treat, and now it is mine. On the odd years I pine. On the even years, when my tree is glutted with the waxy glow of crimson and primrose, I pick baskets of the fruit, drape muslin from the beams of the kitchen, letting the amber juice drip into bowls for days. I then proudly pot dozens of jars, with a sprig of lemon peel adorning each summit.

I even dared to give pots to Richard Corrigan and Simon Hopkinson this year, so good it was. Crab apples should be picked when they are just ripe, but the odd bruise from falling to the ground will not hurt.

Crab Apple Jelly

as much fruit as you can pick
water
unrefined sugar, 450g/1lb for each
  600ml/1 pint of juice

Wash the fruit, put it in a huge preserving pan and just cover with water. Bring to the boil and simmer slowly, covered, until the apples are softened to a pulp. Strain the juice through a muslin or jelly bag into a bowl, suspending it above the bowl and leaving it to drip overnight. You do not want to squeeze or hurry any of the juice through; this will make your jelly cloudy instead of sparkling.

Measure the beautiful pink juice in a jug, and add 450g/1lb of unrefined sugar to each 600ml/1 pint of juice. Bring to the boil, scum and keep boiling until you reach setting point. I start testing after 10 minutes. Put a small saucer in the fridge to cool, then place a teaspoon of boiling juice on the saucer, and put it in the freezer for a couple of minutes. If the liquid on the saucer wrinkles when you push it with a finger, the jelly has reached the setting point.

I scald the jars with boiling water in the sink as I wait for the setting point. Ladle the jelly through a funnel into the jars as soon as you have reached setting point. Cover immediately with cellophane and an elastic band.

I am writing this in January, with two precious jars of crab apple left, and a couple of bramble jelly. Nearly time to make Seville orange marmalade before the last of the jelly has been eaten.

This year, my little mulberry tree fruited for the first time, providing just enough to make a breathtakingly good sorbet and to add to my home-made damson gin. This is an autumn treat of a job: I pick the sloes or damsons in late September, prick them with a fork, add the sugar, gin, kernels from the damson stones, the heart of the fruit, and seal the purple brew in a huge Kilner jar, to shake rumbustiously every week before the first tasting at Christmas. The sweet purple stickiness reminds me of childhood cough linctus – if only that had tasted so good. I filled the last quarter of my jar with mulberries and didn't take the top off until Charlotte and Bill Reynolds of Swaddles Green Organic Farm arrived with my Bronze turkey, goose and ham on Christmas Eve. It was four in the afternoon, and they'd been flat out with Christmas orders for weeks, including 1100 organic turkeys. I sat them down with smoked eel from Michael Brown of Brown and Forrest, home-made granary toast and shot glasses of my mulberried damson gin. Bill was most taken by it and felt suitably mellowed after the first three glasses.

Damson, Sloe or Mulberry Gin

MAKES A LARGE JAR

900ml/1½ pints of damsons or sloes, put them in a measuring jug as you pick, or, if you make mulberry gin, use equal measures of mulberries and gin
350g/12oz unrefined sugar
1.2 litres/2 pints good gin
either half a dozen kernels from inside the damson stones, which you crack open with a hammer, or a few drops of Culpeper's bitter almond essence

Prick the damsons. sloes or mulberries and put them into a large Kilner jar. Add all the other ingredients, seal the jar and give it a good shake. Shake every week until Christmas, when you may strain and bottle the gin. The fruit will be delicious with a bit of the sticky purple linctus eaten with some homemade vanilla ice cream.

This recipe also works well for 'moonshine', which Stephen Markwick of the brilliant restaurant Markwick's in Bristol makes. Moonshine is vodka based, filled with cherries and a lot of the kernels from the cracked cherry stones.

a lingering end

4

Francesco Zanchetta's peerless rendering of this classic Italian pudding. Make this the night before you want it so the cream has time to bind with the layer of biscuit and the flavours develop.

Tiramisu

SERVES 6

1 organic egg and 3 organic egg
    yolks
50ml/2fl oz white wine
50ml/2fl oz Marsala
2 tbsp Amaretto, use Cognac and
    a drop or two of Culpeper's
    bitter almond essence if you
    can't get Amaretto
100g/3½oz unrefined vanilla
    caster sugar
225g/8oz mascarpone cheese
1 tsp espresso coffee powder

For the biscuit layer:
175g/6oz Italian savoiardi biscuits,
    or good boudoir biscuits
3 small cups of espresso coffee
1½ tbsp caster sugar
2 tbsp Marsala
2 level tbsp best cocoa powder for
    sifting over the top, I use Green
    and Black's

Whisk together the egg yolks and whole egg, white wine, Marsala and Amaretto in a double boiler; I have my grandmother's old enamel one. The top pan should not touch the water simmering in the bottom pan. Whisk until the mixture becomes very thick, you are making zabaglione. Once it is firm and fluffy, remove the bowl from the pan and carry on whisking for a few more minutes. Now add the sugar, which will dissolve very quickly. Gently fold in the mascarpone with the espresso powder, and then beat everything together for another minute or so to lighten the cream.

Mix together the cups of espresso, sugar and Marsala in a dish deep enough to soak the biscuits. Dip in the biscuits so that they absorb the liquid but do not start to break up. Hot coffee helps.

Cover the base of a large, shallow rectangular dish with a layer of soaked biscuits, laid tightly together in the same direction, then pour over half of the cream before adding a second layer of biscuits, placed at right angles to the layer beneath. This helps to hold the tiramisu together when you serve it. Cover with the rest of the cream and sift the cocoa powder thickly over the surface. Cover and chill in the fridge overnight.

Chocolate

This could so easily turn into a chapter, a book, a magnum opus. I am, let us say, not immune to the pleasures of chocolate, and only grateful that there is no closed season for it. If there were, the term stockpiling would hardly be sufficient. I greet the discovery of a new bar, cake, pudding or ice cream as just that, an important discovery for the happiness and wellbeing of man, but I would not want to burden those of a dissimilar disposition with the finer details that clearly identify and typify the truly obsessed. Instead, I offer you a token few of my latest recipes, including a few classics and long-time favourites, without which many a Sunday lunch or dinner for friends and family would have been infinitely the poorer.

This is a magical cake, which you can make without the raspberries if you are of the purist chocoholic bent, or simply don't agree with chocolate and fruit, which some don't. You can make the cake well in advance. It will keep for a week in a tin, and then add your ganache. This cake is flourless, but moist with freshly ground almonds.

Chocolate and Raspberry Pudding Cake with Chocolate Ganache

SERVES 8—10
preheat oven to 170°C/325°F/Gas 3

4 organic eggs, separated, plus one
    whole egg
175g/6oz vanilla caster sugar
225g/8oz best bitter chocolate,
    minimum 70% cocoa solids,
    I use Green and Black
150g/5oz blanched almonds,
    freshly ground
1 heaped tsp ground coffee
200g/7oz fresh raspberries

For the ganache:
225g/8oz dark chocolate
125ml/4fl oz double cream

Whisk the egg yolks and egg together with half the sugar, until pale and doubled in volume. Melt the chocolate in a double saucepan. Whisk the egg whites, adding the sugar a bit at a time, until they are at the satiny, soft peak stage. Add half of them to the egg and sugar mixture, folding them in gently. Add the chocolate and the rest of the whites, folding as you go. Then do likewise with the almonds and coffee. Last of all, add the raspberries, which need folding in with extreme gentleness so that they don't break up.

Scrape the mixture into a greased and floured 20cm/8in springform tin, with a circle of greased greaseproof paper laid on its base, and bake for 30 minutes. Then turn the oven off and leave the cake in for another 15 minutes or until a skewer comes out clean from the centre. Remove from the oven and leave to cool in the tin.

Scald the cream in a small pan, remove from the heat and stir in the broken up chocolate. Cover the cake with the ganache and leave to cool.

A delicious birthday cake, which needs little more than a perfectly made vanilla ice cream with fresh Madagascan vanilla pods.

Chocolate Mocha Cake with Irish Whiskey

MAKES A 20CM/8IN CAKE
preheat oven to 180°C/350°F/Gas 4

175g/6oz dark chocolate, minimum 70% cocoa solids
4 tbsp freshly made strong mocha coffee
2 tbsp Irish whiskey
85g/3oz unrefined vanilla sugar
125g/4oz unsalted butter, soft enough to cream
3 organic eggs, separated
50g/2oz almonds, freshly ground
a few drops of Culpeper's natural bitter almond essence
50g/2oz plain flour, sifted

For the icing:
50g/2oz best bitter chocolate
2 tbsp Irish whiskey
50g/2oz unsalted butter

Butter and flour a 20cm/8in cake tin. Melt the chocolate in a double boiler with the coffee and whiskey. Remove the top pan and allow them to cool. Cream together all but a tablespoon of the sugar with the butter until it is pale and fluffy, then beat in the egg yolks, one at a time. Whisk the egg whites with a pinch of salt to soft peak stage, then add the last tablespoon of sugar and beat to firm peaks. Blend the chocolate mixture into the creamed butter and sugar with a rubber spatula, then stir in the ground almonds and bitter almond essence. Fold in a spoonful of the egg white, followed by a spoonful of flour, and continue until it's all blended in.

Scrape the mixture into the cake tin and bake it in the centre of the oven for 25–30 minutes. A skewer should come out clean. Cool in the tin for 10 minutes, then run a knife round the edge of the tin and turn the cake out on to a rack.

Ice it when it is completely cool. Melt the chocolate and whiskey in the top of the double boiler until satiny smooth. Remove from the heat and beat in the butter, a tablespoon at a time. Stand the bowl over iced water and continue to beat, otherwise the butter and the chocolate will separate. You can always add a little cream if this happens – whisk and the mixture will cohere. Spread the icing over the cake, leaving a rough finish.

This is a fabulous pudding, which you turn out in a block rather like a gold ingot and cut into thin slices. I found very good organic Spanish chestnuts to make it with; they come vacuum packed and the flavour is strong enough not to be overpowered by the chocolate. Disarmingly simple to make.

Chocolate and Chestnut Marquise

SERVES 10

3 x 200g/7oz packs of vacuum-packed chestnuts, the best you can find
125g/4oz unsalted butter, melted in a pan
125g/4oz unrefined vanilla sugar
200g/7oz best bitter chocolate, minimum 70% cocoa solids
1 tbsp Cognac
1 tbsp water
4 organic eggs, separated

Put the chestnuts in a food processor with the melted butter and all but a tablespoon of the sugar. Blend until well mixed. Melt the chocolate in a double boiler with the brandy and water, add it to the chestnut mixture and blitz briefly. Stir in the egg yolks one by one, then whisk the egg whites to soft peak stage. Add the remaining tablespoon of sugar and whisk until stiff. Stir the first tablespoon into the chestnut mixture, then fold in the rest as well as you can; the mixture will be very thick and sludgy at this stage. Plop it into a loaf tin, which you have greased lightly with an unobtrusive oil such as almond oil, and smooth down the surface. Leave to cool and put it in the fridge when cold.

I think this is best eaten after a day or two, so you can make it in advance. It will turn out beautifully on to a flat dish. Serve with pouring cream, to which you can add a tablespoon of freshly made coffee if you like. A couple of slices each are all you will want. The other route would be to serve it with a whipped, sugared crème chantilly. Killer.

Sally Edwards was forbidden by her customers to take this pudding off the menu at her River Café in Taunton. I found it very difficult to steer a different pudding course as a result. It is simply one of the best pudding cakes I have ever come across, and it needs no more than a yielding spoonful of crème fraîche and a pile of purple berries to smarten it up.

Chocolate Espresso Cake

SERVES 8—10
preheat oven to 190°C/375°F/Gas 5

185g/6½oz unsalted butter, diced, plus extra for greasing the tin
185g/6½oz best dark chocolate, broken into pieces
50ml/2fl oz very strong freshly brewed coffee
6 eggs, separated
185g/6½oz unrefined caster sugar
185g/6½oz almonds, blanched, roasted and coarsely ground

Melt the butter and chocolate together with the coffee in a bowl over a pan of barely simmering water.

While they are melting, cream the egg yolks and sugar in an electric mixer until pale and light, about 8–10 minutes. Continue to whisk, adding the melted chocolate and butter. Stop the machine, remove the whisk and fold in the almonds with a metal spoon. In a clean glass or metal bowl, whisk the egg whites to stiff peaks. Stir a spoonful of egg white into the chocolate mixture to lighten it before folding in the rest.

Grease the sides of a 25cm/10in springform tin and line the base with a circle of buttered greaseproof paper. Pour in the mixture and bake for 20 minutes. Turn the oven down to 170°C/325°F/Gas 3 and continue cooking for a further 40 minutes.

Remove the cake and leave in the tin set on a rack until completely cool. Turn out of the tin and remove the paper. Delicious served with crème fraîche as a cake or pudding.

Quite the best, just don't overcook them,. Brownies are meant to have a 'sad' centre, above which there is a thin, dry, slightly crunchy crust.

Rich Chocolate Brownies

MAKES 12—16 SQUARES
preheat oven to 180°C/350°F/Gas 4

200g/7oz best bitter chocolate, minimum 70% cocoa solids
125g/4oz softened unsalted butter
225g/8oz unrefined vanilla caster sugar
2 eggs and 1 yolk
4 tbsp freshly made strong coffee
150g/5oz plain flour
1 tsp baking powder
a pinch of salt
a handful of fresh whole hazelnuts

Line the bottom and sides of small roasting tin or gratin dish, about 30 x 22 cm/12 x 9 inches, with foil. Gently melt the chocolate in a double boiler or in a bowl over, but not touching, simmering water in a pan. Cream the butter and sugar until really light and fluffy, I do this in the KitchenAid. Add the eggs, one at a time, then the extra yolk, with the mixer running. Pour in the melted chocolate then the coffee. Remove the mixing bowl to the work surface and sift in the flour, baking powder and a pinch of salt.

Pour into the tin, then push hazelnuts into the top of what you will later cut into 12–15 squares. Bake for about 25 minutes. Test with a skewer, you don't want it to come out completely clean, but the mixture should not feel raw. It will go on cooking when you take it out of the oven. Leave to cool before you cut the mixture into squares and remove them from the tin.

Quite the best, too, so which ones are you going to do? I suggest you try them both. Size is your business, but this mixture fills a small roasting tin.

Rich Chocolate Chip and Hazelnut Brownies

MAKES 12—16 SQUARES
preheat oven to 180°C/350°F/Gas 4

300g/10oz unrefined caster sugar
4 eggs
225g/8oz unsalted butter
85g/3oz Green and Black's organic cocoa
85g/3oz plain flour
125g/4oz roasted hazelnuts
125g/4oz cooking chocolate chunks. The Chocolate Society do them in bags, 70% cocoa solids

Grease the roasting tin. Beat the sugar and eggs together really well, until they have thickened and the sugar has totally dissolved. Melt the butter and pour it into the sugar and egg mixture. Sieve the cocoa and flour together into the mixture, then melt the chocolate in a bowl over hot water and stir it in.

Put the hazelnuts and chocolate chunks in a Ziploc bag, and whack it as hard as you dare with a rolling pin, keeping things a little chunky. The nuts will be more pulverized than the chocolate. Fold into the mixture and scrape it into the baking tin. Bake for about 25 minutes. Test with a skewer. You don't want it to come out completely clean, but the mixture should not feel raw.

Leave to cool before you cut the mixture into squares and remove them from the tin.

Our second lunch at Riva in Barnes the other day, was, I think Simon Hopkinson would agree, true to form, as perfect a symphony as the first last year. The three movements were rather shorter and more eclectic than our previous one – far too long and shamelessly greedy to go into here – but this time it was the week before Christmas and a little self-inflicted abstinence was the plan. The fritto misto that the exceptionally talented chef Francesco Zanchetta made for us consisted of the airiest and crispest of golden batters, encasing everything from a single sage leaf to squid, prawns and the most divinely battered balls of salt cod, one of my favourite things in the world. Then Simon suggested the fresh ricotta gnocchi with chanterelles. I was powerless to resist, what with the joy of having Simon unbossily absolving me of all decisions, and NOT insisting that we had to have something different. That, too, was about as delicious as you could ever imagine it to be from the simple description above. I was not going to eat pudding. Well, that lasted about a minute, until Simon got into conversation with Francesco about his budino. It turns out that Simon has been trying to make a chocolate budino as stratospherically delicious as Francesco's for some time now, and still hasn't quite succeeded. Undaunted and single-minded, he is still refusing the recipe, trying to see if he can create the same silken-textured, creamy chocolate pudding, tremblingly light, the gelatine barely holding its rich, soft, smooth soothingness together. You think I exaggerate? Go to Riva and try it for yourself. And, as Simon insisted I did, accompany it with a white slice of equally trembling and perfect panna cotta. Simon refused the recipe again. I asked for it and have been trying equally hard to reach Francesco's perfection with his minimal instruction, but I will give you what I have arrived at to date. And then Simon insisted that I try the tiramisu, that trat dessert that took over the trolley in all Italian restaurants when the zuppa inglese was finally consigned to the morgue. None so good as this. You will never be sniffy about tiramisu again if you make Francesco's (see page 234). As to the moral of the story, vis à vis Simon struggling on without the recipe and me taking it home with me, I would have thought it rather obvious. He is, of course, the better cook.

Budino

MAKES 7

225g/8oz bitter chocolate, 70%
   cocoa solids
1 short espresso, or the equivalent
   strong small cup of fresh coffee
100g/3½oz caster sugar
500ml/18fl oz milk
2 egg yolks
4 leaves of gelatine soaked in
   2–3 tbsp of water for about
   10 minutes

Melt the chocolate with the espresso in a double boiler. Take it off the heat and whisk in the egg yolks. Heat the milk with the sugar until it is dissolved. Add the milk and sugar mixture little by little to the chocolate, whisking all the time, without creating any foam. Once the gelatine has completely dissolved, add it to the mixture and continue whisking. Pour into small moulds, I used my little plastic steamed-pudding moulds. Allow them to cool and leave to set in the fridge.

You can serve them several hours or a day later. A palate knife worked around the moulds enables you to plop them out onto plates. Thin pouring cream is a must. It slicks the chocolate tops beautifully before cascading down the sides.

I served these at my New Year's dinner as well as the clementine, passion fruit and muscat jelly, and Nick and Sally Welsh were in raptures. My budinos were good, but they weren't as good as Francesco's. Mine seemed to be more solid, less quakey. I will try one leaf of gelatine less next time.

A simply delicious chocolate pudding that you may serve hot or cold, depending on your mood and what timing suits you. Both are equally good, although the cold tends to be richer, since I add a layer of lightly whipped cream and finely grated chocolate to shroud the chocolate beneath.

Hot or Cold Chocolate Pudding

SERVES 6—8
preheat oven to 200°C/400°F/Gas 6

150g/5oz bitter chocolate,
    70% cocoa solids
150g/5oz unsalted butter
1 tsp of pure vanilla extract
150ml/5fl oz of warm water
125g/4oz vanilla caster sugar
4 organic eggs, separated
25g/1oz self-raising flour
cream for serving

Grease a 2 litre/3–4 pint soufflé dish. Melt the chocolate, butter and vanilla in the top of a double boiler over simmering water. Add the warm water and sugar and keep stirring until all the sugar has dissolved. Pour the mixture into a bowl and stir in the egg yolks one by one. Stir in the sifted flour and whisk until the mixture is free of lumps. Whisk the egg whites to stiff peaks, stir the first tablespoon into the mixture, then fold the rest lightly in with a metal spoon.

Boil a kettle, put the soufflé dish inside a roasting tin and pour in scalding water to come half way up its sides. Cook for 10 minutes, then turn the oven temperature down to 170°C/325°F/Gas 3 and cook for 30 minutes more.

Serve hot with thin pouring cream, Jersey or Guernsey unpasteurized if you can find it, or leave to cool completely. To serve the cold version, softly whip 300ml/10fl oz of double cream, cover the pudding with it, and finely grate a dusting of bitter chocolate over the surface. Serve at room temperature – the pudding is lighter that way than if you chill it in the fridge.

This recipe doubles up perfectly, so if you have a party, just make double the amount in a larger soufflé dish.

This is one of the best winter Sunday lunch puddings – incredibly simple to make and it will burble away on the stove top while you tackle the joint. Being flourless, it is a whole lot lighter than you would suspect a steamed pudding to be, and not something any child or grown-up could say 'no' to. Another of my cousin Deborah's good puds.

Steamed Nut and Chocolate Pudding

SERVES 8

100g/3½oz softened butter, plus
   extra for greasing
100g/3½oz vanilla caster sugar
6 eggs, separated
100g/3½oz hazelnuts, ground
100g/3½oz organic plain
   chocolate, chilled
2 tbsp brandy
a pinch of salt
whipped cream for serving

Butter and sugar a 1.5 litre/2½ pint pudding basin. Cream the butter until soft, add the sugar and beat until fluffy and light. Add the egg yolks one at a time, then fold in the ground hazelnuts. Grate the chocolate on the coarse side of a grater or on the big disc of a food processor. Fold the chocolate into the mixture with the brandy. Whisk the egg whites with the pinch of salt until stiff and fold into the chocolate and nut mixture

Pour into the sugared and buttered bowl. Cover with foil and secure with string and steam for 1 hour over simmering water.

Leave to stand for 5 minutes before turning out. Serve with whipped cream with a little extra brandy in it.

Another wonderful recipe from a recent marathon cooking weekend with my friend George Morley, her husband Shawn and small son Charlie. Usually George and I, unreformable greedies, decide who's going to cook what and when, and what we're going to be drinking with it, in slavering telephone conversations. As the two bossiest women either of us know ever to set foot in a kitchen, it is all the more extraordinary that we never seem to come to blows. Greed and mutual respect are no small levellers here, and the culinary laboratory of the kitchen hums with our fairly suspect brand of caustic wit as we dissect everything from bone to body politic over many a fine glass and hot stove. George found this particular recipe the weekend she came down to 'guest' on my television series. I think I probably did the guesting that day. She had found the recipe in an American book, *Walking on Walnuts* by Nancy Ring. I devised the biscuits to go with it, using the last of my fabulous roast hazelnuts from Piedmont. A zen-like combination.

If you need further endorsement, here it is – courtesy of an article written by the illustrious historian Paul Johnson in his *Spectator* column. The subject, 'A rhapsody on puddings that would not have disgraced Belshazzar's chef'. At the end of the piece he writes: 'The other day I dined at the home of Tamasin Day-Lewis, the *Daily Telegraph* expert, and was served the best ice cream I've ever eaten, made of burnt orange according to a most complex and esoteric recipe. I don't know what Richard II would have made of it, but I had three helpings – unheard of!' Praise indeed, but how on earth do I top it next time?

Burnt Orange Ice Cream

SERVES 6—8

quantities are in US cups — we used an ordinary teacup

2 tbsp sugar

1 cup double cream

1 cup full cream milk

2 tbsp grated orange zest

2 cups freshly squeezed orange
  juice, George has also made it
  with blood oranges

¼ cup + 1 tbsp Cointreau

¼ cup + 2 tbsp sugar for the
  caramel

¼ cup egg yolks, about 10 large
  ones

Place the 2 tablespoons of sugar in a mixing bowl. In a medium saucepan, scald the cream and milk with the orange zest, then steep them together off the heat with a lid on the pan for about 30 minutes.

Simmer the orange juice and Cointreau until reduced to one cup. Whisk into the cream mixture and strain, then return it to the pan and keep warm over a very gentle heat. In another pan caramelize the ¼ cup plus two tablespoons of sugar until very dark (just past the colour of an Irish setter). Do not stir at any time. Swirl gently in the pan if necessary to ensure even colour. Remove from the heat, protecting your stirring hand with an oven glove, and immediately temper the caramel with a small amount of the warm orange cream while stirring vigorously. Keep adding cream slowly until the caramel stops bubbling violently. Whisk all of the tempered caramel back into the remaining cream and place on the stove over medium heat to scald once more.

Add the yolks to the sugar in a mixing bowl and whisk together when the cream scalds, but not before. Temper the yolks with the scalded cream by pouring a small stream of the hot cream into the yolks while whisking continuously. Pour back into the pan and return to the stove over medium heat. Stir continuously with a spatula until the mixture thickens to a perceptible custard and a line can be drawn through it with your finger. Cook only until it is just thickened or it will curdle. Immediately strain the finished ice cream base and stir to cool, then churn in an ice cream machine or put into a freezer tray. If you use a tray, remember to stir the setting walls of the ice cream into the middle of the tray after the first hour, and then again an hour or two later, to prevent crystals forming. Serve with the hazelnut and orange biscuits on page 250.

Once you have made the mixture for these delicious biscuits, you can keep it wrapped up like a fat sausage in greaseproof paper in the fridge. Slice it like a salami and cook the biscuits whenever you want them – warm for tea, as petit fours with coffee, or to go with puddings like the burnt orange ice cream on page 249 or a fruit fool.

Hazelnut and Orange Biscuits

preheat oven to 190°C/375°F/Gas 5

200g/7oz unsalted butter
150g/5oz unrefined caster sugar
1 large egg
225g/8oz self-raising flour
finely grated zest of an organic
   orange, use a nutmeg grater
a few drops of Culpeper's sweet
   orange oil
85–125g/3–4 oz whole roasted
   hazelnuts, the freshest you can
   find, bashed into bits with a
   mezzaluna or sharp knife

Cream the butter and sugar thoroughly in a KitchenAid or by hand. Then add the egg, sifted flour, zest, oil and nuts and amalgamate. Form the mixture into two balls and roll each one out on a lightly floured surface with both hands, until you have a sausage about 5cm/2in in diameter. Wrap these in waxed paper and foil, and refrigerate. Overnight is best.

Slice the sausage into as many biscuits as you want, place them on a greased baking tray or two, not touching, and cook in the middle of the oven for about 8 minutes. They should not have coloured significantly. Remember, a minute too far and they will burn.

Using a palate knife, remove the biscuits immediately to a rack. Be careful, they are soft and bendy and can break at this stage, but they firm up very quickly. They should be beautifully crisp and nutty and scented with orange. Serve them warm with the burnt orange ice cream, which you should remove from freezer to fridge 30 minutes before you want to eat it.

You can make this unfussy pudding well in advance, and it is as good in the winter with dried fruit as it is with summer berries or fruits.

Vanilla Cream Pots with Armagnac and Orange Apricots

MAKES 6 RAMEKINS
preheat oven to 170°C/325°F/Gas 3

500ml/18fl oz double cream
100ml/3½fl oz full cream milk
1 fresh vanilla pod with its
    scooped out innards
6 egg yolks
75g/2½oz unrefined
    vanilla caster sugar

Put the cream and milk in a pan, add the vanilla pod and seeds, and bring just to scalding point. Cover the pan, remove from the heat and infuse for 30 minutes or so.

Whisk the egg yolks together with the caster sugar until thick and pale, then remove the pod from the cream mixture and pour the liquid over the yolks, whisking them together. Strain the cream into ramekins, set them in a roasting tin with hot water to come half way up their sides, and cover them with a sheet of greaseproof paper to prevent a skin forming as they cook.

Bake until quiveringly set. They will continue to cook outside the oven. Test after 40 minutes by nudging them. Remove from the *bain-marie* and leave to cool completely.

Three of these apricots in their gloopy, citrussy alcohol make a spectacular top to the vanilla cream pots on page 251. Or you can serve them on their own or with the carrot, apricot and cinnamon cake on page 256. Remember to soak the fruit in half the orange juice the night before you cook it. The dish will keep well in the fridge for several days.

Armagnac and Orange Apricots

SERVES 6

18 dried unsulphured
  organic apricots
200ml/7fl oz freshly squozen
  orange juice
100g/3½oz unrefined caster sugar
100ml/3½fl oz water
a few drops of Culpeper's sweet
  orange oil (optional)
the peel of an organic orange,
  all pith removed, sliced into
  matchstick shreds and
  blanched in boiling water
  for a minute
Armagnac, Cognac, Cider Brandy
  or Calvados

Soak the apricots overnight in half the orange juice. Next day, put the rest of the juice into a pan with the sugar, water and shreds of blanched peel. Simmer for 10 minutes, then add the apricots and their juice and simmer until tender, about 15 minutes. Cool them in a glass bowl, then add a generous slug of alcohol and stir it in well.

If you are keeping the fruit in the fridge, bring it back to room temperature again for half an hour before you place two or three apricots with some juice and peel on top of each vanilla cream.

This is the lightest of cakes, made with potato flour, the ricotta sieved to aerate it. I add a touch of Grand Marnier and orange flower water to the mixture, and serve it alongside strawberries and clotted cream in the summer.

Orange-scented Ricotta Cake

SERVES 8
preheat oven to 180°C/350°F/Gas 4

85g/3oz unsalted butter
150g/5oz vanilla caster sugar
2 large organic eggs
grated rinds of half an organic
    orange and lemon
3 tbsp potato flour
1½ tsp baking powder
a pinch of salt
450g/1lb ricotta. If you are lucky
    enough to find fresh, drain it
    through a muslin-lined sieve
    overnight
50g/2oz organic raisins soaked in a
    little hot water to plump up for
    15 minutes
2 tbsp Grand Marnier or
    Cointreau
2–3 tsp orange flower water
icing sugar

Beat the butter and all but a tablespoon of the sugar together until pale and creamy, then add the eggs continuing to whisk. Add the zests, potato flour, baking powder and salt. Push the ricotta through the small disc of a mouli or sieve, and blend into the other ingredients. Add the plumped-up raisins, Grand Marnier or Cointreau, and sprinkle over the orange flower water. Butter a springform tin, then scatter the rest of the sugar into it and roll it around the base and sides, discarding any extra.

Scrape in the cake mixture and bake in the middle of the oven for 55 minutes, or until a skewer comes out clean; leave to cool. Turn out on to a plate, and sprinkle over a little unrefined icing sugar if you like. This is a habit that I refuse to get into, it is so overworked on restaurant puddings, alongside sprigs of this and that and solitary fanned fruit. If in doubt, leave well alone.

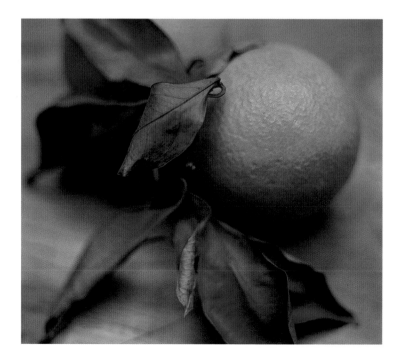

I can't pretend I reach for the suet regularly, even in a cold snap, but once or twice a year when the mood strikes, there is no substitute. If you are loath to part with your own marmalade, shop-bought will do, but go for a quality one such as Thursday Cottage or Bay Tree.

Steamed Apple and Marmalade Pudding

SERVES 6

about 1kg/2¼lb Bramley apples
juice of a lemon
200g/7oz self-raising flour
a pinch of salt
85g/3oz beef suet
50g/2oz muscovado or molasses sugar (depending on quite how dark and treacly you like things)
6 tbsp good, bitter marmalade

Peel, core, quarter and cut the apples into thickish wedges, then sprinkle them with lemon juice to prevent them from discolouring. Put the flour into a bowl, add a pinch of salt and the suet, then add water, a tiny bit at a time, and mix to a stiff dough. Roughly 6 tablespoons of water should do, but go easy, you don't want a sticky ball of slime.

Divide the dough into two pieces, one three-quarter lump, the other the remaining quarter. Roll the large one out first and fit it into your buttered 1-litre/1¾-pint pudding basin. Roll the apple in the sugar, then add the marmalade and coat thoroughly before piling into the pudding basin. Roll out the small piece of dough, wet the edge of the pastry in the basin, and stick the pastry top to it, pressing them together to seal tightly.

Cover with pleated greaseproof, then foil, and tie. Place the pudding in a large, heavy-bottomed pan and pour in scalding water to come halfway up the sides of the basin. Cover with a lid and steam at a simmer for at least 2 hours – 2½ will be fine. Turn the pudding out on to a large plate and serve with home-made custard. Flavour the custard with a bit of Seville orange juice.

This is a recipe I adapted from the winning entry to a competition I held in my *Daily Telegraph* column after my trip to India. The entrants had to devise a pudding to complement one of Hill Station's spice ice creams. Malcolm Kennedy won with this delicious cake, which is not too aggressively or diffusely spiced. It works wonderfully with my stem ginger and spice ice cream (page 256), and with the Armagnac and orange apricots (page 253) as a third element. That way you just need a thin slice of warm cake, always great with ice cream.

Carrot, Apricot and Cinnamon Cake

SERVES 8—10
preheat oven to 180°C/350°F/Gas 4

3 tsp ground almonds
150g/5oz unsalted butter
150g/5oz light muscovado sugar
2 eggs
2 tsp ground cinnamon bark
6 tbsp freshly squeezed orange
    juice, and the zest of two
    oranges
300g/10oz self-raising flour
1 tsp baking powder
a pinch of salt
125g/4oz organic carrot, grated
85g/3oz unsulphured dried
    apricots, chopped

Butter a 1.5 litre/2½ pint gugelhopf tin or fluted mould, and dust it with ground almonds. Cream the butter and sugar in a KitchenAid or by hand until light and fluffy, then whisk in the eggs. Add the cinnamon, orange juice and zest, then sieve in the flour, baking powder and salt, and fold in well. If the mixture is heavy and hasn't quite achieved dropping consistency, add more orange juice. Stir in the grated carrot and apricots.

Scrape into the prepared mould, tap on the work surface to eliminate air bubbles and smooth the top. Bake in the centre of the oven for 1–1¼ hours, or until a skewer comes out clean. Cool in the tin for 10 minutes, then turn out on to a rack and serve while still warm.

It is the frisson of very hot with very cold that does it. These doughnuts were the runners-up in the competition and they worked beautifully with green cardamom ice cream, as they do with spiced ginger ice cream. The tiny doughnuts double in size as they fry and are then rolled in sugar, cinnamon and allspice, an inspirational detail.

Mrs Golumbina's Hot Spicy Doughnuts with Fresh Mangoes and Lime

35g/1½oz unsalted butter
150g/5oz granulated sugar
crushed seeds of 3 or 4 green
   cardamom pods
2 eggs, well beaten
500g/1lb 2oz flour
150ml/5fl oz full cream milk
1 tsp ground cinnamon
½ tsp ground allspice
vegetable oil for deep frying
1 ripe mango, sliced
1 lime

Cream the butter into 85g/3oz of the sugar, then stir in the eggs, the flour and the crushed cardamom seeds. Add the milk bit by bit until you have a soft dough that leaves the side of the bowl.

Divide the dough and roll it into small, walnut-sized balls. Drop them into very hot oil for about 4 minutes. Keep spinning them as they cook until they are golden all over. Remove and drain on kitchen towel. Cook in batches so you don't overcrowd the pan and lower the heat.

Spread the remaining sugar, cinnamon and allspice on a plate. Roll the cooked doughnuts lightly in the mixture until completely covered.

Serve with slices of fresh mango, over which you have squeezed the juice of a lime, and a scoop of spiced ginger or green cardamom ice cream.

I first ate this pudding as an undergraduate. I was lucky enough to have a boyfriend who was also a keen cook. He had found the recipe in one of his mother's tomes under the heading 'lemon bomb pudding' before I ever came across it in Jane Grigson's classic *English Food*. I guess the lemon does explode like a bomb, sending a brackish-black moat of sugary liquid around the dome of suet. The term rib-sticking was made for it. As students, it was perfect – cheap and brilliant to leave for four hours in our little 'gyp' room, where we had a small Belling stove, while we got to grips with *Pericles* or *Gawain and the Green Knight*. Both demanded something epic to tuck into afterwards.

Sussex Pond Pudding

SERVES 6

225g/8oz self-raising flour
125g/4oz suet
125g/4oz slightly salted butter
about 150ml/5fl oz milk and water
125g/4oz molasses or demerara
    sugar, depending on how black
    and how treacly you can take it
1 large organic lemon

Mix the flour and suet together in a bowl. Add the half milk, half water to make them into a soft dough. You will need about 150ml/5fl oz. Roll the dough out into a large circle, and then remove a quarter with a knife to use as a lid.

Butter a 1.5 litre/2½ pint pudding basin, drop the three-quarters piece of dough into it and press it together to line the basin. Put half the chopped butter into the basin with half the sugar. Prick the lemon all over with a fine sharp skewer or larding needle to help the juices escape. Place the lemon on top of the butter and sugar and cover with the remaining butter and sugar. Roll out the remaining quarter of pastry and lay it on top to seal the filling inside.

Cover in the usual way, making a string handle, then lower the pudding into boiling water in a large saucepan, making sure the water comes halfway up the pudding basin, and cook for 3–4 hours. Turn the pudding out on to a large plate with plenty of room for the moat; you will have to ease it with a palate knife first. Make sure everyone gets some of the lemon, all of which will be edible. Clotted or thick cream, naturally.

Will there ever be a successor to the decadently becaloried sticky toffee pudding? I think this is as close as it gets, and I like it equally well with or without the nuts. What I prefer about this pudding is the fact that when you turn it out you have a tidal moat of butterscotch pouring down from its summit, coating everything in sight. Slightly different principle to the sticky toffee sauce that basks underneath the sponge of the original.

Steamed Apricot and Pecan Pudding with Butterscotch Sauce

SERVES 6—8

For the sauce:
200g/7oz light muscovado sugar
125g/4oz unsalted butter
200ml/7fl oz organic crème
    fraîche
1 tsp organic vanilla extract

For the pudding:
200g/7oz unsulphured organic
    dried apricots, chopped into
    small pieces
1 tsp bicarbonate of soda
300ml/10fl oz boiling water
175g/6oz vanilla caster sugar
50g/2oz unsalted butter
1 egg
200g/7oz plain flour
1 tsp baking powder
85g/3oz pecan nuts, bashed up
    but not crushed to death

Melt all the ingredients for the sauce together in a saucepan. Let them bubble for a further 3 minutes or so before pouring them into the bottom of a large, greased pudding basin.

Pour the boiling water over the apricots and bicarb and leave to cool. Cream the sugar and butter until light and fluffy, then beat in the egg. Sift over the flour and baking powder, and throw in the pecan nuts. Stir in the apricot mixture, and scrape into the pudding basin on top of the butterscotch sauce.

Cover with foil and secure with string, then steam in a saucepan of water that reaches halfway up the pudding for 1½ hours. Check that the water level remains constant throughout. Turn the pudding out on to a large, warmed serving plate, not too flat for the moat of butterscotch, and serve with more crème fraîche if you dare.

Another of those lovely pudding cakes, you can also make this with pears. More pudding than cake, it can be served with some crème fraîche laced with Somerset Cider Brandy, Calvados or rum.

Caramelized Apple Cake with Calvados Crème Fraîche

SERVES 8—10
preheat oven to 180°C/350°F/Gas 4

1kg/2¼lb sharp eating apples such as Coxes
225g/8oz unsalted butter plus an extra 50g/2oz to cook the apples in
50g/2oz good runny honey, I use Seggiano chestnut honey
225g/8oz unrefined icing sugar
4 eggs
225g/8oz plain flour
½ a sachet of dry yeast
a pinch of sea salt
demerara sugar

Peel the apples and cut them into small dice. Brown them in the butter, adding the honey after a few minutes

Remove from the heat and drain the juice from the apples, keeping it to pour over the cake later. Cream the 225g/8oz of butter and the icing sugar until white and fluffy, then whisk in the eggs, one by one. Add the yeast, sifted flour and salt and fold in the apples.

Grease a large springform tin and line the base with a disc of greased greaseproof. Sprinkle a thin veil of demerara around the sides. Pour in the mixture and scatter a bit more demerara over the surface of the cake. Bake for about 1½ hours, or until a skewer comes out clean.

Cool for 15 minutes before removing from the tin. Serve warm with the crème fraîche and a small jug of the apple juice.

Of all nursery puddings, this has to be the best and most comforting. It should not be known under any other name; it is a classic and should be treated as such. The other lovely thing about it is that it was the first pudding my nine-year-old daughter Miranda made by herself when I was away filming one Sunday. She followed the recipe to the letter, and my brother Daniel pronounced it 'as good as your mother's'. Just as it should be.

Queen of Puddings

SERVES 6

preheat oven to 180°C/350°F/Gas 4

125g/4oz day-old brown bread
    breadcrumbs
1 heaped tbsp unrefined vanilla
    caster sugar
grated zest of an organic lemon
600ml/1 pint Channel Islands or
    full cream milk
50g/2oz unsalted butter
4 large eggs, separated
a jar of best-quality apricot or
    raspberry jam or bramble jelly
125g/4oz vanilla caster sugar

Put the breadcrumbs into the deep buttered dish you intend to cook the pudding in, with the vanilla sugar and lemon rind. Scald the milk with the butter, stir them into the crumbs and leave to cool for 10 minutes. Now beat in the egg yolks one at a time. Bake in the oven for about 25 minutes until the custard has set.

Heat the jam gently with a teaspoon of two of water, and pour it over the custard. Whisk the egg whites until stiff, stir in a spoon of sugar, then whisk in half of the remaining sugar until it is satiny. Fold in all but a spoon of the remaining sugar, pile the meringue on top of the pudding, and sprinkle the rest of the sugar over the top. Put back in the oven for about 15–20 minutes or until the meringue is golden and crisp. Serve hot with plenty of cold, thin cream. You may make the pudding up to the meringue stage a few hours earlier if it suits you.

If you still find a degree of childish pleasure in dunking a warm toast soldier into a softly boiled egg and watching the crocus-coloured yolk splurt down the sides of the egg cup, the chances are you also love crème brûlée: the tap with the back of the spoon on the mahogany surface; the splintered shards of glassy, bitter sugar as the thick ivory cream breaks through the barrier; the combined tastes and textures. This autumn I had a glut of apples and thought their sharp-scented fragrance and a hint of spice could transform the classic brûlée. There was always the danger that the apple would destroy the custard's unctuousness, but liquid they were not. They were divine.

Spiced Apple Brûlée

SERVES 6—8
preheat oven to 190°C/375°F/Gas 5

4 medium-sized cooking apples
600ml/1 pint organic double
   cream
a little piece of cinnamon bark,
   or 1 tsp ground cinnamon
5 cloves
5 egg yolks
unrefined caster sugar
demerara sugar

Core the apples and score them around their circumference with a knife tip. Place them on a baking tray, pour on a little cold water and bake them in the oven until soft right through.

Meanwhile, scald the cream in a saucepan just to boiling point. Peel the apples, making sure you have de-cored all the toenaily bits, and chuck the purée in the food processor. Grind the cinnamon bark and cloves in a mortar and add them to the apple. Add the egg yolks and process briefly until everything coheres. Add caster sugar to taste, but leave the purée tart, because you are going to brûlée the top with demerara sugar. Lastly, pour the hot cream into the food processor with the blade still running.

Spoon the apple mixture into ramekins and place them in a roasting tin. Pour boiling water around the ramekins to come halfway up their sides, and cook them on the middle shelf of the oven for about 40 minutes. The custards should be set, but with a tremble. They will take longer than conventional custards because of the liquid content of the apples, but hold your nerve.

Remove from the tin and cool, then put them in the fridge overnight. In fact, they will keep for several days if you want to get ahead. Sprinkle a thin layer of demerara sugar over the surface of each ramekin and spray with a mist of water to help the torch scorching. Bubble with a blow torch, using a mild flame as close as you can get to the surface. Once you have a beautiful, even mahogany-coloured top, leave to cool before serving.

There are times when only the best, childhood-memory food will do, and you want something you could cook almost blindfold and one-handed. The three sugars add flavour and texture to the top, and the orange-oily spiced sugar turned into the fruit to macerate delivers a keen whiff of the Orient that is somehow right for the time of year. This is a winter pudding.

Spiced Three Sugar Crumble

SERVES 6—8
preheat oven to 190°C/375°F/Gas 5

8 apples, I used 6 firm cookers
   and 2 sharp eating apples
a blade of mace, 6 cloves and
   a couple of small pieces
   of cinnamon bark
4 tbsp or so of unrefined caster
   sugar
the finely grated zest of an
   organic orange
175g/6oz organic white or
   wholemeal flour
50g/2oz each of unrefined
   granulated, light muscovado
   and demerara sugar
125g/4oz unsalted butter

Peel the apples, quarter and core them. Cut them into slices and place them in the bottom of an earthenware dish. Grind the spices together in a mortar — fresh spices make all the difference, the ready ground have lost their intense flavour. Add the caster sugar to the spice mixture in the mortar and stir to mix well until the sugar is freckled with brown. Add the fine zest of the orange, and stir it in, then pour the mixture over the apples and turn them well to coat. Doing this an hour or so in advance of cooking really helps the spice rub to penetrate.

Process the flour, sugars and cold butter cut into small pieces briefly, or do this by hand, until the mixture is sandy textured. Pile over the top of the apples, smooth the surface and cook for 45 minutes until browned, with little geysers of bubbling juice escaping here and there. Rest for a few minutes before serving with thin pouring cream.

Great cold, too, with a scoop of vanilla or the stem ginger and spice ice cream (page 268). You can prepare the pudding several hours in advance of cooking it.

This is a lovely pudding-cake, the sharp, orange orbs of Cape gooseberry bursting on to the tongue, the sponge moist with almonds. Use Shipton Mill's soft pastry and cake organic white flour. It's made from English organic wheat which is soft to grind, with lower protein levels, so is good for cakes and pastry. Perhaps because of their decorative quality, with their veiny, dry-textured leaves, Cape gooseberries are not always taken seriously as an ingredient. Yet their acid sharpness and explosion of flavour would grace a gooseberry sauce for mackerel, or even a scented summer fool. Experiment.

Upside-down Cape Gooseberry and Almond Cake

MAKES A 20CM/8IN CAKE
preheat oven to 170°C/325°F/Gas 3

350g/12oz Cape gooseberries,
   weighed after removing
   their leaves
200g/7oz unrefined caster sugar
200g/7oz unsalted butter
200g/7oz organic ground almonds
a few drops vanilla extract
3 organic free-range eggs
finely grated zest and juice of
   an organic orange
1 tbsp crème fraîche
125g/4oz Shipton Mill's soft pastry
   and cake organic white flour
1 tsp baking powder
a pinch of salt
demerara sugar to sprinkle

Butter a 20cm/8in springform cake tin. Cover the base with a layer of Cape gooseberries, leaving just under a third of them to add to the cake mixture.

Cream the sugar and butter until light and fluffy, then stir in the ground almonds and vanilla extract. Beat in the eggs, one at a time, fold in the orange zest and juice, then the crème fraîche, sifted flour, baking powder and salt. Fold the remaining gooseberries into the mixture. Sprinkle a bit of demerara sugar over the layer of gooseberries in the tin, then plop the mixture over them and smooth it down with a rubber spatula.

Bake in the middle of the oven for 1 hour and 10 minutes, but check with a skewer every five minutes after 1 hour. Leave to cool in the tin on a rack until just warm, then turn out upside down on to a large plate and serve warm with crème fraîche.

I wanted to come up with a Christmas ice cream, full of warming spices, that would coldly slide from the summit of your pudding or pies, but would also work well with crumble. I puréed the globes of ginger through a mouli, but it would be easier to blitz them in a blender with the custard and cream base. The very finely chopped bits of ginger are a matter of taste. I like the texture; you may prefer to have a silken-smooth ice cream.

Stem Ginger and Spice Ice Cream

SERVES 6—8

450ml/16fl oz full cream or
    Channel Islands milk
2 vanilla pods, split and the
    insides scraped out
6 organic egg yolks
175g/6oz unrefined caster sugar
325ml/10fl oz double cream and
    310ml/11fl oz crème fraîche, or
    all double cream
6–8 globes of stem ginger,
    put 6 in the blender
    to begin with
1 tbsp ginger syrup
2 very finely chopped globes
    of stem ginger
6 or 7 cloves and a few little bits
    of cinnamon bark crushed
    together in a mortar

Scald the milk with the split vanilla pods and their innards. Whisk it into the egg yolks and sugar that you have put into a bowl. Return the mixture to the pan, and cook it over a low heat, whisking as you go, until it thickens perceptibly. Do not allow the mixture to boil, you do not want it to curdle into scrambled egg.

Immediately the mixture has thickened, remove from the heat and whisk in the creams thoroughly. Whizz in the blender with the whole globes of ginger, ginger syrup and half a teaspoon of the spice mixture and taste until you have the right strength. The ginger should predominate, but you want a musky breath of spice.

Churn in the ice cream maker for 30 minutes and then add the tiny ginger bits to the setting mixture. You can put the mixture in a ice tray and freeze, but remember to stir the setting walls of the ice cream into the middle of the tray after the first hour, and then again an hour or two later, to prevent crystals forming.

Little warm shells of spicy sponge, spiced madeleines are delicious with the stem ginger and spice ice cream or the poached Armagnac and orange apricots. You will need to buy a madeleine tray to get the classic shape.

Spiced Madeleines

preheat oven to 180°C/350°F/Gas 4

225g/8oz ground almonds
125g/4oz plain flour
200g/7oz unrefined caster sugar
350g/12oz unsalted butter, softened
150g/5oz runny honey
300g/10oz egg white
a pinch each of 5-spice, cinnamon, nutmeg and star anise
1 tbsp mixed grated orange and lemon zest

Mix the ground almonds, flour, sugar and spices in a large bowl, then add everything else and b eat together well. Put in the fridge for 20 minutes.

Grease some madeleine moulds or bun trays and pour in the mixture. Bake for 10–15 minutes, when a skewer should come out clean. Turn out and leave to cool on a wire rack.

I serve the following two ices together in the summer, the contrast of pistachio green and pale peachy orange, of water and cream ice, both delicate and subtle. You may find the idea of ice cream served in a melon shell kitschly redolent of those frozen atrocities of orange and lemon sorbets that are the province of the 80s' trat or the more contemporaneous Indian restaurant. I would disagree, on the grounds that it is really about the quality of what is inside it. And if you place your scooped-out melon on some pretty leaves it should offend neither the eye nor the good-taste arbiters.

Charentais Water Ice

SERVES 6

125g/4oz vanilla caster sugar
225ml/8fl oz water
2 Charentais melons
lemon and/or lime
1 egg white

Simmer the vanilla caster sugar with the water for a few minutes. Liquidize enough melon pulp to give you 300ml/10fl oz of juice, two melons maximum. Add the cooled syrup slowly, tasting as you go, then sharpen with a spritz of lemon juice, and, if you like, one of lime, which makes melon taste more melony (and, incidentally, mango more mangoey).

Freeze until the outside is set, but the middle still slushily liquid. Gently fold in a stiffly whisked egg white before returning the mixture to the ice tray and to the freezer. You may make this a couple of days before you wish to serve it, but it does tend to lose flavour after that.

Galia Melon Ice Cream

SERVES 6

1 Galia melon
125g/4oz unrefined vanilla caster
   sugar
4 egg yolks
Kirsch
lemon juice
300ml/10fl oz of double cream

Cut a lid off the top of a Galia melon and remove the seeds through a sieve with a bowl placed under it to catch the juice. Carefully scoop out the flesh and stew it gently in a pan with the juice and the unrefined vanilla caster sugar for 2–3 minutes. Blitz in the blender briefly, return it to the pan with 4 beaten egg yolks and cook over a very gentle heat until it thickens.

Cool the mixture, then add a splosh of Kirsch and a good squeeze of lemon juice to taste. Fold in the whipped but slightly slack double cream, and freeze in your ice cream machine or in an old-fashioned tray. If you use a tray, remember to stir the setting walls of the ice cream into the middle of the tray after the first hour, and then again an hour or two later, to prevent crystals forming.

When the ice cream has set, scoop it out in balls and return it to the melon shell, the base of which you may have to shave slightly with a knife so that it will stand upright. Place the filled melon on a white dish lined with fig leaves or any large leaves you happen to have in the garden, and serve.

Magpie that I am, it was while watching a heat of *Masterchef* that I registered one of the contestants cooking a rhubarb and passion fruit tart and I began to wonder about the sanity of pairing these two intensely tart, sharp ingredients together. Reckoning on the softening effect of muscovado sugar, cream, and a proper home-made vanilla-ey custard, I got to work. In fact I got to work twice, the first time with whole chunks of rhubarb, the second with a briefly mashed purée. It was a triumph, the mashed version even better than the jewelled, since the little frozen pieces of rhubarb didn't release their taste so well. With mark 2, both fruits rang out strong and clear. The best ice cream I have dreamed up to date. A clean-fruited pudding that you can make at the end of January when the first fragile wands of forced rhubarb appear and the rigours of Christmas make it all the more desirable.

Rhubarb and Passion Fruit Ice Cream

SERVES 8
preheat oven to 150°C/300°F/Gas 3

8 thin wands of rhubarb
light muscovado sugar, about 4
    tbsp
4 large or 6 small passion fruit
500ml/18fl oz full cream or Jersey
    milk
1 vanilla pod
6 egg yolks, save the whites for
    macaroons to serve with the ice
    cream if you like
125g/4oz unrefined caster sugar
300ml/10fl oz double cream,
    Jersey if possible

Chop the rhubarb into small chunks, turn it in the sugar in a baking dish and bake in the oven until softened, about 20–30 minutes. Test for sweetness. Drain and reserve the juice, you can pour it over the ice cream or drink it! Mash the rhubarb with a fork. Halve the passion fruit, scoop out the contents into a small pan and heat very gently until warm, which makes the fruit easier to sieve. Keep the juice and the seeds separately.

To make a custard, first scald the milk with the split vanilla pod and its innards, then pour the hot milk over the well-whisked egg yolks and sugar, whisking as you go. Return the mixture to the pan and continue to whisk over a gentle heat until you have a thickened custard. Decant into a bowl to cool. Whisk the cream until thickened but by no means rigid. Fold the cream into the cooled custard, then stir in the passion fruit juice and rhubarb. Finally, fold in a dessertspoon of passion fruit seeds, more would overwhelm with crunch. Churn in the ice cream maker and freeze, or freeze in an ice tray. Remove from the freezer and place in the fridge 20–30 minutes before you want to serve it.

Macaroons

MAKES ABOUT 30
preheat oven to 190°C/375°F/Gas 5

175g/6oz ground almonds,
    Spanish organic ones are the
    best
300g/10oz unrefined caster sugar
3 egg whites
20g/¾oz flour or arrowroot
vanilla extract
rice paper or baking parchment
a handful of split almonds

Mix the ground almonds and sugar in a bowl, add the egg whites, and cream together thoroughly. Add the flour or arrowroot and flavour to taste with vanilla extract, a few drops.

Place the rice paper or baking parchment on baking sheets, and spread the mixture out in little rounds with a teaspoon. Press a split almond into the centre of each one and bake for about 20 minutes. Cool thoroughly on a rack before storing.

Apple and Carrot Shortbread

MAKES ABOUT 20 WEDGES
preheat oven to 180°C/350°F/Gas 4

50g/2oz semolina
175g/6oz unbleached white flour
¼ tsp baking powder
a pinch of salt
150g/5oz soft, unsalted butter
100g/3½oz unrefined caster sugar
50g/2oz carrot, grated
25g/1oz apple, grated
milk

Sift together the semolina, flour, baking powder and salt. Cream together the butter and sugar until light and fluffy. Throw the grated carrot and apple into the flour mixture, then fold into the creamed butter. Knead into a soft dough. Rest for half an hour in the fridge.

When you're ready to cook the shortbread, roll into 23cm/9in discs, 1cm/½in thick, and mark into wedges. Fork the edges, brush over a milk wash, and bake on a non-stick surface for about 10 minutes. Leave to cool before cutting.

The Jelly

Curiously, I crave jelly as much in midwinter for its refreshing, fruited zestiness as I do when there are piles of soft-berried summer fruits to play with. Christmas is a great time for jelly, as is the New Year, when the palate is jaded and wearied from the rich, buttery, creamy, sugary, fatty delights of feasting. I cannot understand why most people don't seem to bother with jellies, and why they have become a bastardized childrens' party food, quivering, sugared lumps of primary-coloured hue and phoney fruitiness, which come set in dinky party plates with shop-bought ice cream. I have been making different jellies throughout Christmas, from the jokily frivolous Buck's Fizz on Boxing Day, to orange, grenadillo and Muscat, and, unanimously the best, a clementine, passion fruit and Muscat jelly. Come the blood orange season, I mean to experiment with spice, too – a sunset-coloured, blood orange jelly spiked with cardamom. Ice cream if you must, something home-made, but I think a clean palate, no biscuit, no sponge, no cream is best. A good jelly takes no longer than 10 minutes to make, even if you are squeezing an orchard of oranges. Just remember not to experiment with pineapple. There is an enzyme in the fruit that prohibits it from setting.

I know champagne isn't cheap, but you've got the rest of the bottle to drink and no other killer ingredients to buy – and this is for Christmas, or birthday, or something special

Buck's Fizz Jelly

SERVES 6—8

600ml/1 pint of Champagne
just under 600ml/1 pint of freshly
    squeezed organic orange juice
8 leaves of gelatine, broken in half
    and soaked in 2–3 tbsp of cold
    water for 10 minutes

Measure the champagne and pour it into a bowl. Put the orange juice into a small saucepan with the leaves of soaked gelatine and their water – 8 sheets should set 1.2 litres/2 pints of liquid, but check the packet. Gently heat the orange juice, stirring as you go to dissolve the gelatine completely. You do not want the liquid to become very hot or it won't taste so fresh, but using a wooden spoon, make sure that there isn't a stringy trace of gelatine to be seen. Pour the orange and gelatine mixture into the champagne, stir it all together, it will fizz as you do, and then pour everything through a sieve into a jelly mould. Mine is big enough for 1.7 litres/3 pints, but I never seem to make a jelly quite that big. Leave to cool, before putting in the fridge to set.

You can make a jelly from four hours to two days before you want to eat it. It will keep for longer in the fridge, but the freshness of the fruit starts to diminish. Turn out by dunking the base half of the mould briefly in boiling water and inverting the jelly on to a plate, or serve from the mould.

On a recent trip to the Far East I got hooked on exotic fruits for breakfast. They don't seem quite so attractive away from their native tropical island, served icy cold like the weather you come home to. But when I returned, I found the tangerine-shelled grenadillos, with their milky, moonstone-white fruit, gluey and black seeded, and turned them, with a delicious organic Muscat and some oranges, into jelly.

Orange, Grenadillo and Muscat Jelly

SERVES 6—8

2 grenadillos

8 sheets of gelatine soaked in 2—3 tbsp cold water for 10 minutes

a 37.5 cl bottle of Bonterra organic Muscat, or something similar, poured into a measuring jug

8—10 organic oranges squeezed to make the level of liquid just under 1.2 litres/2 pints

Halve the grenadillos and scoop out the innards and seeds. Heat them gently in a pan and sieve into a jug – it is easier to separate seed from fruit if it is warm.

Put the gelatine and its soaking liquid into a small saucepan with the orange juice. Heat through gently, stirring as you go. Make sure the gelatine is completely dissolved and then pour the contents of the pan into the measuring jug with the Muscat and grenadillo fruit and stir everything together.

Pour the mixture through a sieve into a jelly mould, leave to cool, then set in the fridge for four hours to two days.

This was the triumph. I served it after the New Year's goose, with the either/or option of a divine chocolate budino (see page 245). Well it wasn't an option really; both were impossible to resist. I used large, somewhat underripe passion fruit. The skins had not crinkled and the sharpness won through gloriously. The sweet clementine and fruity muscat flavours were not clouded and were a marriage of three that transported. Sugar unnecessary.

Clementine, Passion Fruit and Muscat Jelly

SERVES 6—8

3 large, underripe passion fruit
about 20 organic clementines
a 37.5 cl bottle of Bonterra organic
    Muscat, or something similar,
8 sheets of gelatine soaked for 10
    minutes in 2–3 tbsp cold water

Scoop the insides of the passion fruits into a small saucepan, and heat to warm so that the seeds will separate more easily from the fruit. Sieve them into a jug with the muscat. Squeeze the clementines until the jug has just under 1.2 litres/2 pints of liquid in it.

Stir in the gelatine, and pour the liquid into the saucepan, heating it through very gently to just warm enough to dissolve the gelatine completely. Pour the mixture through a sieve into the jelly mould, cool and then put in the fridge.

The jelly will be ready to eat from between four hours to two days later, depending on when you want it. Serve with some thinly sliced oranges.

Raspberries and redcurrants, fortuitously, ripen together in late July and to my mind are THE summer pudding fruits. They also make a magical jelly, with little hanging lanterns of redcurrants suspended in the jelly alongside bruise purple blueberries and soft seeded raspberries. A heap of fruits around the plate and you have a summer pudding as toothsome to the very young as it is to the very old. And the fruit is all raw, even in the jelly. I find it a near sacrilege to cook midsummer fruits.

I use individual plastic bowls, the lidded steamed pudding kind, from which the jellies turn out with minimum resistance, so there are no last-minute panics. You can, of course, use a large mould or glass bowl.

Raspberry and Redcurrant Jelly with Summer Berries

MAKES 7

450g/1lb fresh raspberries
150g/5oz redcurrants
unrefined icing or caster sugar to
    taste, about 4 tbsp
6 sheets of leaf gelatine
water
an extra punnet each of
    raspberries and redcurrants and
    a punnet of blueberries

Soak the gelatine for 5 minutes in 2–3 tablespoons of cold water. Blitz the fruits in a food processor, then sieve them into a measuring jug. Sweeten to taste, stirring in the sugar to dissolve. Err on the tart side. Top up with water to the 900ml/1½ pint mark, but remember to fall short of it by the same number of tablespoons of water you have got soaking the gelatine. Heat the fruit liquid gently until hot, stir in the gelatine in its liquid, and stir off the heat until the gelatine has totally dissolved.

Pour the mixture into the wet moulds and leave to cool. The liquid will start to thicken as it cools. Then pop in the berries one by one, about three raspberries, six blueberries and four or five redcurrants to each bowl. Put in the fridge to set.

Eat a few hours or up to two days later. To turn out, dip the base of each bowl in boiling water for 10 seconds, go round the edge of the bowl with a knife point, turn upside down and squeeze. Arrange on a large dish with extra fresh berries or on individual dishes.

Suppliers

The Ark Chicken Company
Roosters of Babylon, Silverton,
Exeter, Devon EX5 4DT
Tel/Fax: 01392 860430
Email: info@arkchicken.co.uk
Top quality, organic guinea fowl,
quail and several kinds of chicken

Baker and Spice
46 Walton St, London SW3 1RB
Tel: 020 7589 4734
Bread, cakes, wonderful pastry

Brown and Forrest
The Smokery, Bowdens Farm,
Hambridge, Somerset TA10 0BP
Tel: 01458 250875.
Fax: 01458 250875
Huge range of smoked foods,
including the best smoked eel

The Fine Cheese Company
29/31 Walcot Street,
Bath BA1 5BN
Mail order: 01225 448748
Wide range of British, Irish,
French and Italian cheeses,
biscuits, chutneys, jams, relishes
and wine. Also agents for
Seggiano products

Furness Fish, Poultry and Game Supplies
Stockbridge Lane, Ulverston,
Cumbria LA12 7BG
Tel: 01229 585037.
Fax: 01229 582485
Brown shrimps, fish, smoked fish
and meats

Hill Station
Stanier Road , Calne, Wiltshire
SN11 9PX
Tel: 01249 816596.
Fax: 01249 816597
Email: info@hillstation.co.uk
Website: www.hillstation.co.uk
Excellent ice creams and sorbets

Sally Edwards
The Crescent, Taunton, Somerset
TA1 4DN
Sally's café serves wonderful food
at lunchtime and occasional
dinners

Shipton Mill Ltd
Long Newnton, Tetbury,
Glos GL8 8RP
Tel: 01666 505050.
Fax: 01666 504666
Email: enquiries@shipton-mill.com
Stock more than 20 kinds of flour,
including organic Irish soda,
three malts and sunflower, spelt,
light and dark rye, and can supply
by mail order.

Somerset Cider Brandy Company
Pass Vale Farm, Burrow Hill,
Kingsbury Episcopi, Martock,
Somerset TA12 5BU, UK.
Tel: 01460 240782.
Fax: 01460 249220
Website: www.ciderbrandy.co.uk
Traditional cider and cider brandy

Somerset Lamb Direct
Bittescombe Manor, Upton,
Wiveliscombe, Taunton,
Somerset TA4 2DA
Tel: 01398 371387.
Fax: 01398 371413
Website:
www.somersetfarmdirect.co.uk
Traditionally reared, properly
hung lamb and mutton as well as
beef, pork and poultry

Swaddles Green Organic Farm
Hare Lane, Buckland St Mary,
Chard, Somerset TA20 3JR
Tel: 01460 234387.
Fax: 01460 234591
Email: orders@swaddles.co.uk
Website: www. swaddles.co.uk
Wonderful meat, poultry, hams,
sausages, and a range of cooked
dishes, including puddings, cakes
and pies

Swedish Affar
32 Crawford St, London W1H 1PL
Swedish pickled herrings and
other products

Graeme Wallace
Wallace's of Hemyock, Hill Farm,
Hemyock, Devon EX15 3UZ
Tel: 01823 680307.
Fax: 01823 680017
Website: www.naturalmeat.co.uk
The best venison

Index

A

Achari Paneer 134
aïoli 163
Ajo Blanco con Uvas de Malaga 70
Akri Bhindi, Crisp Okra 132
almonds
  Almond Macaroon Cake 220
  Anchoiade de Croze 60
  Carrot, Apricot and Cinnamon Cake 256
  Chocolate Espresso Cake 241
  Chocolate Mocha Cake 238
  Chocolate and Raspberry Pudding 237
  Macaroons 274
  Romesco Sauce 87
  Spiced Madeleines 269
  Upside-down Cape Gooseberry and Almond
    Cake 266
  White Gazpacho 70
Anchoiade de Croze 60
anchovies
  Anchoiade de Croze 60
  Grillade of Lamb Breast 188
  Grilled Peppers 21
  Hard-boiled Eggs with Tapenade 58
  Peperoni alla Siciliana 28
  Piemontese Peppers 24
  Roast Stuffed Monkfish 182
  Sun's Eye, or Sologa 15
apples
  Apple and Carrot Shortbread 274
  Caramelized Apple Cake 261
  Parsnip and Baked Apple Soup 74
  Roast Chined Loin of Pork 110
  Sillsalad 46
  Spiced Apple Brûlée 264
  Spiced Three Sugar Crumble 265
  Steamed Apple and Marmalade Pudding 255
apricots
  Armagnac and Orange Apricots 253
  Carrot, Apricot and Cinnamon Cake 256
  Daube of Pork with Apricots 148
  Steamed Apricot and Pecan Pudding 260
  Vanilla Cream Pots 251-3
Armagnac and Orange Apricots 253
Artichokes, Globe 55
aubergines
  Caponata 30
  Parmigiana di Melanzane 27
  Roasted Aubergine, Red Onion and Tomato
    Salad 120
  Sicilian Pasta Pie 200
  Smoky Aubergine and White Bean Purée 31
avocados
  Chilled Crab, Cucumber and Avocado Salad 210
  Cucumber, Avocado and Fennel Sambal 45
  Guacamole 50
  Jersey Royal, Chicken, Green Bean, Egg and
    Avocado Salad 153

B

bacon
  Broad Beans with Serrano Ham 57
  Cabbage and Bacon Soup 75
  Country Terrine 17
  Guinea Fowl 95

Jambon Persillé 170
  Leg of Lamb Braised 160
  Lentil and Pasta Soup 82
  Pollo alla Cacciatore 93
  Potato, Leek, Bacon, Sage and Cheese Gratin 206
  Roast Cod 151
Balsamic and Shallot Dressing 55
Bateyr Hara Masala 140
beans
  broad
    Broad Beans with Serrano Ham 57
    Iced Broad Bean Soup 66
    with Tomato Cream 64
  butter, Chinese Slow-Braised Belly Pork 117
  cannellini, Smoky Aubergine and White Bean
    Purée 31
  green, Jersey Royal, Chicken, Green Bean, Egg
    and Avocado Salad 153
  haricot, Leg of Lamb Braised 160
beef
  Beef and Prune Tagine 192
  Bigos, or Hunters' Stew 190
  Salt Beef 186
  Steak and Kidney Pie 123
beetroot
  Chilled Beetroot Soup 66
  Medallions of Venison 154
  Sillsalad 46
  Sun's Eye, or Sologa 15
Bigos, or Hunters' Stew 190
biscuits see cakes and biscuits
Bloody Mary, Homemade 34
blueberries, Raspberry and Redcurrant Jelly 280
Bourride of Chicken 162
brandy butter 218
bread 172-9
  Focaccia 179
  Malted Grain Loaf 174-5
  White loaf 177-8
  Wholemeal Caraway rolls 16
Broad Beans with Serrano Ham 57
Buck's Fizz Jelly 276
Buckwheat Kasha 191
Budino 245
butternut squash
  Gnocchi di Zucca 203
  Roasted Aubergine, Red Onion and Tomato
    Salad 120
  Roasted Butternut Squash with Wild or
    Chestnut Mushrooms and Cream 52
  Spice-roasted Red Onion or Butternut Squash 204
Butterscotch Sauce 222

C

cabbage
  Bigos, or Hunters' Stew 190
  Cabbage and Bacon Soup 75
  Colcannon 159
  Stuffed Cabbage in the Troo Style 124
cakes and biscuits
  Almond Macaroon Cake 220
  Apple and Carrot Shortbread 274
  Caramelized Apple Cake 261
  Carrot, Apricot and Cinnamon Cake 256
  Chocolate Espresso Cake 241

Chocolate Mocha Cake with Irish Whiskey 238
  Chocolate and Raspberry Pudding Cake 237
  Drenched Ginger and Lemon Cake 224
  Hazelnut and Orange Biscuits 250
  Lemon and Cardamom Cake 223
  Macaroons 274
  Malt and Apple Loaf 226
  Mrs Golumbina's Hot Spicy Doughnuts 257
  Orange-scented Ricotta Cake 254
  Parkin 222
  Rich Chocolate Brownies 242
  Rich Chocolate Chip and Hazelnut Brownies 243
  Sesame and Roquefort Biscuits 211
  Spiced Madeleines 269
  Upside-down Cape Gooseberry and Almond
    Cake 266
Caponata 30
Chaa Meat 137
Chaas, Buttermilk flavoured 131
Charmoula 128
cheese
  caciocavallo, Sicilian Pasta Pie 200
  cottage, Achari Paneer 134
  cream
    Pierogi 191
    Smoked Salmon 53
  feta
    Piemontese Peppers 24
    Puy Lentil, Feta, Roast Tomato and Onion
      Salad 150
    Roasted Aubergine, Red Onion and Tomato
      Salad 120
  Gruyère
    Chicken Savoyarde 96
    Focaccia 179
    Tomatoes baked 33
  mascarpone
    Smoked Salmon 53
    Tiramisu 234
  mozzarella
    Pancakes 197
    Parmigiana di Melanzane 27
    Sicilian Pasta Pie 200
  Parmesan
    Gratin of Turkey 161
    Parmigiana di Melanzane 27
    Penne with Roasted Squash 205
    Sicilian Pasta Pie 200
    La Torta di Porri 209
  ricotta
    Cold Cucumber and Ricotta Mousse 62
    Orange-scented Ricotta Cake 254
  Roquefort, Sesame and Roquefort Biscuits 211
  Potato, Leek, Bacon, Sage and Cheese Gratin 206
chestnuts, Chocolate and Chestnut Marquise 240
chicken
  Bourride of Chicken 162
  Chicken Charmoula 128-9
  Chicken Savoyarde 96
  costolette alla milanese 101
  Gratin 161
  Jersey Royal, Chicken, Green Bean, Egg and
    Avocado Salad 153
  Mantuan Chicken Dish 194
  My Thai Chicken 145

Oriental Noodle Salad 118
Pollo alla Cacciatore 93
Roasted Chicken and Leeks 98
Tarragon and Garlic Chicken 99
with Tomatoes, Olives, Mustard and Gruyère 33
chicken livers, Spiced Chicken Livers 18, 20
chickpeas
Chickpea Soup with Pasta 80
Falafel 180-1
Roasted Aubergine, Red Onion and Tomato
Salad 120
Salad of Hot Chickpeas 61
Chinese Slow-Braised Belly Pork 117
chocolate 236-47
chorizo
Paella de Cerdo 147
Sopa de Ajo 83
chutney 136, 138
Civet of Hare with an Aillade 107
Clementine, Passion Fruit and Muscat Jelly 278
cod
Baked Cod with Greek Potatoes 102
Codcakes 184-5
Roast Cod with Braised Puy Lentils and Roasted
Vegetables 151
Colcannon 159
Cold Cucumber and Ricotta Mousse 62
Country Terrine 17
courgettes
Courgette, Pine Nut and Sultana Salad 90
Griddled Courgettes 89
Roasted Aubergine, Red Onion and Tomato
Salad 120
couscous 128-9
crab
Chilled Crab, Cucumber and Avocado Salad 210
Crab Apple Jelly 228
Crème Fraîche Tartare 127
cucumber
Chilled Crab, Cucumber and Avocado Salad 210
Cold Cucumber and Ricotta Mousse 62
Cucumber, Avocado and Fennel Sambal 45
Gazpacho 68

D
Damson, Sloe and Mulberry Gin 230
dressings 118, 203
Balsamic and Shallot 55
Coriander, Red Chilli and Ginger 150
Herb Mayonnaise 153
drinks
Damson, Sloe and Mulberry Gin 230
Home-made Bloody Mary 34
duck
Bigos, or Hunters' Stew 190
Rillettes de Tours 23

E
eggs
Hard-boiled Eggs with Tapenade 58
Jersey Royal, Chicken, Green Bean, Egg and
Avocado Salad 153
Pancakes Layered with Mozzarella di Bufala and
Tomato Sauce 196-7
Pancakes Layered with Pesto and

Mozzarella di Bufala 199
Piperade 32
Tiramisu 234
Tortilla Española 56

F
Falafel 180-1
fennel
Braised Squid with Leeks, Fennel, Orange, Chilli
and Red Wine 105
Cream of Fennel Soup 79
Cucumber, Avocado and Fennel Sambal 45
Smoked Salmon with Saffron-braised Fennel 53
fish 38-46, 87, 102, 126, 151, 156
see also named varieties; seafood
Focaccia 179

G
game 93, 107, 115, 116, 161
see also named varieties
garlic
aïoli 163
Civet of Hare with an Aillade 107
Sopa de Ajo 83
ginger
Coriander, Red Chilli and Ginger Dressing 150
Drenched Ginger and Lemon Cake 224
Stem Ginger and Spice Ice Cream 268
Gnocchi di Zucca 203
goat, Chaa Meat 137
Gratin of Turkey (Chicken, Guinea Fowl,
Pheasant) 161
Guacamole 50
guinea fowl 36, 93
Gratin 161
Guinea Fowl with Puy Lentils, Lardons and
Marsala 95

H
haddock, smoked, Spiced Kedgeree 207
hake, Roast Hake Steaks with Poor Man's Potatoes
156
ham
Broad Beans with Serrano Ham 57
Piperade 32
see also prosciutto
hare, Civet of Hare with an Aillade 107
Harissa 193
hazelnuts
Hazelnut and Orange Biscuits 250
Rich Chocolate Brownies 242
Rich Chocolate Chip and Hazelnut Brownies 243
Romesco Sauce 87
Steamed Nut and Chocolate Pudding 247
herrings 138
Grilled Herrings with Sweet Smoked Paprika
and Coriander 40
Sillsalad 46

I
ice cream
Burnt Orange 249
Galia Melon 271
Rhubarb and Passion Fruit 272
Stem Ginger and Spice 268

J
Jambon Persillé 170
jelly 275-80
Jersey Royal, Chicken, Green Bean, Egg and
Avocado Salad 153

K
Kedgeree, Spiced 207
Ketchup, Home-made 185

L
lamb
Barley Broth 76
Bigos, or Hunters' Stew 190
Chaa Meat 137
Charmoula 128
Grillade of Lamb Breast 188
Irish Stew 159
Leg of Lamb Braised with Haricot Beans 160
Stuffed Vine Leaves 26
see also mutton
leeks
Bourride of Chicken 162
Braised Squid 105
Colcannon 159
Potato, Leek, Bacon, Sage and Cheese Gratin 206
Roasted Chicken and Leeks 98
Scallops and Steamed Leeks 38
La Torta di Porri (Leek and Rice Pie) 209
lemons
Chicken Charmoula with Preserved Lemons
128-9
Drenched Ginger and Lemon Cake 224
Lemon and Cardamom Cake 223
Organic Seville Orange Marmalade 214-15
Preserved 129
Roast Stuffed Monkfish 182
Sussex Pond Pudding 258
lentils
Guinea Fowl with Puy Lentils, Lardons and
Marsala 95
Lentil and Pasta Soup with Smoked Bacon 82
Moong Dal Tarka 135
Puy Lentil, Feta, Roast Tomato and Onion Salad
150
Roast Cod with Braised Puy Lentils and Roasted
Vegetables 151
lettuce, Thai Lettuce and Pea Soup 72
limes
Codcakes with Kaffir Lime Leaves 184-5
Mrs Golumbina's Hot Spicy Doughnuts with
Fresh Mangoes and Lime 257
liver
chicken, Spiced Chicken Livers 18, 20
pig's, Country Terrine 17

M
mackerel, Marinated Mackerel with Potato Salad
41
mangoes, Mrs Golumbina's Hot Spicy Doughnuts
with Fresh Mangoes and Lime 257
Mater Tikki 141
melons
Charentais Water Ice 270
Galia Melon Ice Cream 271
Mincemeat, Home-made 219

monkfish
  Monkfish steeped in Saffron Milk 87
  Roast Stuffed Monkfish 182
Moong Dal Tarka 135
mulberries, Damson, Sloe and Mulberry Gin 230
Muscat
  Clementine, Passion Fruit and Muscat Jelly 278
  Orange, Grenadillo and Muscat Jelly 277
mushrooms
  Bigos, or Hunters' Stew 190
  Roasted Butternut Squash with Wild or
    Chestnut Mushrooms and Cream 52
mutton
  Barley Broth 76
  Chaa Meat 137

O
okra, Akri Bhindi 132
olives
  Hard-boiled Eggs with Tapenade 58
  Peperoni alla Siciliana 28
  Pheasant Legs Stewed with Green and Black
    Olives 116
  Tomatoes baked with Olives, Mustard and
    Gruyère 33
onions
  Puy Lentil, Feta, Roast Tomato and Onion Salad
    150
  Roasted Aubergine, Red Onion and Tomato
    Salad 120
  Spice-roasted Red 204
oranges
  Armagnac and Orange Apricots 253
  Braised Squid with Leeks, Fennel, Orange, Chilli
    and Red Wine 105
  Buck's Fizz Jelly 276
  Burnt Orange Ice Cream 249
  Carrot, Apricot and Cinnamon Cake 256
  Hazelnut and Orange Biscuits 250
  Orange, Grenadillo and Muscat Jelly 277
  Orange-scented Ricotta Cake 254
  Organic Seville Orange Marmalade 214-15
  Roast Boned Leg of Pork with a Spiced Orange
    Rub and Orange Sweet Potatoes 108

P
Paella de Cerdo con Chorizo y Espinaca 147
Palak Aloo 142
Pancakes
  Layered with Mozzarella di Bufala and Tomato
    Sauce 196-7
  Layered with Pesto and Mozzarella di Bufala 199
Parmigiana di Melanzane 27
Parsnip and Baked Apple Soup 74
passion fruit
  Clementine, Passion Fruit and Muscat Jelly 278
  Rhubarb and Passion Fruit Ice Cream 272
pasta
  Chickpea Soup with Pasta 80
  Lentil and Pasta Soup with Smoked Bacon 82
  Oriental Noodle Salad 118
  Penne with Roasted Squash, Prosciutto, Sage and
    Parmesan 205
  Risoni with Seafood and Roasted Vegetables 201
  Roasted Chicken and Leeks with Lemon and

Tagliatelli 98
  Sicilian Pasta Pie 200
pastry
  filo, La Torta di Porri 209
  Slow-roasted Tomato Tart 49
  Steak and Kidney Pie 123
  Tomato and Prosciutto Tarts 48
peas
  Baked Cod with Greek Potatoes 102
  Thai Lettuce and Pea Soup 72
pecan nuts, Steamed Apricot and Pecan Pudding
  260
Peperoni alla Siciliana 28
peppers
  Grilled Peppers 21
  Harissa 193
  Peperoni alla Siciliana 28
  Piemontese Peppers 24
  Piperade 32
  Poor Man's Potatoes 156
  Risoni with Seafood and Roasted Vegetables 201
  Rouille 73
pheasant
  Gratin of Pheasant 161
  Pheasant Legs Stewed with Green and Black
    Olives 116
  Pheasant and Pomegranates with Jewelled
    Bulgur 115
  Pollo alla Cacciatore 93
Pierogi 191
pine nuts, Courgette, Pine Nut and Sultana Salad
  90
Piperade 32
pomegranates, Pheasant and Pomegranates 115
pork
  Bigos, or Hunters' Stew 190
  Charmoula 128
  Chinese Slow-Braised Belly Pork with Butter
    Beans 117
  Country Terrine 17
  Daube of Pork with Apricots 148
  Paella de Cerdo 147
  Pierogi 191
  Rillettes de Tours 23
  Rillons, or Confit of Belly Pork 22
  Roast Boned Leg of Pork with a Spiced Orange
    Rub and Orange Sweet Potatoes 108
  Roast Chined Loin of Pork with Baked Apples
    and Cider Gravy 110
  Spiced Pork Meatballs with Guacamole 50
  with Tomatoes baked with Olives, Mustard and
    Gruyère 33
  sausages, Stuffed Cabbage in the Troo Style 124
potatoes
  Baked Cod with Greek Potatoes 102
  Colcannon 159
  Crushed New Potatoes with Olive Oil and
    Thyme 89
  Focaccia with Potato, Thyme, Gruyère and
    Crème Fraîche 179
  Heston's Mashed Potato 166
  Heston's Pommes Dauphinoise 167
  Jersey Royal, Chicken, Green Bean, Egg and
    Avocado Salad 153
  Marinated Mackerel with Potato Salad 41

Mashed Potatoes 164
  Mater Tikki 141
  Palak Aloo 142
  Potato, Leek, Bacon, Sage and Cheese Gratin 206
  Roast Hake Steaks with Poor Man's Potatoes 156
  Salmon Fishcakes with Crème Fraîche Tartare
    126
  Sillsalad 46
  Tortilla Española 56
prawns
  Oriental Noodle Salad 118
  Risoni with Seafood and Roasted Vegetables 201
  with Tomato Cream 64
preserves
  Crab Apple Jelly 228
  Organic Seville Orange Marmalade 214-15
  Spiced Redcurrant Jelly 227
  Tomato Chilli Jam 212
prosciutto
  Broad Beans with Serrano Ham 57
  Penne with Roasted Squash, Prosciutto, Sage and
    Parmesan 205
  Tomato and Prosciutto Tarts 48
prunes
  Beef and Prune Tagine 192
  Bigos, or Hunters' Stew 190
puddings
  Almond Macaroon Cake 220
  Budino 245
  Caramelized Apple Cake with Calvados Crème
    Fraîche 261
  Charentais Water Ice 270
  Chocolate and Chestnut Marquise 240
  Chocolate Espresso Cake 241
  Chocolate and Raspberry Pudding Cake with
    Chocolate Ganache 237
  Christmas Pudding 217
  Hot or Cold Chocolate Pudding 246
  Parkin 222
  Queen of Puddings 262
  Spiced Apple Brûlée 264
  Spiced Three Sugar Crumble 265
  Steamed Apple and Marmalade Pudding 255
  Steamed Apricot and Pecan Pudding 260
  Steamed Nut and Chocolate Pudding 247
  Sussex Pond Pudding 258
  Tiramisu 234
  Upside-down Cape Gooseberry and Almond
    Cake 266
  Vanilla Cream Pots with Armagnac and Orange
    Apricots 251-3
  see also ice cream; jelly
pumpkin see butternut squash

Q
quail
  Bateyr Hara Masala 140
  Grilled Quail with Balsamic Vinegar 36

R
rabbit, Rillettes de Tours 23
raspberries
  Chocolate and Raspberry Pudding Cake 237
  Raspberry and Redcurrant Jelly 280
redcurrants

Raspberry and Redcurrant Jelly 280
Spiced Redcurrant Jelly 227
rhubarb, Rhubarb and Passion Fruit Ice Cream 272
rice
Paella de Cerdo 147
Risotto with Lemon 100-1
Spiced Kedgeree 207
Stuffed Braised Breast of Veal 149
Stuffed Vine Leaves 26
La Torta di Porri 209
Rillettes de Tours 23
Rouille 73

S
saffron, Smoked Salmon with Saffron-braised
Fennel 53
sage
Penne with Roasted Squash, Prosciutto, Sage and
Parmesan 205
Potato, Leek, Bacon, Sage and Cheese Gratin 206
salads
Chilled Crab, Cucumber and Avocado Salad 210
Courgette, Pine Nut and Sultana Salad 90
Jersey Royal, Chicken, Green Bean, Egg and
Avocado Salad 153
Oriental Noodle Salad 118
Puy Lentil, Feta, Roast Tomato and Onion Salad
150
Roasted Aubergine, Red Onion and Tomato
Salad 120
Salad of Hot Chickpeas 61
Sillsalad 46
salami, Sicilian Pasta Pie 200
salmon
Ceviche of Wild Salmon with a Cucumber,
Fennel and Avocado Sambal 44
Salmon Fishcakes with Crème Fraîche Tartare
126
Smoked Salmon with Saffron-braised Fennel 53
sauces
Béchamel 197
Bretonne 152
Butterscotch 222, 260
Crème Fraîche Tartare 127
Home-made Ketchup 185
Lemon and Caper 182
Maltese 38
Romesco 87
Thai Dipping 185
Tomato 197
Scallops and Steamed Leeks with Sauce Maltese 38
seafood 38, 45, 118, 201, 210
see also named varieties
Shrimps, Potted 42
Sicilian Pasta Pie 200
Sillsalad 46
skate, with Caponata 30
sloes, Damson, Sloe and Mulberry Gin 230
Soca 81
Sologa (Sun's Eye) 15
Somerset Cider Brandy, Brandy or Rum Butter 218
Sopa de Ajo 83
soups 66-83
Baked Sweet Potato and Roasted Cherry Tomato
Soup 78

Barley Broth 76
Cabbage and Bacon Soup 75
Chickpea Soup with Pasta 80
Chilled Beetroot Soup 66
Cream of Fennel Soup 79
Gazpacho 68
Green Salad Soup 67
Iced Broad Bean Soup 66
Lentil and Pasta Soup with Smoked Bacon 82
Parsnip and Baked Apple Soup 74
Sopa de Ajo 83
Sweetcorn Soup with a Rouille 73
Sweet Potato and Coriander Soup 75
Thai Lettuce and Pea Soup 72
White Gazpacho 70
spices 130-43
spinach
Green Salad Soup 67
Paella de Cerdo 147
Palak Aloo 142
Puy Lentil, Feta, Roast Tomato and Onion Salad
150
Roasted Aubergine, Red Onion and Tomato
Salad with Chickpeas, Feta and Spinach 120
Salad of Hot Chickpeas 61
Stuffed Braised Breast of Veal 149
squash *see* butternut squash
squid
Braised Squid with Leeks, Fennel, Orange, Chilli
and Red Wine 105, 162
Risoni with Seafood and Roasted Vegetables 201
Sun's Eye (Sologa) 15
sweet potatoes
Baked Sweet Potato and Roasted Cherry Tomato
Soup 78
Gnocchi di Zucca 203
Roast Boned Leg of Pork with a Spiced Orange
Rub and Orange Sweet Potatoes 108
Roasted Aubergine, Red Onion and Tomato
Salad 120
Sweet Potato and Coriander Soup 75

T
Tadkeywala Dahi 143
Tapenade 58, 64
tomatoes
Baked Sweet Potato and Roasted Cherry Tomato
Soup 78
Caponata 30
Gazpacho 68
Homemade Bloody Mary 34
Homemade Ketchup 185
Piemontese Peppers 24
Piperade 32
Puy Lentil, Feta, Roast Tomato and Onion Salad
150
Roasted Aubergine, Red Onion and Tomato
Salad 120
Romesco Sauce 87
Sicilian Pasta Pie 200
Slow-roasted Tomato Tart 49
Tomato Chilli Jam 212
Tomato Cream 64
Tomato and Prosciutto Tarts 48
Tomato Sauce 197

Tomatoes baked with Olives, Mustard and
Gruyère 33
Tortilla Española 56
tuna, Hard-boiled Eggs with Tapenade 58
turbot, Baked Turbot with Sauce Bretonne 152
turkey, Gratin of Turkey 161

V
Vanilla Cream Pots 251-3
veal, Stuffed Braised Breast of Veal 149
vegetarian dishes
Achari Paneer 134
Cold Cucumber and Ricotta Mousse 62
Globe Artichokes in Balsamic and Shallot
Dressing 55
Gnocchi di Zucca 203
Mater Tikki 141
Moong Dal Tarka 135
Palak Aloo 142
Pancakes Layered with Mozzarella di Bufala and
Tomato Sauce 197
Pancakes Layered with Pesto and Mozzarella di
Bufala 199
Parmigiana di Melanzane 27
Puy Lentil, Feta, Roast Tomato and Onion Salad
150
Risotto with Lemon 100
Roasted Aubergine, Red Onion and Tomato
Salad 120
Roasted Butternut Squash with Mushrooms and
Cream 52
Salad of Hot Chickpeas 61
Slow-roasted Tomato Tart 49
Smoky Aubergine and White Bean Purée 31
Spice-roasted Red Onion or Butternut Squash
204
Tadkeywala Dahi 143
Tomato Cream 64
Tomatoes baked with Olives, Mustard and
Gruyère 33
Tortilla Española 56
venison
Bigos, or Hunters' Stew 190
Medallions of Venison with Spiced Beetroot,
Cornichons, Tarragon and Sour Cream 154
Roast Haunch of Venison 155
Steak and Kidney Pie 123
Vine Leaves, Stuffed 26

W
water ice 270
watercress
Chilled Crab, Cucumber and Avocado Salad 210
Green Salad Soup 67
Sauce Bretonne 152

Acknowledgements

I almost dread writing this bit more than the horror of conceiving the introduction that will give the book its shape and form and send it on its way. But this bit I dread for different reasons. First, it's like putting the book to bed, as curiously recalcitrant a thing, I find, as a small unwilling child. Second, I have said it all before, and several times now, since I have had the great good fortune to work with the very same individuals on this book as on the last. And, in most cases, the previous two as well.

What I would like to say, and this is in no small measure due to the main protagonists, is that they have done it again. They have produced an even better book, and that is because they are now even better at their jobs than they were this time last year, and the book reflects that. If I had detected even the slightest sense that David Loftus, the most talented photographer I have worked with, was going to coast this book and rely on what we had achieved in the past, it would have been time to try someone new. But the joy of working with David is that he isn't like that. We can talk through the look of a book, and go on developing it until the last shot. I wanted something more abstract, less reliant on endless brush strokes of colour than a lot of the current cook books, but something that allured through its glamorous simplicity and beauty, and still made you want to scrape the food off the page. David, you have shot the most beautiful pictures of my food yet, not always easy with me as cook and with the insanely short schedule we had to work to, but made a trifle easier by the beautiful pots, bowls, plates and linen lent by the lovely kitchen shop Divertimenti.

Susan Haynes, my editor, is, like the best football supporter, always at the match cheering and shouting from the terraces and utterly loyal and committed to the game. She treats the emergent work with a degree of love and care that goes well beyond the confines of professionalism. She really minds about the end result and its attaining, which, in turn, forces authors to give of their best. Thank you for being as good an editor as you are a friend.

This time, the publisher, Michael Dover and his wife Ruth invited us to their house to shoot the photographs. Michael's support, advice and encouragement have always been of the best, but this time, the joys of his lovely kitchen and garden have made the feel of the finished book what it is. It wouldn't have been the same without his generosity. And all for a few leftovers that we hadn't hoovered up with our customary greed. Michael, I owe you a serious Dover Dinner.

George Capel, my agent, is chief cheerleader. She listens to the earliest ramblings of an idea, then encourages, cajoles and enthuses as the glimmer takes shape and the fledgling flies. How lucky I am, knowing that each doubt, uncertainty and questioning is met with serious attention, an honest response and her inimitable sense of fun.

David Rowley's cooking has probably not improved during the shoots for this book, due to the degree of unseriousness with which his attempts at whisking and stirring were taken. But it is not every art director who will come on a shoot and be told that he is there to do more than eat and primp. His is the brilliant eye that has conceived the shape and form of *Good Tempered Food*, alongside designer Nigel Soper, and I know how lucky I am to have both of them for their sensitivity, attention to detail and ability to capture the visual beauty and style that is the essence of the book.

Jinny Johnson has, yet again, edited the text intelligently, coherently, minutely in a way that is always a pleasure rather than a chore, and helped cook for the shoots, making herself so indispensable that it would now be impossible to imagine doing them without her. Bar the chocolate cake that is. She is a first-class cook and skilled navigator, clearing a path through any culinary imprecision and suggesting just where suggestion is needed.

TAMASIN DAY-LEWIS, MAY 2002

First published in the United Kingdom in 2002
by Weidenfeld & Nicolson
an imprint of the Orion Publishing Group
Wellington House
125 Strand
London WC2 0BB

Photographs by David Loftus

A CIP catalogue record for this book is available from the British Library
ISBN 0 297 84306 0

Design director David Rowley
Editorial director Susan Haynes
Designed by Clive Hayball and Nigel Soper
Edited by Jinny Johnson
Proofread by Gwen Rigby
Index by Elizabeth Wiggans

Pots, bowls, plates and linen used in the photographs were kindly lent
by Divertimenti, 139-141 Fulham Road, London SW3 6SD
Tel: 020 7581 8065. Fax: 020 7823 9429. E-mail:
fulham@divertimenti.co.uk